Career Satisfaction and Success

A Guide to Job and Personal Freedom

Bernard Haldane

With a Foreword by
Peter F. Drucker

Revised and Enlarged Edition

JIST Works, Inc.
720 North Park Avenue
Indianapolis, Indiana 46202

Copyright©1996 by Bernard Haldane

Published by JIST Works, Inc.
720 North Park Avenue
Indianapolis, IN 46202-3431
Phone 317-264-3720 Fax 317-264-3709
E-mailJIST Works@AOL.Com

Cover Illustration: Fresh Design, Teri Capron

Library of Congress Cataloging-in-Publication Data

Haldane, Bernard.
    Career satisfaction and success : a guide to job and
personal freedom / Bernard Haldane ; with a foreword by
Peter F. Drucker.—Rev. and enlarged ed.
      p. cm.
    Includes index.
    ISBN 1-56370-200-2
    1. Job satisfaction.   2. Success.   I. Title.
    [HF5549.5.J63H27   1996]
    659.14—dc20   95-20685
                                                        CIP

Printed in the United States of America

99 98 97 96   1 2 3 4 5 6 7 8 9

Earlier editions copyright©1974, 1981 by AMACOM, a division of
American Management Associations, New York; and copyright©1988 by
Bernard Haldane.

ISBN 1-56370-200-2

To

JEAN

companion, teacher, critic,
friend, facilitator, and wife

Foreword

BERNIE HALDANE has, for twenty-five years or more, pioneered in finding human strength and in making it productive. Long before it became fashionable, Mr. Haldane realized that placing people is the most important help one can give them, whether they work in an organization or for themselves. And understanding what one is good for and what one therefore should try to strengthen and develop is the key to self-development. But, from the beginning, Bernie Haldane has gone beyond philosophy, has been the practical guide, the helping hand, the pathfinder. This book distills his experience, his achievements, his knowledge, and his wisdom. It is more than a "guide to the perplexed"—it is a guide to achievement and self-fulfillment, especially in the modern organization.

Peter F. Drucker
Business and Management
Philosopher

Preface
to JIST's Revised
and Enlarged Edition

Are job satisfaction and success possible in this turbulent time of downsizing and mergers? "Know your core strengths," says management guru Peter Drucker. In this book they are called "motivated skills."

Fifty years of exploring how people use and don't use their energies (skills are energies, some of which really demand expression) has revealed how a person can influence his or her future. One national survey showed that managers believe that productivity could increase by 40 percent if people were in jobs they did well and enjoyed doing.

The possibility of such a change is shown by agreement among social scientists that people rarely apply as much as 20 percent of their potential. If 10 points of their unused 80 percent were shifted, their 20 percent of applied potential would increase by half to 30 percent.

If only 2 points of the 80 percent were added to the 20 percent of applied potential, that would mean as much as a 10 percent increase in one's applied potential.

How might you increase your potential by 10, 20, or more percent? The steps to take are given in this book.

It begins by recognizing that you have ups and down, and that the usual way to improve one's position is by "learning from mistakes." This means "finding out what you did wrong and never doing that again." A simple chart shows that when you are in the "downs," you are likely to have limited vision. While you are "up," when you are high on a hill or mountain, your vision is wonderful; you can see so many paths that you are likely to overlook or discount some. But you sure can see more than when you are in the valleys of your life.

Many—perhaps most—career problems arise when people are in the valleys of their lives, when they are feeling low and feel unable to see ways of rising over their difficulties. That's really when they need to review times when they were near their highs, when they feel free to view from on high. It's a lot easier to say than to do, but not difficult with the aid of steps given in this book.

These steps have been organized into different programs for different purposes, for executives, for kids and young adults in school, for those coming out of drug treatment and prisons, for the deprived and refugees who need culture bridging help, for women and the military who need transition assistance and recognition of their contributions to everyday society.

And some have been popularized in best-selling books like *What Color Is Your Parachute?* (Bolles), *Do What You Love* (Sinetar), *The Truth About You* (Arthur Miller), and others.

This is a basic book about career management and career advancement within an organization. Primarily, it is directed toward the person, and secondarily toward management.

Essentially, this is a manual of ideas and proven procedures, ways to determine one's own strengths, to set goals and attain them, to find renewal when slowdowns occur, to manage stress and change careers, and to select high-performance employees. Good workbooks give procedures to follow and systems to use. So this is a practical, results-oriented book, as well as a book for periodic reference, at least yearly.

To check its practicality, you might take just one chapter that interests you and work your way through it. You'll find it to be distilled common sense based on experiences with many thousands of men and women— simple, but not easy to do. Building career satisfaction into your life requires good planning, and that takes time—just about a week of time with the aid of this book.

You *can* have career satisfaction, and certainly you deserve it. It must be done your way, in cooperation with others. And your way is quite different even though the principles applied are the same. The principles are in these pages. The opportunity is here to create your own system that accentuates *your* gains and cuts *your* losses. All of us can do that, and all of us can gain by doing it cooperatively. You can increase your productivity by about 20 percent, with less stress, so both you and your employer gain—and so does the community of people you serve, and your family. By using this book, you can obtain those kinds of benefits.

I was born in England and came to the United States when I was eighteen after earning the First Certificate of the Royal College of Surgeons. I hoped to continue my education so that I could heal people's bodies, but U.S. medical colleges wouldn't accept my British certificate. Eventually I got into reporting and writing as an editor of the *New York Journal of Commerce*. There I was asked by my professional Society for the Advancement of Management to volunteer and create a placement counseling program for our members returning from World War II. This led me to research how people gain employment, find ways through the mess of applications, interviews, and biases that screen out job seekers.

There were no career development counselors at that time, but the writing of some who benefited from my volunteer work created a demand that led me to resign from the newspaper and become an entrepreneur.

Now, almost fifty years later, nearly sixty offices around the world carry my name (I retired from the company, Bernard Haldane Associates, twenty years ago). My decades of volunteer and research work with the University of Washington helped bring me the "distinction" of appearing on videotape in every prison in the state of

Washington. Just last year, 1994, I received commendations and awards from nine professional associations, including an award which reads: "In recognition of your lifelong work in establishing adult career development as a profession."

At 84, I feel I have lived a good life, given much, and have more to give. I am grateful for commendations from Presidents Kennedy and Johnson saying, "Programs such as yours supplement the public effort to provide men and women with job alternatives and new futures." And, "Progress in helping people use their highest skills not only helps the individual worker but also the entire country."

I believe that the ideas and procedures given in this book can help you and others to find more—much more—of the meaning and self-expression you really want.

For this new and enlarged edition, I felt the need for a new chapter (Chapter 15) because of today's rapid economic change and new needs people have. There are no more permanent jobs. Continuing careers are based on one's core strengths and how they may be developed and adapted to accelerating change. And there is new research, developed over recent years in the University of Washington, with some funding through the National Science Foundation.

The process of identifying one's motivated skills, Dependable Strengths, significantly increases one's self-esteem, motivation to achieve, internal locus of control, mental health, and self-efficacy, the studies by doctoral students reveal.

Associated research has shown that people in strength classes substantially reduce the time it takes to find a job; and they learn new things about themselves and increase their potential. Chapter 15 is also concerned with how a person can attract job offers—be a job magnet.

The effort required (about a week of time) to gain job satisfaction, a sense of fulfillment and recognition of the best that is in you, is a worthwhile effort. The grandchildren of some of my clients tell me how well it has worked for their grandparents. I'm for you. The Great Spirit is for you. This book is for you. My heartfelt wish is that you may prevail over all the obstacles that somehow come into each person's life. Live with fulfillment!

Bernard Haldane, Ph.D.
Seattle, Washington

Acknowledgments

Several men and women have directly influenced me in the writing of this book. Many more have been helpful less directly. I would like, in particular, to thank Jean Haldane for her spiritual and Organization Development knowledge. A nationally recognized professional, she, with her patience and encouragement, has contributed to the contents of this book.

There were several times when my best writing expediters were Michael Gilman, Tai Chi expert and masseur; Dr. Shou Chun Ma, acupuncturist; and Dr. Michael Evans, physician.

Bill Olcheski gently bullied me into finishing the original chapters so that he could discuss them with me and work them over. He kept my nose to the grindstone. David Noble, my new and enlarged edition editor, persistently nudged me to get on with it; I am grateful!

The contributions of many persons who helped me in earlier days, thus enabling me to build the groundwork for this book, should be mentioned. These include Katherine Schick and Dr. Norman Vincent Peale, who helped me live through the traumas associated with my first book in 1959; my Quaker friend and mentor, Thomas Gaylord Herendeen; a pioneer career counselor, Dr. Holmes W. Merton; and University of Washington Professor Jerald R. Forster, who directed seven years of research into my procedures.

Thank you all for your inspirations.

Contents

Part I Perspectives for Employees

Our great mistake is to neglect the cultivation of those virtues a person has, and try to exact from each person virtues he does not possess.

—Hadrian (A.D. 76–138)
Roman emperor (A.D. 117–138)

Know Your Strengths— The Way to Job Success

Traditional beliefs about how to identify the talents of working people are outmoded. They don't meet today's needs. As a result, millions of workers, managers, and professionals feel locked into their jobs and plagued by frustration.

Many of them believe that their supervisor is responsible for their plight. Truth is, the supervisor often feels as locked in as the employee.

The growing awareness of this problem by both employees and employers makes it possible for each of them to do something about it. The end result could be happy, efficient workers and supervisors who are reaping the rewards of increased job satisfaction.

A quick look at industry and government upgrading policies shows why the problem exists for both workers and supervisors.

Supervisors generally are locked into goals they had no part in setting. They have no reliable system for knowing the best skills of the people who work for them, so they hold tightly to people who seem to be of most help in reaching department goals.

Much of the time the structure of organizations discourages upgrading employees and making better use of their talents. Supervisors often don't have the option of enabling their subordinates to use and develop their talents. Instead, supervisors are required to do better with the employees working under them. It is reasonable to assume they will try to hold onto their best performers—even when those subordinates are unhappy in the jobs to which they are assigned.

Each person has uniqueness and excellence. But almost all of us are trained to take for granted some of our best skills and talents, and even encourage others to overlook them. For this reason, many people accept the belief "No one really knows oneself." To this they add, "No one can see oneself objectively."

Those are ancient, traditional beliefs. They also are invalid. They make it difficult for a person to know his or her best self. When people try to arrive at such self-knowledge, the closest most come to that is the creation of two lists—a list of strengths and a list of weaknesses—as if balance were desirable. There is something better, however.

The individual who is not afraid to try can gain self-knowledge as a growing, progressing being. That person can identify a pattern of inner motivation. This makes it possible to take charge of one's own life and career development and, with the cooperation of others, influence the course these will follow.

That individual can identify personal excellence and rechannel its direction. This helps the person beat most career-shock problems that are likely to hit one person in five every year as jobs become obsolete at a faster and faster rate.

Understanding Job Freedom

Let's look now at job freedom—what it is all about and why it is important to you.

First, you should know that the rate of technological change in our nation means that most people will have to change careers at least five times in their working lives, and change jobs more often than that. Reports on that come from the Harvard Business School, the University of Maryland, the U.S. Labor Department, Jean-Jacques Servan-Schreiber, and many other authoritative sources. This change rate means greater opportunities for most people, and it should be approached as a welcome challenge rather than as a threat.

> **66** *A person with job freedom knows personal strengths and how to use them well, how to adapt them to meet changing conditions, and in what proportion to develop them to enhance job satisfaction and progress.* **99**

Knowing and Communicating Personal Strengths

A person with job freedom knows his or her personal strengths and how to use them well, how to adapt them to meet changing conditions, and in what proportion to develop them to enhance job satisfaction and progress. This individual knows also how to communicate what these strengths are to a supervisor and how to get the supervisor's cooperation in finding opportunity for them to be expressed.

Who Should Read This Book?

This book is addressed to the 75 million professional and management men and women who are regularly employed; it describes ways to cope with or overcome job frustrations, set goals and meet them, negotiate for a promotion or a lateral transfer, and get a raise. Because this book is also for supervisors, it includes a supervisor's guide to cooperation with subordinates.

How Should You Identify Your Motivated Skills?

The procedures are simple, but they take time. They include no statistical instruments. They do use the *System to Identify Motivated Skills*, which will be referred to mostly as "SIMS" from here on.

This system helps you identify experiences in which you have used those skills or "dependable strengths," and it enables you to explore those experiences so you can see which strengths have reliably helped you achieve job satisfaction and grow.

As you become familiar with your strength patterns, you begin to feel release from the traditions that have blocked you from job freedom.

Removing Blocks to Job Freedom

Job titles, for instance, are one of the biggest blocks to job freedom. This is especially true if job titles include the names of the activities attached to the jobs. It is obvious that being a valedictorian, winning an essay contest, and winning a spelling bee are quite different things. It is not as obvious that each of these experiences uses words, memory, and competitiveness in different ways.

Once you are aware of the strengths you have used in different ways, job titles themselves are put into proper perspective. You lose your fear and awe of them—and perhaps also some of your desire for the status they seem to carry.

With this new outlook, you become more interested in, and more able to express, more of the best that is in you— more of your strengths.

By getting yourself out of the deep freeze of job title attachment, you are in a better position to examine the many opportunities around you. Blinders that have limited your viewing of these opportunities are removed.

Unhampered by job titles and aware of your strengths, you become less concerned about structured forms of progress and more interested in opportunities to "do your thing."

This can mean less frustration and more job satisfaction for you, and a greater contribution of your strengths to your employer. Self-knowledge also is likely to stop you from wasting time looking for the kinds of "opportunities" that could only increase your frustration.

Understanding Your Strengths as Motivated Skills

Your strengths, the ones that are used repeatedly in experiences that turned you on, I call *motivated skills*. You will have other skills that are perhaps just as great when they are briefly used, but I call them *unmotivated skills* because you feel turned off when you use them.

An unmotivated skill is just as real as a motivated one, and you may even do better with it for a short while. But using it just doesn't give you a lasting sense of satisfaction. More important, you can be easily distracted when using an unmotivated skill. An appeal to one of your real strengths will easily take you away from the task that uses your unmotivated skill.

For example, a young man I know found this out some years ago when be was working in his garden. He was uninspired by weeding and pruning, but made up his mind to do a first-class job nevertheless. When he was about halfway through, the telephone rang. It was a friend who wanted to discuss an auto repair problem—an area in which our friend had great strength and was highly motivated. He quickly forgot about the yard work, and it was almost an hour before he reluctantly and unenthusiastically returned to the pruning shears.

From time to time, we all have to do jobs that use our unmotivated skills. But, unless we know what those skills are, we are likely to be trapped frequently into doing the same kinds of things because someone has seen us using them well.

The more intelligent you are, the easier it is to be confused about your motivated and unmotivated skills and to be loaded down with assignments that invite more and more frustrations. Most people have this confusion, and the longer they are unaware of the difference, the longer they will have frustrations associated with their work and their personal activities.

Once you know what your strengths, or motivated skills, are, that knowledge sticks with you. It gives you greater freedom to choose the activities you are willing to undertake. It also increases your ability to cope with things you have to do but don't enjoy.

Case History—
A Corporate Controller

Take, for instance, the case of a brilliant man of 35, the controller of a large corporation. He had a good salary and had worked his way up to his present position after getting his master's degree in accounting. But he was very frustrated, and his anxieties were at a point where psychiatric consultation was essential. The doctor suggested that the person receive career counseling.

He wasn't given tests, and he wasn't asked about his problems. Instead, he was asked to talk about some childhood experiences in which he had thoroughly enjoyed his activities. He also was asked to describe an experience that had happened during the last five years which really seemed to give him satisfaction and enjoyment. He told of raising funds for a Boy Scout drive. He had headed the team; dreamed up the plan; worked out the steps for each participant to follow; and orchestrated the drive, which proved to be a financial success and raised more funds than any other drive in the history of the community.

His earliest two experiences of achievement were at ages 8 and 11. At 8 he had started selling magazines and got his friends to help him distribute them. By the time he was 11, the route had grown to the point where he had seven paid helpers.

At 11 he had sold that business to a friend and teamed up with another friend whose father had given him a small printing press. Our controller had, at age 11, organized and built a printing business around that press.

He had done the selling, his buddy the presswork, and together they had kept themselves in pocket money plus little extras all through grammar school. When they went on to different high schools, the partnership ended.

While in high school, he had sold photographs for the yearbook and for parties. His success and skill in selling had kept several of his photographer friends busy meeting the demand.

In college he had been the only student to have three concessions operating during his freshman and sophomore years. When asked how he had managed all the activities, he replied: "I just got them organized." He had hired other students to help him and had made out very well for himself.

Then, at the suggestion of his father, a professor had gotten hold of him and said: "You've got brains enough, so you don't need to be a peddler, a salesman for the rest of your life. You can be a professional man." The convincing argument had prompted this young man to focus on accounting. His first degree came through cum laude. The money he had earned as a combination salesman-businessman financed continuing education through his master's degree.

He had been recruited by a big firm while in college, gotten married, had children, stayed with the firm, and moved up to his position as controller.

In his free time he had volunteered for every community activity that involved selling or promotion of any type. He had sold tickets; he had organized groups to sell tickets. He had raised funds; he had organized groups to raise funds for many community activities. He had worked for community betterment projects and organized groups to promote them, then lobbied successfully to have them accepted by the city council.

And, all this time, he had been becoming increasingly job-frustrated. While often commended for his controller work, he had always been glad when the week ended, but somewhat resentful at having to go to work in the mornings. Because he had seen many other executives suffer the same feelings, he thought frustration was normal. Only when his home life had deteriorated substantially did he bow to his wife's insistence and discuss his problems with a psychiatrist.

After he was referred for career counseling, it was soon apparent that at least some of his frustrations were due to his being in a figures-and-paperwork job rather than in a selling and people-persuading job.

Counseling helped him think through how he could switch within his company to an activity in the sales department where his accounting skills would still be useful. He, on his own, suggested some private studies in marketing techniques and strategy. A program developed for him led to his becoming regional sales manager for the company within two years. The company had lost a man who was about to become a disaster in his controllership but had gained a person who proved to be happy and highly productive in sales management.

If you have frustrations, your situation probably will not be like the one just described or the example that follows. Because of your own uniqueness, you will need to do something special to meet your particular needs.

The preceding case and the one described in the next section give you clues to the recognition of your self-motivated skills or strengths. The procedures outlined elsewhere in this book show you how to make personal, reliable use of the information you assemble about yourself. When you get together the data about yourself, you will find it relatively easy to assess your own career situation, no matter where you work.

Case History—
An Unemployed Card Designer/Ceramist

Mary had been unemployed for a very long time. She had held only two or three jobs during a five-year period, and each had lasted less than a month. Government specialists had given her psychological tests, and welfare placement experts were able to get her jobs only as a wrapper or a packer in a department store. She did not have a high school diploma or formal training for any occupation. Because of her harelip, she tried to avoid speaking to people. Yet, one week after entering a program for identifying motivated skills, she had a self-supporting job that virtually meant running her own business.

Mary could read and write. She listed experiences where she felt she did things well, things she also enjoyed doing.

Then she stood before a group and outlined her problem: "You've got to help me get a job. I'll go crazy if I stay on welfare any more."

Examination of her "turned on" experiences already had revealed possibilities in the art field, but, like so many people, she generalized with her facts.

She was asked: "What do you do now to stop yourself from going crazy?"

She replied, "I design and make greeting cards and place cards for people who are kind to me and my kids and sometimes give us meals. I also like to do ceramics."

She was invited to bring samples of her cards and ceramics work to the next meeting of her strengths-identification workshop. The group members indicated willingness to buy some of the pieces. They also indicated their belief the items could be sold through gift or department stores.

Mary had to be trained to approach the buyers in such shops. She went to one of them a few days later and displayed her wares. She was hired, at $10 an hour, to handle special orders. Two months later she was promoted and given an assistant.

Nine months later she still was successful in the job, and it seemed unlikely that she would ever need to return to public welfare.

The two preceding case histories illuminate a number of points:

1. There are no hidden talents.

2. We often have talents that we hide from ourselves for a variety of reasons.

3. Examination of your positive experiences, the ones that enabled you to feel "turned on," can reveal a pattern of strengths.

4. When you are aware of the pattern of your strengths, you become open to new opportunities and free to combine them in different ways.

5. For most people these new opportunities may be with their present employers and are obtainable.

6. Awareness and use of your strengths give you greater flexibility or adaptability and also greater job security.

7. This increased knowledge of yourself, your uniqueness, enables you to prepare for and manage the development of your own future.

Strength Identification Does Not Solve All Problems

Don't draw any hasty conclusions. The identification of motivated skills is not a solution to all problems. There are many ways to approach self-understanding. One long-neglected area, now being recognized more and more, is the area of a person's strengths.

When my strength approach to career advancement began some 50 years ago, it was a lonely road, and the work often was ridiculed.

Now, leaders in psychiatry, behavioral sciences, business, and government frequently are reporting that a person is much more than one's own problems, mistakes, and weaknesses; they urge the search for strengths.

Resisting Self-Knowledge to Avoid Responsibility

Some individuals would rather not know what is strong about them, the strengths that point to growth and reveal potential. A greater degree of responsibility is required to take hold of success rather than to stay in the safe area of complacency and complaint. This tolerance for frustration can itself become a skill, a means to avoid letting out the reins and moving toward self-realization and job satisfaction.

> **66***Many individuals would rather not know what is strong about them, the strengths that point to growth and reveal potential. A greater degree of responsibility is required to take hold of success rather than to stay in the safe area of complacency and complaint.* **99**

A Lesson from Alice in Wonderland

Consider the following mythical conversation between the Mad Hatter and Alice in Wonderland. I've provided this conversation as a way to illustrate the problem most of us have in evaluating our strengths.

MAD HATTER: We only go around in circles here in Wonderland, but we always end up where we started. Would you mind explaining yourself?

ALICE: Well, grown-ups tell us to find out what we did wrong, and never do it again.

MAD HATTER: That's odd! It seems to me that in order to find out about something, you have to study it. And, when you study it, you should become better at it. Why should you want to become better at something and then never do it again? But please continue.

ALICE: Nobody ever tells us to study the right things we do. We're only supposed to learn from the wrong things. But we are permitted to study the right things *other* people do. And, sometimes, we are even told to copy them.

MAD HATTER: That's cheating!

ALICE: You're quite right, Mr. Hatter. I do live in a topsy-turvy world. It seems as if I have to do something wrong first in order to learn from that what not to do. And then, by not doing what I'm not supposed to do, perhaps I'll be right. But I'd rather be right the first time, wouldn't you?

Almost all of us are trained to expect and respond to failure. "Learn from your mistakes; profit from them," we are told.

Preferring Failure to Success

Over the centuries, this pressure to learn from our weaknesses has influenced most people to try to fail. This condition is basic to Dr. Eric Berne's book *Games People Play* and his transactional analysis system. A new viewpoint can change the focus on failure to a focus on self-realization.

> 66 *Theologian Paul Tillich commented on the failure focus along these lines: 'Many people prefer enslavement to liberation because it relieves them of the need to make decisions.'* 99

The story of one man, Jim, demonstrates beautifully the drive to fail, clothed in the garments of success.

Case History—The Drive to Fail

Jim got a new career. At 28 he moved from assistant manager of a small-items store to printing salesman. He called on a friend at the end of the second week. "This sale will help me make my quota and earn $400 in commission for the week," he said.

His willing friend first asked Jim what he knew about printing, varieties of paper, and typefaces. Jim admitted he knew nothing of the subjects and claimed he was so busy with calls on potential customers that he didn't have time to worry about such details.

The friend asked: "How much do you aim to sell next week?" Jim replied that he was hoping to earn $800 weekly, so he had to get printing orders worth $8,000 in the next week. When the friend asked what Jim felt his chances were of attaining his goal, Jim said: "Not too good. But I'm certainly going to try."

"And how about the following week?" the friend asked. "I'm going to try for the $8,000 again, even if I don't make it. And I'm going to keep on trying." He was beginning to sound a bit belligerent at this point. "You always told me to aim high, and that's what I'm doing."

"Can't you see, Jim," his friend asked, "that you are aiming to fail? You say you are too busy to learn your trade. You

know that customers from whom you can get larger orders will ask you about paper varieties and typefaces, but you are not taking time to learn about your business. And, from what you say, you are going to drive yourself to call on potential customers even though you know it is unlikely that they will give you the volume of orders you want.

"You are working at building a habit of failure, when you could just as easily build a habit of success."

Jim was not too ready to agree. "If you can tell me how to get the business and income I want, don't hold out on me," he said.

The process that was outlined for him helped him earn more than $50,000 in the first year. In brief, Jim set himself a monthly quota averaging—for the first three months—a 10 percent monthly increase over the preceding period.

In the time gained through planning and not overpressuring himself, he learned the elements of the printing business and was able to counsel his customers on their needs. He found he had less need to call on outsiders for help.

This process helped him develop a habit of reaching his goals and sometimes surpassing them. At the end of the first quarter, he planned for a substantial increase in sales based on his ability to offer better service. His new goal was reasonable, and he attained it.

After the first year, Jim took a new look at himself, identified his self-motivated skills, and started back to college for his master's degree in marketing.

Not everyone is as fortunate as Jim. Because misery loves company, most people console each other for failure to achieve self-realization. They commiserate with one another about their frustrations and almost completely misread the guidance systems built into their own life stories.

Learning from Experience

Everyone has frustrating and bad experiences along with good ones. Perhaps space flights with the space shuttle and its "electronic brains" can give clues to learning from experience. All space vehicles have built-in error factors, with self-correcting mechanisms. These elements do not function when the vehicle is directly on course, but must be tested early in flight to ensure that they are working. Consequently, a rocket is launched "off course," and its direction is controlled through error-factor corrections. In other words, when an error is detected, it is used as an aid to change the direction of flight. No attempt is made to study the error, except for the information it can give for course correction.

You could liken this to a man waking up in a strange, dark room and trying to grope his way to the door. The traditional approach would have him try to beat the wall down if he touched that first. He would keep trying to get through at his first point of contact.

The cybernetic, or "rocket," approach would have him accept that first touch as an indicator that he must move in a different direction. What complicates the traditional approach is the rigidity of old structures, old ideas about try, try, try again—but in the same old way.

These old ideas are what really caused the tragedy of unemployment for space scientists and engineers in the early 1970s, for auto industry workers during the 1980s, and possibly for medical doctors in the 1990s. There is a great deal of difference between holding onto your strengths while changing the way they are applied and holding onto your job title even if it extends unemployment and brings career and psychological disaster.

Using Self-Understanding as the Path to Career Freedom

The response to "failure" in this day and age must be change. The response to growth blocks, now and in the future, must be a system that removes or gets around those blocks. When you know and are able to use this system, of which the identification of dependable strengths is a basic part, you have a high degree of career freedom. You appreciate how to cope with frustrations and obstacles; you are concerned with understanding the elements that enable you to feel "turned on" by your work; you gain for your own use a process that helps you handle the interpersonal relationships that can ease and speed your development, or at least slow down the pace of your frustration.

Most people do not need to quit their employers in order to enjoy job satisfaction. But they do need secure employment, reasonable assurance of continued income as a result of their efforts, and opportunity to move within their organizations so that both self-actualizing opportunities and growth may be a part of their lives.

The following chapter details the major obstacles traditionalists have put in the way of the self-understanding that is essential to career freedom. It also gives theoretical supports for the processes described in subsequent chapters.

Consequently, if you want to go on with the process of discovering and integrating all your strengths, you might want to skip Chapter 2 now and come back to it later. Whether you do this or not will depend on how much of a theorist or a pragmatist you are.

Just about everyone has job frustrations. Traditional ways of dealing with them have failed to increase job satisfaction. Burnout and career shock, caused by the need to change vocations and jobs, as well as by early retirements, are increasing.

Career shock can be reduced or eliminated when you know your strengths and are open to changing the way they are applied—and when you lose your attachment to job titles.

Most of us have been trained to relate to failure rather than self-realization. The error factors in life can be used, as they are in the space shuttle, as aids to a safe shift in direction—usually within the organization where you are now employed.

Unrest of spirit is a mark of Life.

—Karl Menninger (1893–1990)
American psychiatrist

Overcome Resistance to Change

Nearly everyone wants to grow, but almost no one wants to change. Most of us want the benefits of change, but few of us search for ways to cooperate with the process of change. It follows, therefore, that theories, rationalizations, and practices have been developed to support "antichange" attitudes.

But change does go on, despite the fog of "facts" and projections that provide enough information to ensure that when progress is made, it passes through "quicksandlike" territory. A progressive labor department executive put it this way: "Of the many places that can muddy the waters on employment facts, the U.S. Department of Labor is the most productive and consistent."

This chapter identifies some of the sand traps and outmoded traditions, highlights some outstanding contributions for workforce progress, and gives a theoretical background for ways to identify motivated skills.

New Approaches for Workforce Progress

Among the most positive terms in the language of human progress are *organizational development; job enrichment; management by objectives*, which is related to the first two; and *human resources development* (HRD). All of them aim to increase job satisfaction and performance by intelligent involvement of employees in the goals and decision making of their employers. Many companies are using these systems on the basis of modern behavioral science research.

> **66** *Among the most positive terms in the language of human progress are* organizational development; job enrichment; management by objectives, *which is related to the first two; and* human resources development *(HRD). All of them aim to increase job satisfaction and performance by intelligent involvement of employees in the goals and decision making of their employers.* **99**

The really good systems ask each person to contribute ideas and to consider personal goals as they relate to an organization's goals. The latest literature says employees should be given at least a day's notice of decision-making meetings that will require taking their own goals into consideration. More and more work is relatively short-term team tasks where employers "hope" the best capabilities of each employee will complement the others. The literature gives little indication of attempts by organizations to help employees know their own best strengths and potential, factors essential to intelligent personal goal setting.

Wherever it is implemented, the System to Identify Motivated Skills adds that factor of self-knowledge. Not every company wants to promote self-knowledge, however. An example would be a company that successfully uses biographical-data patterns to identify persons with management potential—an approach that seems similar to SIMS—but does not permit employees to see the outcome of the company's analysis of that data. The company regards its process a trade asset and keeps it secret from other organizations and even from its own employees.

Organizational Dynamics

Organizational development (OD) is concerned with the processes that help people be more open and honest with one another. It helps them relate more effectively, gain greater insight into their own feelings, look at disagreements and conflicts as aids to improved understanding and more effective cooperation, and work together to solve problems.

OD enables people to be more effective in their team relationships and task performance. It facilitates cooperation with change as a means of gaining its benefits, and it helps people learn through mutual experiences.

OD designs frequently include methods to help groups clarify and set goals and plan for attainment of intermediate objectives. The process sometimes helps employees change behavior in order to be more representative of their own self-image. But the literature reveals no strategy to help individuals know their own strengths or self-motivations. It is all group- or organization-centered.

Institutions that use OD have management practices that are light years away from the traditional pyramid of power. Perhaps 8 million of the 150 million employees in the United States have felt the enriching impact of this new style of management. Virtually all those who have report more job satisfaction. The employers say labor turnover is lower and attendance is better. Both factors lead to reduced costs and higher productivity.

Pioneer Contributors to Organizational Development

The pioneer contributors to OD strategies include B. F. Skinner, Abraham Maslow, David McClelland, Douglas McGregor, Frederick Herzberg, Eric Berne, and Leland Bradford. The early stages of their research coincided with the early development of the System to Identify Motivated Skills. Each of them complements and reinforces the others.

Skinner's Programmed Learning Theory

B. F. Skinner (1904–1990), an American psychologist, experimented with programmed learning. His experiments led him to suggest that desired (productive) behavior be reinforced, recognized, commended, or rewarded. In programmed learning the person studies a small bit, is asked a question to test the learning, and is rewarded for a correct answer. The individual then advances to a more complex bit of learning. This process is repeated until the total of the desired learning is attained.

With the System to Identify Motivated Skills, as the next two chapters will show, a person's own experiences become a programmed "textbook." Those who participate in this method recall experiences in which they did well and from which they earned recognition and reward. By bringing these up to date, they are able to see how they contributed to their own programming. They become alert both to their inner motivation to continue and to what they can do to make further progress.

Maslow's Hierarchy System

A major contribution from Abraham Maslow is his hierarchy of needs, or values. Under his system, people work first to meet their physical and safety needs, then to meet their needs for self-esteem and self-actualization. Almost all persons in management and the professions are concerned primarily with seeking the latter two. "I want to be able to do my thing," is a cry for self-actualization. Perhaps one in five can truly claim fulfillment through work.

From time to time, most of us taste fragments of fulfillment. Then we say, "Too good to be true" or "Can't last
long." Should these be self-fulfilling prophecies, in which
what you think may happen becomes more likely to
happen because of your behavior, these great periods
somehow pass, and we drift again into the daily grind or
rat race. The System to Identify Motivated Skills provides
incremental knowledge about the self, which makes it
more likely that a person's period of fulfillment will occur
more often and last longer.

McClelland's Research on Achievement Motivation

David McClelland smashed many old psychological traditions when he reported research findings in his book *The
Achieving Society*. In essence, he found that "hero styles"
influence the children of that society, and they grow up
seeking to copy those styles. Thus Horatio Alger novels
many years ago helped inspire the rapid industrial growth
of the United States. In India, where priestly searchers for
Nirvana long provided the hero style, industrialization
and living standards have been slow to grow; in recent
years this has changed.

McClelland has taken his theories into developing nations.
Staffs trained by him, in both India and Mexico, have
helped change levels of desire for achievement. Classes
conducted by these staffs begin by testing the level of
achievement "need" among participants. This is done by
having them write interpretations of pictures and count-
ing the words that have "achievement" content. The
students then are told their scores and given exercises
and special lessons designed to increase the number of
achievement-content words in their vocabularies. At the
end of the course, another test, with the same pictures,
usually shows a rise in the number of achievement words
used to interpret the pictures.

It may seem strange, but when this process is kept up, it
often results in greater achievements by the class over the
following years. Although it doesn't work for all the students, it does work for enough of them, so McClelland's
achievement motivation workshops became quite popular.

The vocabulary-changing approach is a helpful influence to changing achievement motivation. The System to Identify Motivated Skills enables a person to recognize experiences which prove that the individual has been and is an achiever.

It helps a man or a woman see and accept his or her own "heroics," his or her own achievements, as well as describe them. It helps each person perceive how to continue to build achievements or even change personally the direction for achieving them.

With the System to Identify Motivated Skills, the assumption is that each person *is* an achiever with a unique career style. When individuals know their own style and pace, they have freedom and inner motivation to develop or change them.

> 66 *With the System to Identify Motivated Skills, the assumption is that each person is an achiever with a unique career style. When individuals know their own style and pace, they have freedom and inner motivation to develop or change them.* 99

A fun-loving teenager of 14, whose parents feared he would amount to nothing, came to our counseling center. He (and his parents) learned that he was deeply motivated to achieve in areas associated with entertainment—and that his school pranks, which got him expelled, were an outflow of his inner drives. Eight years later he started what is now a small chain of entertainment stores selling records, books, related instruments, and games. Currently, just over 30, he is planning his first London stage production, a musical.

His parents were shocked by the encouragement that the System to Identify Motivated Skills gave him—to do more of being himself, to be a showman. They tried to suppress this interest in much the same way as did the father of the unhappy controller mentioned in Chapter 1.

McGregor's Views on Organization Structure

Douglas McGregor was more concerned with the individual in an organization structure, particularly in relationships with supervisors. His "Theory X" dramatizes the dictator type, the domineering executive who usually is unwilling to listen to criticism or even to other people's ideas. This personality type tells subordinates what to do and cannot conceive of delegating any authority. In fact, this kind of executive discourages communication between employees and supervisors.

His "Theory Y" poses the "democratic manager," the individual who encourages employees to participate in helping to accomplish—and even helping to plan—what should be accomplished.

McGregor suggests that this approach brings out the best in both the supervisor and subordinates, improves the productivity of both, and gives both greater job satisfaction. Today hundreds of consultants are helping organizations establish participative management procedures as an aid to greater effectiveness.

The Theory Y manager is a concerned communicator who deliberately builds a climate that encourages cooperation and participation, especially as long as participative management is not confused with permissiveness. Usually it is not.

There are, however, situations in which an autocratic manager's style becomes essential. Even in the most enlightened examples of participative management, there comes a time when the individual with final responsibility may have to slam the desk and say, "This is the way it must *be done."*

A story about McGregor, after he became a college president, goes like this. "Do you have Theory Y management at the university?" he was asked. "It isn't pure," he is said to have replied. "When you're in this kind of job, you quickly learn there are times when conditions call for what appear to be arbitrary decisions."

When managers are concerned with McGregor's participative management style, they should not be required to assume that everyone is in a job that is self-actualizing, the one which is right for that individual and permits that person to make the greatest contribution. Yet there is a tendency to assume that people in certain jobs are actually in the right jobs. Too often this assumption is wrong.

Dogmatism in theory of any kind tends to produce dogmatic practices. When the issue is the conduct of human beings, it may be wise to regard behavior as determined more by current conditions.

The Greeks charged, "Know thyself," but—as most know—they believed that full self-knowledge was virtually unattainable, something that could be hoped for but not achieved. When accepted dogmatically, as happens too frequently, this precept results in individuals not trying to know themselves.

Through the studies leading to the System to Identify Motivated Skills and by the use of this time-tested process, you can come much closer to knowing your best self.

> *I once achieved a kind of fame when I was quoted in* Forbes' *Think, a book of quotations, and an Oldsmobile dealer magazine. The quotation was this: "If you want to get the best out of a person, you must look for the best that is in him or her." When managers do not know the best in themselves, they cannot be expected to look for it in others.*

Theory Y managers need to know the pattern of the best in themselves, which the System to Identify Motivated Skills will help them clarify. Then they gain the kind of comfortable self-esteem, not conceit, that encourages them to facilitate application of the expertise possessed by each of their subordinates. Effective participative management is achieved by recognizing and encouraging the use of the best in each person.

> 66 *Effective participative manage-ment is achieved by recognizing and encouraging the use of the best in each person.* 99

True, Theory Y managers tend to be more effective, but that may often be because they are concerned communicators and their attitude encourages cooperation. Many Theory X managers also do well. Good management attitudes do encourage people to try harder; but, until their "best" is identified, their best cannot be used intelligently.

The climate for doing your best is a try-harder climate, but it is different from one in which the motivated best in each person is known to both the supervisor and to the subordinate. In a number of organizations, all supervisors and employees have used the System to Identify Motivated Skills to help identify the best in themselves. They then work together to find ways to apply their best skills— through job enrichment, job modification, team efforts, and other ways. This includes being patient when things don't work out as quickly as desired.

Herzberg's Job-Enrichment Research

Frederick Herzberg's research has led to job-enrichment approaches. His work parallels that of Maslow, but where Maslow starts with the individual employee, job enrichment starts with the employer.

Maslow's hierarchy of needs indicates that people work first to meet their physical and safety needs. When these are assured—and only then—they feel free to seek satisfaction of some of their social needs. When these are reasonably assured, they look for work to give them self-esteem and self-actualization. People are inner-motivated when they feel self-actualized; then they continue to develop their potential.

Herzberg theorized that elements of a job that motivate

and satisfy an employee are dimensions of motivation different from those that dissatisfy and "de-motivate" that individual. He found that challenges, more responsibility, and more authority are "satisfiers." Money, environment, and tight supervision are among the "dissatisfiers." The latter, in a negative dimension, stimulate alienation, absenteeism, and lowered productivity.

He distinguishes *job enrichment* from *job enlargement*. He said, in essence, that if you add to a meaningless job a second meaningless operation, you enlarge the job and double its meaninglessness. A simple example of job enrichment would be empowering a typist to correct letters and sign them, instead of having, as in the past, a supervisor correct and sign the letters. The typist will need additional training, but the supervisor will have more time to do higher-level work.

Enrichment changes would be more effective if they were reinforced by the individual's own knowledge of the skills the person is self-motivated to apply, the things the individual is truly good at. Also valuable is knowledge of the skills people are *not* motivated to apply—even if they are well trained in the techniques of their use.

Berg's Criticism of Education

Ivar Berg has made a special contribution in this area. His book *Education and Jobs: The Great Training Robbery* reports research studies and case histories which disprove the general belief that more education necessarily makes a person more effective on the job. He concludes that employers have been misled on that concept.

Two of the many examples given relate to teachers (the rising educational credentials of teachers have not halted the deterioration of urban education) and air traffic controllers (education is not a major factor in daily performance of this demanding, decision-making job).

Government, business, and industry spend billions each year to support the education and training of people. What a benefit it would be if managers were aware of a person's motivated skills and could informatively select and approve requested training and educational costs. The person would not be misled on the value of a particular course, and thus could seek wisely the courses that would lead to opportunities for self-actualization.

Berne's Transactional Analysis System

Eric Berne is a psychologist whose book *I'm OK, You're OK* became a best-seller. He developed an approach called Transactional Analysis (T/A) for understanding human behavior. In many ways, his conclusions support the System to Identify Motivated Skills.

Berne points out that infants, with their dependency on parents and other grown-ups for guidance and help, are persistently conditioned to believe that others are right (are OK), and that they (the infants) are not right (are not OK). This attitude tends to be encouraged through early school years, when parents, teachers, and others are required to show or teach children what is "right" in many areas of activity, thinking, speaking, and writing. These conditioned attitudes frequently cause adults to relate in childlike ways. Berne's T/A system is designed to help the individual recognize that as an adult dealing with other adults, the person can feel, "I'm OK and you're OK."

As indicated in the discussion about Skinner, the System to Identify Motivated Skills clarifies the strengths a person has developed, applied, and reinforced. It affirms the individual's "OK-ness" without overlooking weaknesses, mistakes, and failures. It is effective in identifying the reality of a person's feeling that he or she is OK with regard to many activities.

Bradford's Laboratory Training Approach

Leland Bradford is among the pioneers of laboratory training, a process designed to help people learn from experience about their behavior and feelings and also to give them a chance to experiment in changing their behavior. His work with the National Training Laboratories, of which he was a founder, expedited the arrival of organizational development strategies. One of his great contributions, the Training Laboratory, or *the sensitivity train-*

ing concept, creates a community in which people are free to express their feelings, practice being open and honest with each other, and increase each other's effectiveness.

This oversimplified description of a laboratory experience permits disclosure of an important element that can make these experiences more valuable to many people. The element is self-knowledge of skills or strengths and the impact such knowledge provides when goals, plans, and behavior changes are to be considered.

Men and women who have participated in both T-lab and SIMS career workshops have often described their experiences this way: "The lab makes me aware of my feelings in a way that enables me to be more alive, to be more aware of what is going on; without taking away from that, the SIMS workshops gave me a different dimension of self-understanding so that my feet are on the floor and I know where I am going."

The SIMS Theory of Individual Excellence

Basic to the System to Identify Motivated Skills approach is the theory of individual excellence. It was several years after I developed and began using its techniques, as a professional counselor and amateur behaviorist, that it dawned on me to look for the principles underlying them. Development of this theory and the recognition of its principles have led to substantial expansion of the areas in which the System to Identify Motivated Skills has already proved useful. The assumption supporting the theory is this:

Each person has some form of excellence within that seeks expression.

Flowing from this is the probability that the person's excellence will be expressed more through experiences felt as achievements or successes than through other varieties of experience.

Assuming that personal excellence has many component parts (skills, talents, or strengths), the experiences likely to hold the greatest concentration of these components are an individual's greatest achievements.

It follows that examination of many experiences felt to have been one's greatest achievements can be expected to reveal a pattern of skills common to several of those achievements. These inner-motivated skills are likely to be central in future achievements, even though the experiences themselves may be very different because the skills can be developed and combined in different ways.

These motivated skills clamor for expression. When they have insufficient outlet, they tend to "act frustrated" and cause stress of many kinds.

Personal problems, job conflicts, and frustrations generally arise when someone is in a position that requires little use of motivated skills. Such a situation forces the individual to use too many unmotivated skills. Frustrations also come when a supervisor is ignorant of another's strengths or competencies.

Several strategies designed for different purposes using the System to Identify Motivated Skills approach are revealed later. First we need to deal with some attitudes, traditions, and practices that tend to block human relations progress and cooperation with change.

Some Obstacles to Better Employment Programs and Information

Government Employment Programs

Over the years, I have observed many times that the government provides a well-intentioned web of obstacles to employment through its many "programs." In a number of cases, the obstruction is created by funding to academic, governmental, and other bureaucratic institutions rather than to businesses or not-for-profit organizations that actually work with the unemployed. As a result, vast sums of money are spent on things that don't really have much real impact on employment.

An example of this is the system of "unemployment" offices in each state. While they go by different names, each state is required to list job openings, administer unemployment compensation claims, and provide job search assistance to job seekers. Although a few states do provide meaningful assistance to job seekers, many offices simply are not staffed or funded to do so. While job seekers are led to believe that they will be referred to job openings through these offices, they typically know of only 5% of the job openings in an area. Most offices do not have the staff to provide even brief career counseling, and most job seekers get virtually no individual help from these offices other than unemployment checks.

Most universities, high schools, and government-funded employment programs are no better. Few provide meaningful training on how the labor market works or on how to get a job. What information that is provided is often incorrect, old-fashioned, or downright damaging. Often the "professional" staff who are trusted to provide this information are poorly trained or misinformed and are incapable of providing good advice to others.

Traditional Job Application Forms

Job application forms deserve special attention because millions of them are completed each year. Their existence in that volume, as well as their general sameness, causes most people to believe that what they ask represents what should be asked.

When you look at job application forms with a sense of history and an understanding of today's need, their incompleteness and content become incomprehensible. Application forms in general use today are not far removed from the old factory hiring-gate process. In the old days it was a buddy's introduction that got the factory foreman to invite an applicant through the gate. Today most application forms continue to give proportionately more space to "credentials" data—relatives, place of birth, schools and locations—the "stuff" that enables an employer to make an "objective" security check.

When it comes to work history, the space provided and the questions asked reveal purposes inconsistent with the name of the form. You are not asked what you do well and enjoy. Again you are asked for security check data: name and address of employer, supervisor's name, job description, and salary. Does the form ask what kinds of things you did best while in that job, or which parts of it you enjoyed most?

One of the application form's problems is illustrated by what happened when a regional group of government personnel officers met to develop an "updated" job application form. A newcomer, representing the younger personnel officers, suggested enlargement of the space allotted for the description of job duties and responsibilities. The senior participant said, "No use doing that. You'll just be giving more space for them to try and do a snow job. They all lie anyway, so why give them more space in which to do it?" The senior officer won.

Job application forms were designed as an aid to security checks during World War 1, not as aids to identification of skills that enable a person to do a job well. Neither purpose is well served when a single form is used to accomplish both objectives. To do so is similar to having the form say to the supervisor, "I vouch not only for the loyalty of this individual but also for the quality of the person's work."

The traditional job application form contributes little to the task of selecting the right person for the job. It has contributed to downgrading the fine men and women who make up the personnel profession. It has influenced job applicants to accept wrong assignments repeatedly, to accept job frustrations as being their fate, to see their jobs as providing little more than a way to earn money, to seek ways that will "beat" the job application system.

With relatively few exceptions, personnel professionals do not have high status in their organizations. Yet they are concerned and capable, with little authority. Certainly they are undeserving of the image represented by an advertisement in the *New York Times*. "DO YOU HATE PEOPLE?" read the caption. "Here is an opportunity to reject nine out of ten people you meet. Employment interviewer wanted."

Years ago I discussed practical changes in job application forms with a leading consultant firm and two professional researchers with the U.S. Civil Service Commission. The consulting firm implemented our discussion within three years and introduced it to some of its clients. My suggestion was that realistic employment data can be obtained by asking applicants to describe briefly what they felt were their greatest formal or informal contributions on their different jobs. I said this data is more significant than the description of a worker's duties and responsibilities. A person's feelings about the different parts of a job—which parts bring personal satisfaction and which parts the person regards as done best—provide information that bears on the individual's productivity and potential.

The Federal job application form SF 171 attempts to introduce this point by asking for "accomplishments on the job," overlooking completely the strong possibility that most people would read that as "What does your employer say you did well?"

The impact of the government employment specialists on job application forms deserves mention. Their attitude was demonstrated at a panel meeting for management interns.

I served on the panel with a government executive responsible for many operations of the U.S. Employment Services (USES).

I passed around one of its forms used to register workers with little education. The lines on the form were arranged for typewriter use, barely one-eighth of an inch apart. I pointed out that such registrants were likely to write with large letters and would have to cramp their style—almost to the point of unreadability—in order to use the form. This, I maintained, would tend to show their "fitness" for the dead-end jobs commonly offered beginners and the unskilled.

Seven years ago, when I first suggested that widening the space between the lines would [facilitate] writing and help improve the employability of these people, I was told the form could not be enlarged because that would make obsolete thousands of filing cabinets around the country. I overcame the shock of that and redesigned the form so that it folded and could fit the cabinets. But nothing has happened since then.

The executive responded, "I felt sure you'd mention that one. I'm pleased I can report that the change you suggested was approved four years ago. But we have not yet been able to locate the executive who can authorize the new forms."

All the interns laughed, but they didn't really think that was funny.

Traditional Views about Education

One of the myths of career planning is that a college or high school education is a passport to success. Don't interpret this as an attack on education. I was about to say that education never hurt anyone, but evidence is mounting that it has hurt the careers of some people. What is certain is that the impact of present-day education on employability and advancement is not nearly as great as previously supposed.

Ivar Berg says education is a major contributor to employee dissatisfaction. In a preface to Berg's book, Eli Ginzberg wrote that the continuing rise in educational requirements for jobs represents a bias that contributes to malfunctioning of the industry and government labor markets. He says, "The data [Berg's] proves overwhelmingly that the critical determinants of performance are not increased educational achievement but other personality characteristics and environmental conditions."

The **Wall Street Journal** *once reported on an experiment that highlighted the impact of job application forms and educational specifications. Its researchers developed data on the backgrounds of great engineering inventors who did not have college degrees. The list included Thomas Edison and Henry Ford.*

With essential name changes, this data was organized, giving the applicants' ages as 24, and put on standard job application forms and in résumés at a national engineering convention employment exchange section. Each of the more than 200 personnel recruiters received the data. Only one of the geniuses was offered an interview, and the invitation said that his experience warranted an interview but his educational background was weak and only engineers with a degree were being hired at the time.

A few years before that I had been one of 200 people attending a conference arranged by the mayor of New York City on youth employment problems. I pointed to the background of Thomas Edison, who did not complete elementary school, and suggested that employers look more vigorously for skills besides educational attainments. A personnel executive from an insurance company gave a sharp retort: "We can't afford the time to look for another Edison."

This is in line with current policy in many major companies whose studies show that about 80 percent of their managers graduated in the upper half of their college classes. Because of this track record, they have stopped interviewing college students who were not in the top half of their classes.

An engineer-student at Rensselaer Polytechnic Institute graduated at the bottom of his class. He was given no interviews by Corporation Personnel visiting the R.P.I. placement department. It turned out that he was too busy to pay attention to getting grades. He had designed, built, and managed the R.P.I. TV station; he worked two summers as consultant on communications for the State Throughway Authority; he sold hearing aids and earned $500 weekly to pay his way through college. The self-discovery process given in this book helped him get a pay rate 30 percent above the average for his class.

In the 1930s Walter Gifford of AT&T unintentionally downgraded 90 percent of college graduates. A study given to him showed that the company's most successful and productive professional and management personnel were in the top 10 percent of their graduating classes. He announced this to the world and started a rush for the top 10 percent. What he didn't find out until much later was that the statistics were collected from the research operation of Bell Scientific Laboratories and were not representative of the company as a whole.

Berg reports several research studies showing that high school graduates sometimes outperform college graduates in a variety of occupations.

One of my experiences, which caused me to lose an assignment associated with one of the first uses of a computer in selecting personnel, is related to the question of high school versus college graduates. The original specifications for one type of scientist were so loose that more than 500 names were spewed out by the machine. I was going over the specifications with some 20 Air Force personnel officers when the requirement for a college degree came up. The morning's newspaper carried a front-page picture of an Air Force colonel and a high school senior. The colonel was telling the student that the rocket the young man had designed on his own had proved operative. He advised the boy to go to college, get his degree, and then apply to the Air Force for a job. "We can use men like you," the colonel was saying.

I asked the group if they really could use such talent. They unanimously agreed they could. Then I said, "Since he already has proved he has the skills, imagination, and initiative you want, why not hire him now? You could use him part-time and pay his way through college part-time." No sale! They were adamant about the need for that sheepskin first.

The reach of job application forms is very long. It touches most other areas of work. The security-check approach is concerned with flaws, with identifying weaknesses.

Traditional Annual Employee Reviews

It "naturally" follows that annual personnel reviews, officially concerned with helping employees improve their careers, should generally become associated with a meeting between an employee and the supervisor so that the supervisor can point out the employee's weaknesses.

While I was consultant to the U.S. Air Force on career development, I was asked to comment on the annual appraisal report each supervisor was required to complete on subordinates. It was a four-page form with all-capital letters at only one point. That question was this: <u>WHAT IS THIS PERSON'S GREATEST WEAKNESS? THERE MUST BE ONE.</u> It also was the only item underscored.

Another experience, this time with the General Electric Company, involved 40 engineering supervisors. A consultant was giving them some exercises in the annual review process. I observed as one of the four groups of 10 tackled this problem orally and in writing.

Five members of each group served as the engineer, and five as the supervisor. They were told: "Using the data on the written pages, develop approaches designed to bring out the best in this subordinate and support or strengthen this person's best skills."

After some 30 minutes of discussion in each group, representatives of the four groups gave brief presentations of their conclusions. Each of the reports began the same way: "This person's weak points are. . . ." or "Areas where this individual really needs improvement are. . . ."

Before giving this assignment, the consultant reported on a study of the aftereffects of annual reviews that center on an employee's deficiencies. "The study shows," she said, "that following these reviews the individual's productivity drops for a minimum of three months."

The difference between that kind of annual review and the SIMS approach is described in detail later. For the present, it is enough to say that the System to Identify Motivated Skills helps employees identify strengths and develop a report to help them discuss how they want to improve or strengthen them. The supervisor discusses each report with each employee and verifies the data; the supervisor and the employees become jointly concerned with making the best use of those strengths throughout the organization.

Traditional Résumés

The evils spawned by the traditional job application form extend to job résumés. The traditional résumé begins with personal and family data, education, Social Security number, and so on, followed by a chronological listing of work experiences. Personnel departments approve of this approach. Obviously it is a traditional job application form slightly rearranged. It reports exposures to experience but not learnings from those experiences.

Just as obviously, supervisors can use only what a person has learned from experiences. The supervisor must think in terms of the future, starting with the present. Job application forms and résumés begin with the present and move into the past, nearly always overlooking whether a job was well done, or which parts of it were most enjoyable to the applicant. Such forms and résumés force guesswork into the hiring process and contribute to job frustrations, absenteeism, and turnover.

Accredited Psychological Tests

A book by Robert L. Thorndike and Elizabeth Hagen titled *10,000 Jobs* reports on a study of several thousand people given similar batteries of psychological tests by the armed forces and followed up over a ten-year period. The conclusion reported is that the predictions made with the aid of these accredited psychological tests were no more dependable than tea leaf readings. Other research has found that the great majority of such tests have a high margin of error.

Employment tests do have value when properly selected and administered, and when interpreted by professionals expert in their field. A series of studies have shown, however, that there is a middle-class bias in words and phrases used in the construction of most employment tests. Because of the controversy over tests, the U.S. Civil Service Commission has stopped using them for personnel selection.

The attempt to be objective or statistical about people is being abandoned. No person is objective. No person is objective about work. The movement has begun toward using subjective techniques like the System to Identify Motivated Skills to identify trends and patterns of behavior that release as well as identify a person's potential.

Building on Personal Successes

We can ask, without fear of disapproval, "What's wrong with me?" We would attract unfavorable reactions by asking, "What's right with me?" It is considered improper to suggest that a person study and learn from personal successes.

"Find out what you did wrong and never do that again" is believed to be a reasonable statement. If someone were to suggest that individuals find out what they did right so they could be sure to do it again, and better the next time, that would be seen as encouraging conceit.

Then there is the "balanced" approach to self-examination. This one calls for two lists—your strengths and your weaknesses or weak points. These are supposed to be balanced against each other to gain "objectivity" about oneself and decide what to do next.

Does industry look for this balance in its operations? Hardly. The growth company is concerned with successful products, not with balanced lists of strengths and weaknesses with the "hope" that unprofitable items will somehow be turned into profitable ones. Growth companies throw unprofitable items out of the line and concentrate on profitable ones.

Industry does almost the same kind of thing teachers do. They help students acquire the profitable "products" of great thinkers, experimenters, and workers. We are encouraged to learn from and build on their successes. But which student of electricity, for instance, would be expected to study the 5,000 mistakes Edison made before developing the electric light bulb? Which student of English would be expected to study the bad writers of Shakespeare's time to learn from their mistakes? We are taught insights of the great philosophers, their concepts that help improve the quality of life—and these emphasize being true to the best that is in you and advocate the release of the best that is in humankind.

The structures built to support and maintain old interpretations of good philosophies have become rigid and traditionalized. These structures are limiting progress and change, often because the meanings of the words have changed with time. G. K. Chesterton once said, "Tradition is democracy of the dead." The old structures often cost too much to maintain.

"Find out what you did wrong and never do it again." "Learn from your mistakes." Teachers and parents everywhere continue to use those statements. Yet they also say: "You get better at whatever you study." That makes it obvious that study of your mistakes should help you become better at making them.

> 66 *"Find out what you did wrong and never do it again." "Learn from your mistakes." Teachers and parents everywhere continue to use those statements. Yet they also say: "You get better at whatever you study." That makes it obvious that study of your mistakes should help you become better at making them.* 99

Historically, two concepts have been confused in the "learn from your mistakes" idea. The first is that you resist learning until after you admit you don't know; the second is that you do learn from experience if you study it.

Usually, it is a mistake or some failure that makes you admit you didn't know. But, since a mistake often is a painful experience, there is a tendency to avoid studying the pain and to move quickly into new activities.

Goal Setting

It is here that the concept of managing by objectives and the SIMS approach to goal setting offer much to complement each other. Incidentally, both find support in the Bible's suggestion that the past and present be considered in the light of desired goals: "Forgetting those things which are behind and reaching forth unto those things which are before, I press toward the mark. . . ."

Unless you know where you're going, it doesn't matter which road you take. Until you have decided on a goal, or the results you want, you cannot plan to attain it. Further, you are not free to change your mind about your goal until you have first made a decision.

> 66 *Unless you know where you're going, it doesn't matter which road you take. Until you have decided on a goal, or the results you want, you cannot plan to attain it. Further, you are not free to change your mind about your goal until you have first made a decision.* 99

If you are to manage your career or your department for results, you need to know not only the results you want but also the strengths, relationships, and attitudes that have brought you to the present situation and then support movement toward your objectives.

The usual approach to goal setting, however, is to estimate the organization's aims and estimate how dependably the available personnel can contribute to reaching them.

The organizational development facilitators help subordinates contribute to goal decision making, but usually the organization goals are the central theme. While individuals may be asked what their goals are, they usually are given neither time to clarify them nor instructions on how to evaluate themselves so that they may intelligently know their own goals. This is where the System to Identify Motivated Skills is making a major contribution.

Concluding Observations

Perhaps this has seemed like an angry chapter. It is more sorrowful than angry—sorrowful because all the personnel and organizational development techniques have been so long in gaining a foothold with institutions, and sorrowful because so many factors seem to have been required to produce the willingness to examine and try needed new human development procedures. These factors include chaos in educational institutions, undependability in product performance, urban violence, and major changes in life-styles.

The time has arrived when people can find opportunities for self-actualizing work. The procedures are available to enable each of us to use conflicts and disagreements as tools for sharpening our understanding and ability to cooperate for mutual as well as independent growth. At the same time, there is with us a huge weight of traditional beliefs that block the opportunities ahead. Those beliefs cannot be destroyed, but there needs to be a refocusing on beliefs that are real for today's world and tomorrow's. This will not be easy.

First, a few individuals in a group or workshop will experience renewal. Then these few will grow individually, into many groups, and within organizations. These groups already are in action. Organizational development and procedures to identify motivated skills are at the core of many strategies, and more are being designed to meet the needs of new groups.

Already included in the SIMS designs is one to aid in adult and youth career planning and guidance. Another seeks to increase awareness and use of individual competencies in a team. Still another is associated with midcareer renewal and the prevention of obsolescence. A fourth helps people recovering from drug/alcohol addiction. A fifth is concerned with the prevention of high school dropouts; a sixth relates to the recharging of persons who lose their jobs because of reorganization, downsizing, changes in technology, mergers, contract cutbacks, discrimination, lack of self-confidence, youth, or age. Another is concerned with the selection of training courses that are most likely to be growth-producing both to the worker and for the employer. The SIMS approach has also been used to identify activities for retiring persons and many others.

These workshops give people incremental knowledge about themselves, extra knowledge that helps them make wiser choices and become more stable in the freedoms that are increasingly theirs. The steps for gaining this knowledge are in the following chapters.

Strength is the starting point for
rebuilding any organization.

— Alfred J. Marrow (1905–1978)
Psychologist, businessman, author

Explore
for Your Strengths

This chapter shows you how to identify your strengths. Once you have followed these procedures and carefully taken the necessary steps, you will not need to explore your strengths again for another three to ten years. It takes time to do the process right, but the payoff will be more than equal compensation for the effort you expend.

Everyone has strengths or motivated skills. The System to Identify Motivated Skills (SIMS) will enable you to do what industry has learned it must do to have sustained growth: It will help you identify your "payoff skills," just as industry must identify its "payoff products." As you know, industry carefully explores the profitability of its products. It reinforces the most profitable or strongest ones and drops the least profitable or weak ones. You have to learn to live with your weaknesses, whatever they are, but industry expects its employees to try to improve their weaknesses. Of a person's strengths, they say simply: "You don't have to worry about them!"

Just as industry gives greatest support to its most profit-able products, so you should reinforce whatever is right about you, your self-motivated skills or strengths.

The right combination of your skills is what makes you valuable to your employer and "alive" to your friends and family.

> 66*The right combination of your skills is what makes you valu-able to your employer and "alive" to your friends and family.*99

The problems evolving from weakness will be dealt with in a later chapter. At this point we are concerned with help-ing you know what's right with you, helping you recognize how you developed what is right with you, the direction in which your right skills or strengths seem to be propelling you, and the power to change direction or accelerate toward the changes you want.

There is a challenge to that self-knowledge. It calls for you to accept the facts you know about yourself as limited to the past. Further, it calls for you to examine yourself, to identify new facts that can take you into a more enjoyable, meaningful, fulfilling future.

Since you really cannot be modest until after you have done something you can brag about, you must avoid boxing yourself in with old-fashioned ideas about mod-esty.

Many facts may be coloring your outlook. They could include such concepts as these: "I don't have the right education or training," or "Someone has it in for me and is blocking my progress," or "My experience is wrong." However true these considerations may be, new facts can be developed to help you clear these hurdles.

A grand old story illustrates the importance of knowing what your true strengths are, what is right with you. It also shows how the viewpoint of one person can, with the best of intentions, block the effectiveness of another. It's the biblical tale of the encounter between David and Goliath.

When King Saul heard the slender shepherd getting ready to challenge the giant call out, "Let me at him," or its equivalent, the king turned to the eager youth and said, "If you're going to make a try against that giant, the least I can do is give you my sword and armor."

Now, the king was a big man, and his armor was heavy. But David was obedient. He put on the armor, picked up the big sword, and found he could hardly move. He quickly dropped the sword, got out of the armor, and probably said the three-thousand-year-ago version of: "Hey, King, let me do my own thing. My strength is with my sling, not with your armor and sword." (Even in those days teenagers probably had little regard for the opinions of anyone over 30.) David then went ahead and did his own thing with all the strengths he knew the Lord had given him.

Virtually all modern business writers urge the identification and use of your strengths—Joe Batten, Peter Drucker, John Gardner, Frederick Herzberg, Abraham Maslow, Harry Levinson, Tom Peters, to name just a few. But they don't tell you how to go about identifying them.

The procedure outlined here for identifying your strengths is going to seem deceptively simple. But don't let the appearance of simplicity fool you. It is both worth while and important that you follow the steps carefully, but the method will not be easy. Just knowing what the steps are does not get you to know your strengths. Nor does that knowledge help you take the steps. When you know your strengths or motivated skills, that information won't even help you know the variety of benefits available.

Accordingly, while the rest of this chapter is concerned with helping you identify strengths, subsequent chapters will provide you with guidelines for using this knowledge to set and attain your goals. You will be shown how to adapt your strengths so that they can meet changing demands, and you will learn to renew and assess your career. You will be able to improve interpersonal relationships, build your career, increase your job satisfaction, and reduce stress on the job.

Understanding the Four Basic Steps

Here is an outline of the four steps you will need to follow:

1. Accept yourself as unique in the kind of excellence always growing in you.

2. Recognize that the elements of your excellence probably have been demonstrated from time to time in your life. This is most likely to have happened in the experiences you feel have been your achievements. (If you do not consider yourself an achiever, if you feel you have not really been successful, you will find some helpful thoughts later in this chapter.)

3. Believe that by carefully identifying and studying your achievements, you will find the pattern of skills and talents you have repeatedly used to make those achievements happen.

4. Concern yourself with using this pattern of your self-motivated skills or strengths, the reliable elements of your special excellence. This pattern of strengths indicates the kinds of career activities that are likely to be a part of your future achievements regardless of your job titles.

Keep in mind that the System to Identify Motivated Skills is not perfect. It is not a solution to all problems. It can help you trace through your own lifetime experiences and identify the skills that have been associated repeatedly with your development.

To oversimplify again, it is like studying and clarifying the best that is in you so that you may be more certain of improving on the best you have done in the past, being your best, and doing your best in the future with emphasis on meaningful, enjoyable, and productive activities.

Defining Achievement

What kinds of achievements should you study? What do you mean by an achievement? Will you give some examples of achievements? How about the person who feels that he or she is not an achiever? These probably are the kinds of questions you are asking now.

When your objectives are job satisfaction and continuing growth, and when your purpose is to be a self-actualizing person, the definition of achievement is this: An experience when you yourself feel you did something well, that you also enjoyed doing, and of which you were proud. When you had such an experience, you made use of some of the best that is in you. Accomplishments, getting things done, are not necessarily achievements, although they could be. An achievement, by our definition, has a feeling quality, an element of joy or satisfaction. Big and little achievements happen throughout life. One that very few people remember is the first time they did something important without the help of an adult—like putting on their own shoes.

Recognizing Kinds of Achievements

Achievement experiences could range from helping out at home or carrying someone's grocery bag at age 8, to performing volunteer work, to saving a person's life. They could include developing and installing a new management system or serving as successful director of a new profit center.

Life provides each person, including you, with opportunities to demonstrate some kind of excellence at different times. The elements of your excellence can be seen by carefully studying achievements you really had.

Nearly all of us have achievements that don't seem to amount to much in the eyes of others. But, by the definition given, it is your personal feeling about the experience that counts. Experience shows that achievements are color-blind and sexless.

Here are some examples of achievements recalled by men and women participating in several SIMS seminars:

When I got my first job . . . Persuading the boss to accept my idea; it saved a lot of time and money . . . When I got my graduate degree . . . Saving someone from drowning . . . Election to a national committee . . . Cooking my first meal for the family . . . Singing in the church choir as a child and winning several talent shows for my singing . . . Turned the company's profit picture around so that it gained 15 points on the stock market . . . Being the first in my family to graduate from college . . . Getting a good bonus . . . My athletic letter for wrestling . . . Organized and ran a successful bazaar . . . Elected president of a civic club, although almost all the members were more than twice my age.

It should be obvious from the list that almost every kind of activity can be someone's achievement. But there are people who do not feel they are achievers, and it is true that many people have been blocked from achieving a good part of the time. It also is true that many people are in jobs that do not fit them and understandably feel they have little to speak of as achievements in their jobs. On the other hand, some people delude themselves in thinking they are achievers, but those people are relatively rare. The next few paragraphs are designed to help those who feel they are not achievers.

If You Think You're Not an Achiever, ...

One client who wanted a career assessment responded to the question about his greatest achievements in this way: "Me an achiever? I've been making trouble for people from the moment I was born. My mother was 18 hours in childbirth with me."

This man was about 43, a graduate engineer who also had graduated from the Harvard Business School. His fourth good job collapsed from under him because of a company merger. His fifth job, at much lower pay, influenced him to compare himself and his record with the averages for Harvard Business School graduates. The comparison showed he was much below average for graduates in his class in status, salary, and satisfaction. He therefore labeled his $35,000-a-year job as both a demeaning experience and a failure. Because of this outlook, it was hard for him to see himself as an achiever.

Like this man, most people who say they are not achievers need to explore their experiences in a different way. There is no simple answer to persons who feel they are not achievers. But the examples that follow indicate some approaches.

The first point is this: Do not compare yourself with others. Certainly do not compare yourself with the average data reported by others.

You might have read many books when you were a child, as Malcolm X did; then you could have been turned off by some adviser or counselor, as he was, so that facility at reading didn't seem like much of an achievement.

On another occasion, while doing research on the use of SIMS as an aid to identifying skills among high school youths, I was working with my staff at the Bronx High School of Science. I asked an attractive girl of 16 what she considered her best subject. She said: "I don't have one." I had been told she had top honors in the school, so I said: "Now, stop kidding me. There must be some subject at which you are the best, some subject you like more than the others."

"No," she said. "I am about the same in all of them, and I do like all of them."

I was exasperated and trying to keep my cool as I asked: "What was your grade in math?" She said, "A hundred." "How about the other subjects?" I asked. "I got a hundred in all of them. I don't have a best subject. I'm first in all of them."

The point in telling this story is that persons with the highest levels of intelligence usually have the greatest possible choice of areas in which they can do well and therefore tend to be confused—until they become clear on the area where they are most highly self-motivated.

Another point brought out by this brilliant girl's case history is that, because being at the top of her class was customary for her, she was unable to take a repetition of that status as an achievement. It is a fact that most people take many of their greatest strengths for granted.

If You Think You're a Nonachiever, ...

Let's look into some other achievements of people who call themselves "nonachievers." You might have had to play Number Two to someone who always managed to beat you out for the credit, so that couldn't count as an achievement. You might have written a lengthy book, which was not published, so you might have a feeling of no achievement there. Perhaps an experience has just given you a sense of fulfillment, perhaps not. Again, you might feel that something you did which was your duty cannot count as an achievement because you were expected to do it.

You can look at it this way: Each day there is something you do that feels more satisfying or closer to being an achievement to you than other things you do that day. Each month and each year, some of your activities give you a greater sense of achievement than others. The experiences you have, the feelings of achievement you have, cannot be duplicated by anyone else.

Your feelings about your experiences make them real to you. Your experiences need not be related to your work.

An example of this is an electric company employee, let's call him Joe, who was sent in as part of an experiment on career assessment. Joe was a capable high school graduate who was tapped by the company as someone whose college education the company would finance. He obtained his degree and was employed by the company as a physicist. After nine years he seemed to be dissatisfied with where he was going, and the company was not sure what to do with him next.

He felt he had not achieved much in his job, but was able to list many achievements in community service. These related primarily to sports activities, such as coaching athletic teams of different kinds; his own participation in athletics; and his involvement in community affairs, which won him the chairmanship of a community program to study the impact of athletics on learning. He really wanted the chairmanship and did much campaigning in the community to win his election.

During the summer, the company assigned him to community relations services on an interim basis. He liked the work and performed it well. The company offered him a permanent staff position, but he refused and resigned. His next job was a promotional position with a leading manufacturer of sports equipment sold primarily to schools. He was happy in it because it provided an opportunity for him to combine his motivated skills in athletics and community contacts.

Joe's lack of a sense of achievement in his earlier jobs was rare because most people do have some achievements associated with their jobs. But the example does illustrate that the person who feels a lack of achievement in a job probably would be able to achieve in another one. Knowledge of yourself, your uniqueness, enables you to choose more wisely the kind of content you want in your job and to negotiate for that content with your present employer.

To begin with, you will need to accept the probability that you do have achievements and be prepared to remember what they are so you can examine them for their content of self-motivated skills.

Looking Inside Yourself

As you go on with this project of self-identification, keep in mind these three things: (1) the purpose is to help you take charge of your own career, gain career freedom, and identify areas for low-stress progress; (2) you initially are looking for a pattern of skills that have been essential in your past achievements and therefore are likely to be essential in bringing about future achievements; (3) an achievement is something you feel you have done well, enjoyed doing, and are proud of.

Seven Questions to Identify Ten Top Achievements

The first seven questions will take you about an hour to complete. There really is no time limit about it, so you don't have to rush. You do need to remember many of your experiences at different times of your life. The sequence of the questions is designed both to help your memory and to enable you to be reasonably objective in this most subjective activity of looking inside yourself.

1. What is the achievement that first comes to your mind? Describe it briefly in the following space and tell your age at the time it took place.

_____

_____

_____

_____

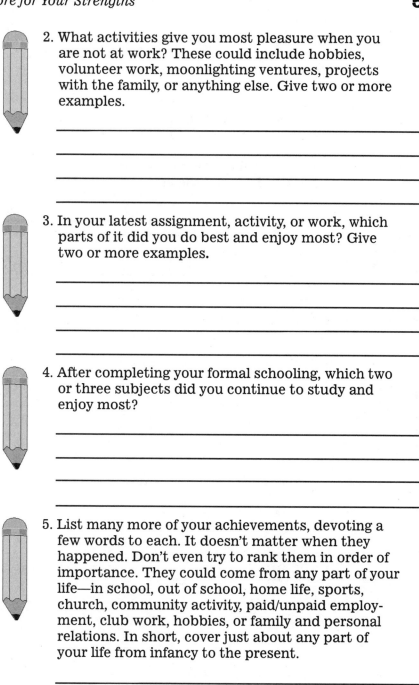

2. What activities give you most pleasure when you are not at work? These could include hobbies, volunteer work, moonlighting ventures, projects with the family, or anything else. Give two or more examples.

_____

_____

_____

_____

3. In your latest assignment, activity, or work, which parts of it did you do best and enjoy most? Give two or more examples.

_____

_____

_____

_____

4. After completing your formal schooling, which two or three subjects did you continue to study and enjoy most?

_____

_____

_____

_____

5. List many more of your achievements, devoting a few words to each. It doesn't matter when they happened. Don't even try to rank them in order of importance. They could come from any part of your life—in school, out of school, home life, sports, church, community activity, paid/unpaid employment, club work, hobbies, or family and personal relations. In short, cover just about any part of your life from infancy to the present.

_____

_____

_____

_____

If you have difficulty remembering, try to think of two or three achievements for each few years in your life. It may be easier if you begin with recent years.

For your convenience, try to list one achievement next to each of the following letters. Put down as many as you can, but come up with at least a dozen.

Work at this for about 30 minutes, take a break, and then come back and expand the list.

a. _____
_____
_____

b. _____
_____
_____

c. _____
_____
_____

d. _____
_____
_____

e. _____
_____
_____

f. _____

_____

_____

g. _____

_____

_____

h. _____

_____

_____

i. _____

_____

_____

j. _____

_____

_____

k. _____

_____

_____

l. _____

_____

_____

m. _____

_____

_____

n. _____

_____

_____

o. _____

_____

_____

p. _____

_____

_____

q. _____

_____

_____

r. _____

_____

_____

s. _____

_____

_____

6. Check the ones you feel are your ten greatest achievements. As you do this, you may think of some important ones that you left off the original list. In that case, simply add them to the list now or put them in the space below.

_____

_____

_____

_____

7. Carefully review the ten you have checked. Find the one you consider most important and write it down after the letter a in the list below. Continue this process until you have ranked the top ten in order of their importance to you.

a. _____

_____

_____

b. _____

_____

_____

c. _____

_____

_____

d. _____

_____

_____

e. _____

f. _____

g. _____

h. _____

i. _____

j. _____

Having completed these first seven questions, you have come a good way into the process that leads to identifying your strengths. But you need to do more before you are sure. You need to have more data in order to identify your strengths clearly and clarify your career goals. If your data is unrealistic, your goals can be fuzzy, and you could be heading for discouragement and failure.

Keep in mind that job freedom means your career is not static. It should continue to develop and grow throughout your working life and even into retirement.

Identifying Job Contributions

At this point a few people can begin to see their patterns of motivated skills. Thoroughness, however, calls for more patience, more exploration, and the collection of more precise data. You need to flesh out the skeleton you have begun to develop and add to it from data taken from only your work experience.

Your special world of work is not only work for which you have been paid. It includes volunteer projects, special assignments both outside and inside the scope of your job description, and other types of activities you feel may have been special contributors to the success of your organization. Accordingly, question 8 will ask you to list two or more contributions associated with each job you have had. This means you include a separate section for each of the different jobs you have held with the same employer. Each new piece of information you provide will help you see your pattern of skills or strengths more clearly.

8. In the column at the left, begin with your present job or most recent one and list the name of your employer, the assignment or a brief job description, and the dates of your employment. In the second column, describe briefly your most significant contributions on that job, as well as the outcome of those contributions. Where the activity is a special, short-term assignment, perhaps only one contribution example can be given; otherwise, try to indicate two or more contributions and outcomes or results. Please number your contributions for each job.

Employer/ Job Outline/Dates	Contributions and Outcomes or Results
_____	_____
_____	_____
_____	_____
_____	_____
_____	_____
_____	_____
_____	_____
_____	_____
_____	_____
_____	_____
_____	_____
_____	_____
_____	_____
_____	_____
_____	_____
_____	_____

Keeping a Career Planning Notebook

You may need additional space; for this purpose you should prepare a career planning notebook. You will need to refer to it from time to time as we move ahead, and you should make additional entries as you progress in the future.

It is probable that you have not carefully studied your ten greatest achievements in the order in which you rated them. This needs to be done for several reasons. Perhaps the most important is the need to think about your motivated skills in a more disciplined way, a way that permits you to project them into the future. Another reason for review is the opportunity it gives you to decide if one or more of the ten should be replaced by some other achievements that have since come to mind or if the order in which you rated them earlier should be changed.

A third reason is to help you recognize that when you do think of achievements in this way, you not only compare them with your best but also tend to think of some past mistakes, weaknesses, and failures. These are not being ignored by the SIMS process. Far from it. Because this process enables you to become more involved with your strengths in depth, you are likely to be more willing to look at and cope with your weaknesses and the causes of past mistakes and failures. That's why you should examine intensively your ten greatest achievements listed in question 7.

Examining Your Ten Achievements Further

Question 9, then, asks you to give more details about each of the ten so that in this process you are enabled to study them in sequence more carefully.

9. Give some details about each of these experiences in a way that will enable you to appreciate the skills you used to make them happen. Describe as clearly as you can what you did and what made it important to you. You also should list your age at the time.

Achievement No. 1

_____

_____

_____

_____

_____

Achievement No. 2

_____

_____

_____

_____

_____

Achievement No. 3

_____

_____

_____

_____

_____

Achievement No. 4

_____

_____

_____

_____

_____

Achievement No. 5

_____

_____

_____

_____

_____

Achievement No. 6

_____
_____
_____
_____
_____

Achievement No. 7

_____
_____
_____
_____
_____

Achievement No. 8

_____
_____
_____
_____
_____

Achievement No. 9

_____
_____
_____
_____
_____

Achievement No. 10

_____
_____
_____
_____
_____

Examining Career Disappointments

You need to look at some of your disappointments, too. So in question 10, you are asked to examine two or more of your greatest disappointments.

10. What have been two or more of your greatest disappointm chronological order; just write down and describe the first two or three that come to your mind as being important.

a. _____

_____

_____

_____

b. _____

_____

_____

_____

c. _____

_____

_____

_____

d. _____

_____

_____

_____

Examining Possible Blocks to the Future

11. Are you satisfied with your career progress at present? If your answer is no, write down two or more things that you feel may have interfered with your past advancement or that could possibly block it in the future.

Identifying Your Pattern of Skills

Now you are ready to begin selecting and putting together the information that shows your strengths.

Verbal Skills

If you are a management or professional person and have a degree or two, you are likely to have observed that the use of words was essential to making three or more of your greatest achievements happen. The use of words, then, is one of the items in your pattern of motivated skills. You may have demonstrated this skill in writing, or in speaking, in the form of intensive reading, or in some other way.

Memory

Memory is another item that may have been instrumental in the accomplishment of several experiences that you listed as your greatest achievements. This, too, would be an important element in your pattern of skills.

Sixteen Groups of Skills

A progressive way of identifying additional items in your pattern of skills is by grouping and classifying them. Here are 16 groups of skills or functions that combine to make up most varieties of jobs. Read through all of them.

1. *Design, color, shape things.*
2. *Calculate, count, keep records.*
3. *Observe, operate, inspect.*
4. *Write, read, talk, speak, teach.*
5. *Have hand skills: fix, build, assemble.*
6. *Analyze, systematize, research.*
7. *Invent, develop, create, imagine.*
8. *Help people, be of service, be kind.*
9. *Have ideas, sense of beauty, foresight.*
10. *Participate in physical, outdoor, or travel activities.*
11. *Manage or direct others.*
12. *Perform independent work; own or collect things.*
13. *Perform music, act, demonstrate.*
14. *Prepare foods, cook, do homemaking.*
15. *Persuade, sell, influence others.*
16. *Participate in science, engineering.*

Selecting and Ranking Certain Groups of Skills

Now check 4 or 5 of the 16 groups that you feel contain skills that must be part of any job you would really like and could do well.

From the groups you have checked, select the one or two items you feel are most important to you and underscore them. Think about them for a little while; then in the space that follows list in the order of their importance to you the items you underscored:

1. _____
   _____
   _____

2. _____
   _____
   _____

3. _____
   _____
   _____

4. _____
   _____
   _____

5. _____
   _____
   _____

6. _____
   _____
   _____

7. _____
   _____
   _____

Evaluating Further Your Selected Skill Groups

You can further evaluate the meaning of the items you have checked in the 16 sections that follow. Each corresponds with one of the groupings. This reading will help you appreciate the importance of listing in order the items you checked. (You will find two more cross-checks toward the end of this chapter and in the one that follows.)

First, here is an indication of the importance of listing the items in the exact order of their priority as far as you are concerned. If, for example, your first and second most important items related to groups 5 and 7, it would indicate that your achievements are mainly concerned with inventing, developing, or creating things that require some sort of hand skill. If the order were reversed (groups 7 and 5), it could mean the opposite—that you use some form of hand skill to invent, develop, or create.

Now read through the group descriptions.

1. **Design, color, shape things.** *These are commonly associated with "artistic" qualities, but the man or woman who cuts leather, hair, paper, or plastic materials to shapes, or selects colors that match or contrast, is not an artist in the usual sense. A surgeon has to know the shape of the organ or other part of the body on which he or she is working. The architect and the engineer must be able to see in their mind's eye the shape they are planning. The pilot must see the shape of the runway to set the plane down right. The bricklayer's ability to erect a straight wall is associated with talent to shape things. The smart dresser has a good sense of design and color.*

It is obvious that item 1 is useful in many different activities. The same thing is true of the other 15 items. Keep in mind how occupations change in content and requirements.

Just a few years ago, for instance, the telephone operator was concerned primarily with words, a good-sounding voice, and patience. Today, with the change from name telephone exchanges to numerical designations, the operator must be more expert in learning and remembering numbers. The requirement has moved from a mainly "words" occupation to a mainly "numbers" occupation— from primarily an item 4 job to an item 2 job.

2. Calculate, count, keep records. *This item is concerned with figures and their different applications. The bookkeeper writes down, adds, subtracts, and otherwise uses figures; mathematical researchers have figures as one of the reasoning tools; the computer programmer works with figures as symbols of simple or complex operations; building contractors and buyers use figures to help them estimate costs, time, and inventories; accountants and budget specialists use figures to help them record and observe business operation trends; actuaries and statisticians use figures to work out risks; economists use figures to help them forecast; homemakers use figures to keep track of their grocery money; and grocery clerks use figures to calculate what a customer should pay for food taken from their shelves.*

If you are very good with figures in one way, it doesn't mean you always will be good with figures in another way. The clerk who can press the right keys on a cash register quickly and accurately may not be able to add or calculate. That individual, however, may be able to press the right keys also on computer keypunch equipment.

3. Observe, operate, inspect. *Many people with good eyesight don't really see much of what goes on around them. The people who notice everything, who seem to be paying attention all the time, are safe operators of automobiles, airplanes, and machines of different kinds. They often are good inspectors, too, if they will concentrate enough.*

Number 3 is common to nurses and crane operators, to newspaper reporters, ornithologists, ball players, textile inspectors, and many others.

4. Write, read, talk, speak, teach. *All these activities involve words. Everyone uses words, of course, but not everyone would want the use of words to be central to his or her career. The crane operator needs few words, while the news reporter's whole job depends on the written or spoken word. Words are important to travel agents, salespeople, interviewers, almost everyone in radio and TV, receptionists, secretaries, most executives, teachers and trainers, dispatchers, advertising writers, and public speakers.*

5. Fix, build, assemble. *You may have a real knack for doing things with your hands. Some people like "big" projects—plumbing, working with heavy machines or bricks, and welding; others might work with small, light objects—woods, plastics, instruments, watches, or electronic components. (It is unusual for a person who likes to work with big, heavy things to like to work also with tiny, lightweight things.)*

Some people like to do this work on their own or with just one or two people at a time; others would just as soon work with people in a team or a group.

Here we are concerned with people who really enjoy repairing things, building or making things, or assembling products of different kinds. Such tasks might include sewing or knitting or fixing up a jalopy; making tools and dies; and working as dental technicians, jewelers, or mechanics. Surgeons, of course, need hand skills; diagnosticians rarely do.

Many technicians who work in laboratories, including certain types of hospital technicians, also fit into this category. Many who fit number 5 also might fit into number 7 as inventors and into number 16 as engineers and scientists.

6. Analyze, systematize, research. *These are the problem-solving, planning, research, and organizing skills. People with these skills want to know the why of things and often the how of things. Analysts tend to break things down into parts; sometimes they observe the parts and organize them into smoothly flowing operations—as systematizers.*

Researchers may be analytical too; yet, they sometimes also belong with the systematizers; they certainly aid both activities. And, while researchers usually work on their own, it is becoming more commonplace for them to work in small "teams."

The why and how qualities go into almost every area of progress. There are scientific systems, economic systems, and educational systems, all of which require analysis and research. The research usually goes further in the effort to find entirely new ways of progress. Researchers are the ones who get credit for the breakthroughs.

When the four-minute mile record was broken, it was done by a runner who had studied and researched the elements inherent in fast running. When the first jet plane was built, it contained an electronic system to help the pilot control the plane. When the wonder drugs started to be developed in greater quantity, they were based on patient analysis, biological research, and planning.

All planning is associated with analysis and research, whether the planning involves a budget, a career, a corporation, or a government forecast. Jobs associated with item 6 nearly always require considerable education or training.

7. Invent, develop, create, imagine. *New products, new ideas, and adaptations of products and ideas—these changes are taking place all the time in all parts of the world. There is constant demand for creative people, those who originate and modify for the better whatever exists either in actuality or in the mind.*

There are little changes and big ones. Someone thought up the idea of putting ridges on paper clips; someone dreamed up the idea of the ceramic nose cone that permits rockets to reenter the atmosphere.

The plumber has to work out different ways to bend or curve pipe around obstructions; the agricultural engineer works on adapting machines to replace unskilled farm labor or ways to use an old machine for a new task. The homemaker must discover new ways to cope with sudden breaks in the flow of electricity, new mixes and frozen food combinations, and new varieties of meals.

The teacher has to adapt to new ways in education, such as multimedia, the educational requirements of the changing job market, and the changed attitudes about education.

Creativity, imagination, inventiveness, adaptation—all are parts of progress in every occupation. These qualities often are needed to help find the right solution to a problem in human relations, as well as in the technical and scientific fields.

In some occupations these four qualities are vital to success; R&D engineers and scientists, technicians in experimental laboratories, creative writers and artists, and surgeons must be highly inventive.

Application engineers are developers of new ways to get things done. Architects are highly creative, as are many kinds of physicists, engineers, and researchers,

8. **Help people, be of service, be kind.** *The human relations occupations come into focus here. This category includes interviewers, nurses, receptionists, social workers, urbanologists, teachers, clergy and church workers, training directors, hotel and restaurant hostesses and headwaiters, social anthropologists, many types of public service jobs (politicians and others), some psychologists and doctors, recreation directors, many lawyers, counselors, and others whose work or business requires them to be dependent on direct people relationships. Enthusiasm, trust in others, and patience with others are part of this item.*

If you want to organize and lead a group, you must be willing to be of service to them. Many managers and executives are effective because of this quality; some are effective by virtue of their own excellence, being respected and blindly followed; some ensure their leadership by stimulating fear, but this is not a dependable or desirable approach.

Many new types of occupations will be opening in these "humanities" areas, especially as they relate to ecology and oceanic exploration, new forms of energy, and computer usage.

9. Have ideas, sense of beauty, foresight. *This item often is associated with number 7, sometimes with number 6, but it is also related to the beauty and harmony of life. Dealers in antique furniture, museum curators, and others who have sensed the greatness of life everywhere are likely to have checked this one.*

Farsighted business leaders and diplomats, outstanding men and women in the advertising field, as well as many of the creative people who are concerned with future programs and progress—these and others are likely to recognize their strength here.

The man or woman with creative or leadership ambitions is likely to have demonstrated some talent along these lines, perhaps through some action that required anticipating future events and planning for them intelligently. Ideas, sense of beauty, and foresight constitute an area that affects development in all occupations, in all industries.

An individual must have an idea before doing anything new, and often before doing anything at all. An idea is not worth much unless you do something constructive with it; then it becomes other than an idea. And sense of beauty— what is beauty to one "artist" may not be beauty to another. Foresight is another intangible; no manager is a success without this quality, a hunch, or intuition, about whether something will turn out right or wrong. Foresight is a capability that can be developed for practical applications. Like the other two, its applications affect the widest variety of occupations.

If you have reliable foresight, or have found your hunches consistently reliable in special types of circumstances, remember that it is a valuable contributor to your progress and success.

10. Participate in physical, outdoor, or travel activities. *Sports and athletics are not the only careers associated with this item. It encompasses the physical movements of people and things. It includes the truck driver along with the enthusiastic world traveler.*

The people who really like physical, outdoor, or travel activities include recreation directors, most people in the construction industry, traffic managers, travel agents, sailors, pilots, policemen, dancers, and many types of entertainers who must be on their feet for long periods.

Civil engineers work on outdoor piping, bridges, dams, and other structures; geologists and mining engineers, miners, airline stewardesses, astronauts, nurses—all are concerned with the movement of things and people, and to this extent all are concerned with item 10.

11. Manage or direct others. *This is the "leadership" item. Check this only if you really have experienced being the leader of a group, a gang, an association, a club, or something similar.*

Frequently this type of person is formally or informally elected to head up an activity. In early years it might be to run a prom or a dance, to head up student activity, or to direct something in the community. Three or more leadership achievements, ones that include managing others, indicate real strength in this item.

Many people dream of being leaders, while the concern here is with actual leadership, on a small or a large scale.

There are many colleges that teach leadership techniques. This is especially true of the nation's military academies, and of university schools of business administration. These techniques sharpen natural leadership talent, which shows up early in life. A study conducted by the

U.S. Air Force showed that more than 96 percent of the world's outstanding executives believe that leadership talent shows up early in life.

12. Perform independent work; own or collect things. *People who want to run their own business, including doctors and many other professional people, should check this one. There are many independent workers—individual researchers and inventors, independent consultants, plumbers who work alone, and others—who also will want to check this item.*

One of the main differences between the independent employee and the successful independent business owner is the way they think about things. The owner tends to think about "my property, my collection, the things I own." That kind of person concentrates on accumulating things, including money, in order to buy more things. Others who do not feel the same way, and that includes most of us, do not take the trouble to learn how to accumulate things for profit or to collect outstanding bills. (Most independent medical doctors now employ professional bill collectors, which helps explain why their earnings head the list among professionals.)

13. Perform music, act, demonstrate. *Shakespeare said we all are players on the world's stage. Some of us are not good at getting up before people and even shy from it, others are "ham actors," and a few are really good performers.*

There are many different kinds of performances, most of which do not take place on a regular stage. Just being tastefully dressed, or the deliberate opposite, is one kind of performance. Demonstrators in stores require performing ability. Receptionists in offices and showrooms must have a good amount of showmanship to do their work well; so must restaurant hostesses. Public speakers and politicians have to put on a show. Demonstration is part of a teacher's work. Briefings on products or reports are another kind of performance.

Let your achievement *facts, not your* dreams, *reveal whether you should check this item. There is no doubt about actors, actresses, and musicians; there is no doubt about twirlers, majorettes, and active class presidents.*

14. **Prepare foods, cook, do homemaking.** *Chefs, food managers, and dietitians are among those who would check this item. If your greatest achievements include cooking, making beds, home care, and baby sitting, you, too, should check this item.*

Clarence Birdseye, the inventor of frozen food processing, was proud of being the only boy in his high school cooking class. A White House pastry cook was extremely happy to tell about his first success in pastry making at the age of seven.

One high school student told of her pride in learning to make a bed with the linen so tight at the corners "you could bounce a penny off it."

15. **Persuade, sell, influence others.** *Obviously the salesperson will check this item. Not so obvious are the student negotiator who influences the administration to change a rule, the man or woman from whom others regularly seek advice and counsel or even consolation, the business manager, the peacemaker between conflicting groups and individuals, the scientist or other employee who "sells" an idea up the line, or the "smoothy" who has a knack for "conning" people.*

The persuasive arts extend to diplomats, clergy, teachers, training directors, business negotiators, politicians of all kinds, public relations counselors, lobbyists, advertising executives, and the whole host of persuaders ranging from the corner peddler to executives who negotiate multimillion-dollar national and international deals. All these and more have as a part of their work the job of persuading, selling, or influencing people.

16. Participate in science, engineering. *Education in these fields offers the best formal training available in the art of thinking for yourself. The history of scientific development shows that more than 5,000 years ago mathematicians were using many of today's mathematical formulas.*

History shows that scientific breakthroughs result when people of vision see beyond the limits of today's facts. So the scientific and engineering occupations are concerned with both the facts and limitations of today's knowledge and the uncovering of new facts that extend knowledge and its application.

Some scientists and engineers are concerned with making better applications of today's facts. These are the applied scientists and engineers, who range from architectural and atomic to zoological. These are the specialists and paraprofessionals in most branches of science and engineering. Some deal with people, some with materials, some with insects and animals or live things, some with rocks and metals—inert things that do not seem to move. (All things, of course, are moving constantly.)

The "applied" men and women usually work on ways to improve the applications of present knowledge as it relates to their field of specialization.

Other scientists and engineers are called "pure." These usually are researchers, the seekers of new knowledge, new types of information, and new natural laws.

Sometimes their discoveries are not appreciated for many years and lie buried in books, research reports, and even in old wives' tales.

The discovery of penicillin, the wonder drug that has saved countless lives, was recorded more than 20 years before its use became routine.

Now leading manufacturers of drugs and chemicals are financing expeditions to study the practices of jungle witch doctors to discover how to identify and use their healing abilities. Many scientists are studying the basics of acupuncture, genetic engineering, and other new areas.

Science and engineering are doorways to the future.

Identifying Your Ideal Career Pattern

When you have read through the descriptions of these 16 items, you can more carefully identify which parts are most important to you. Completion of each step that has been suggested so far will have established nearly all the data needed to sharpen your ideal career pattern. In reality, most people do not attain their ideals, but there is a better chance that you will, and even surpass them, when you know what they are. In addition, when you must make concessions and compromises in your career, it is helpful to know the points from which you are starting.

Recognizing Benefits from the Process

Greater Job Freedom

An example of what can happen, the benefit you can get from going through this process, was related by an executive of a leading computer manufacturing organization when he spoke about his self-imposed early retirement. He followed the basic procedures outlined in this chapter, then went to his boss to discuss modification of his job. He had considered his plan carefully. The changes he suggested would benefit the company as well as him personally. The boss agreed the changes would be beneficial, and they were made.

As a result, this executive said, he experienced his most enjoyable and productive five years with the company. In the interim the company instituted an optional early retirement plan. Our executive was advised, however, that he was expected to retain active status. Before making a final decision, he elected to explore his progress again in the same way he had five years earlier. The data he developed, combined with a financial analysis of the value of his retirement options, influenced him to request early retirement.

As a consultant he has since done some work for the firm he left, has developed several new tools to aid in the development of persons, has traveled extensively with his family, and claims he is enjoying life to a degree he had never before dreamed possible.

It took much courage for a man over 50, earning more than $60,000 a year, to ask for a radical change in his responsibilities. But he saw this step as a more viable way to greater job satisfaction and productivity than remaining within the confines of corporate structure. Both times he found increased job freedom through developing more facts about himself and more understanding of his options. He tested his dreams for reality, dropped his pipe dreams, and moved into greater job freedom.

Take these points with you when you leave Chapter 3: the System to Identify Motivated Skills is not a full, immediate solution. Its principles are easy to understand, but its practice takes time, patience, and careful search. Weaknesses are not overlooked in the search for strengths. Both are road markers that can provide useful direction on the highway to job freedom.

The person who follows the steps outlined in this chapter will select and reselect at least seven times the experiences studied and will therefore substantially reduce the chance of error in the selection used as the base for identifying motivated skills.

Greater Resistance to Bad Advice

When individuals complete this process, their memory will be so strongly refreshed that they will resist bad advice. This needs an explanation.

Such intensive thinking makes you acutely aware of your greatest achievements and sensitive to potentially discordant experiences. This can be compared to using a needle that does not fit the grooves of a record. Instead of good music, you hear a squeal. Inside, you really know what is best for you, what your strengths are. But, as with almost everyone else, your difficulty is recognizing those strengths and using them effectively.

Better Evaluation of Opportunities

Circumstances, habits, your attitudes and those of others, modes of life, and other elements limit your knowledge and alternatives. The sharp increase in self-knowledge that results from using the System to Identify Motivated Skills makes you more alert to, and more able to avoid, opportunities and special assignments that would not use or develop your greatest strengths. You then can turn down those opportunities, seek to modify them, or accept, knowing the failure risks that could be involved.

In short, job freedom means that you are free to take high risks and free to become a self-actualizing person through your work.

So far, the data you have developed has not been exposed to "hardheaded" examination. That is discussed in Chapter 4. There you learn to confirm the strengths you have identified, modify your understanding of them, and clarify those that are most important to your development.

To survive, the individual
must become infinitely more adaptable
and capable than ever before.

—Alvin Toffler, *Future Shock*

Enlarge Your
Attainable Dreams

Knowledge of your strengths is a bridge to the kind of life you want. It enables you to know your management style and how to adapt it to changing conditions. It can make it possible for you to take significant upward or lateral job leaps.

Now that you have identified some of your strengths, you need ways to enlarge your self-knowledge and to determine an attainable goal.

This chapter shows you three ways to do this yourself. A fourth way, of course, is to seek professional guidance. The procedures outlined here are based on my many years of career assessment and renewal work with thousands of professionals and managers.

About one individual in seven has a really good grasp of his or her personal capabilities and potential. Of the many thousands I have counseled, fewer than one percent overstated their capabilities; almost everyone else understated them. Understatement and undervaluation of self are common among men and women of higher intelligence. They often say, "I know my limitations," but they box themselves in with unrealistic self-evaluations.

> **66** *Understatement and undervaluation of self are common among men and women of higher intelligence. They often say, "I know my limitations," but they box themselves in with unrealistic self-evaluations.* **99**

Consequently, they frequently reap a harvest of job frustrations from tackling jobs they can do with little effort. Instead they can seek and accept challenges and opportunities that turn them on.

Preparing a Motivated Skills Chart

The first way to confirm your strengths is to prepare a motivated skills chart. In essence, you take each of your ten greatest achievements, one by one, and place checks opposite the skills, talents, and attitudes you frequently used in accomplishing them. For your guidance you will first find instructions for completing a chart, then a sample chart (page 89), and finally a blank chart for you to fill in (page 90).

Instructions for Preparing a Motivated Skills Chart

1. Review carefully the No. 1 achievement you described in Chapter 3.

2. Read down the list of skills, talents, and attitudes, and in column 1 of the chart check each one that you must have used strongly in order to make that experience happen.

3. The blank item lines at the bottom are for qualities you want to put into the list. A number of people, for instance, have wanted a "Curiosity" line; some have asked for an "Aggressiveness" line; still others have called for a "Recognition" line; and so on. When you add your own line, be sure to check each of your achievements against it.

4. Repeat step 2 for each of your other numbered achievements: column 2 for strongly applied skills, talents, etc., in achievement 2, and so on.

5. Add the number of check marks against each item listed, and put the result in the total column.

6. Assuming you have previously described your ten greatest achievements, circle the items you have checked six, seven, eight, nine, or ten times.

7. The more checks, the more certain you can be of the strengths of that item. Each person usually has four or more items in that top group; this is that person's pattern of strengths. (See the sample chart, which illustrates five achievements and therefore has fewer check marks.)

Achievements Used to Prepare a Sample Chart

The following five top achievements are presented to illustrate how to fill the Motivated Skills Chart with check marks. When you actually do the exercise yourself, you should list seven to ten achievements.

1. After 20 years out of college, I was accepted in an accelerated M.A. program. I reported in detail on my formal and informal education since getting my B.A., developed a study plan aimed at attaining my stated goal, and wrote a six-page report on my philosophy as it relates to my goal. The credits granted will permit me to earn an advanced social science degree within a year while working full-time.

2. Organized myself out of a job. While paid executive director of a national voluntary organization, worked with its board of directors to reach the decision it had outlived its usefulness. Then set up,

directed, and participated in a program that within three years gained the cooperation of its 4,000 members (many of whom I had trained) to merge it into another national organization at a final convention.

3. Designed a university program for mid-career development. Convinced the dean I could strengthen his special course by adding training in team building and problem solving. Designed and led the workshops for his special student body.

4. Trained Girl Scout leaders in how to start and carry on troop programs, health and safety practices, reporting procedures, and interpersonal problem solving.

5. Requested to write article on dramatic presentation techniques I developed. It was published, was well received, and brought me much personal comment.

It is, perhaps, of greatest importance to recognize the strengths that form the penetrating cone of your career style. In the chart you just completed are three or more items carrying the most check marks without which your achievements could not have happened.

For instance, if you are a controller and thoroughly enjoy your job, these three items may be analysis, figures, and observation. If you are a job-satisfied district sales manager, your three may be words, organization, and sales. If you are a national marketing manager, the three items may be ideas, negotiations, and leadership. A newspaper editor's three items may be words, writing, and analysis (a reporter's may be words, writing, and observation).

Attitude-type words in the chart include *energy drive, persevering, practical, things.* Yet the entire profile, as shown by the chart, reflects combinations of attitudes. For instance, curiosity can be derived by combining analysis and observation; a high degree of initiative could become aggressiveness, which, in combination with things and hard practicality, could indicate a style that may ignore people in order to get desired results. The profile on your chart deserves much attention because potentially it can be very meaningful to you.

MOTIVATED SKILLS CHART

INSTRUCTIONS: Start with your No. 1 achievement of your ten greatest achievements. In column 1, check off those items strongly applied in your No. 1 achievement. Do the same with your No. 2 achievement in column 2, and so on with the others. Remember that this sample chart illustrates only five achievements. When you consider ten achievements, all ten columns should have check marks in them.

	1	2	3	4	5	6	7	8	9	10	Total
Analysis											
Artistic					✓						1
Budgets											
Controls											
Coordination		✓		✓	✓						3
Creative			✓		✓						2
Design/art											
Details	✓	✓									2
Energy/drive		✓		✓							2
Economical											
Figures											
Follow-through	✓	✓	✓	✓	✓						5
Foresight	✓	✓									2
Human relations	✓	✓	✓	✓							4
Ideas	✓		✓		✓						3
Imagination		✓		✓							2
Individualist			✓		✓						2
Initiative	✓	✓									2
Inventive		✓		✓	✓						3
Leader		✓	✓	✓							3
Liaison		✓	✓	✓							3
Manager		✓									1
Mechanical											
Memory	✓	✓	✓	✓	✓						5
Negotiations		✓	✓								2
Observation		✓	✓	✓							3
Recognition	✓	✓	✓		✓						4

	1	2	3	4	5	6	7	8	9	10	Total
Organizer	✓	✓	✓	✓							4
Outdoors/travel		✓		✓							2
Ownership											
People	✓	✓	✓	✓							4
Perceptive		✓	✓	✓							3
Persevering	✓	✓	✓	✓	✓						5
Personnel											
Persuasive		✓	✓	✓							3
Planner	✓	✓									2
Policy making		✓									1
Practical	✓	✓		✓							3
Problem solving		✓	✓	✓							3
Production											
Programs		✓	✓	✓							3
Promotion				✓							1
Research	✓										1
Sales											
Service											
Showmanship		✓	✓	✓	✓						4
Speaking		✓	✓	✓							3
Systems/procedures				✓							1
Things											
Training	✓	✓	✓	✓							4
Troubleshooting											
Words		✓	✓	✓	✓						4
Writing	✓				✓						2

MOTIVATED SKILLS CHART

INSTRUCTIONS: Start with No. 1 of your ten greatest achievements. In column 1, check off those items strongly applied in your No. 1 achievement. Do the same with achievement No. 2 in column 2, and so on with the others.

	1	2	3	4	5	6	7	8	9	10	Total
Analysis											
Artistic											
Budgets											
Controls											
Coordination											
Creative											
Design/art											
Details											
Energy/drive											
Economical											
Figures											
Follow-through											
Foresight											
Human relations											
Ideas											
Imagination											
Individualist											
Initiative											
Inventive											
Leader											
Liaison											
Manager											
Mechanical											
Memory											
Negotiations											
Observation											
Recognition											

	1	2	3	4	5	6	7	8	9	10	Total
Organizer											
Outdoors/travel											
Ownership											
People											
Perceptive											
Persevering											
Personnel											
Persuasive											
Planner											
Policy making											
Practical											
Problem solving											
Production											
Programs											
Promotion											
Research											
Sales											
Service											
Showmanship											
Speaking											
Systems/procedures											
Things											
Training											
Troubleshooting											
Words											
Writing											

Participating in a Self-Appraisal Team

The second way to start expanding and sharpening your self-understanding is through the formation of a self-appraisal team. The process was detailed in EGO, a copyrighted game. The "team concept" uses the System to Identify Motivated Skills to help a small group of people (four or five) appreciate one another's strengths and also to support one another. It supplements and can expand the information gained from the chart.

Here is how the process works. Three people you respect listen to you describe a few important experiences you are proud of. They will help you see the strengths that made them happen. You probably will feel very good about what they say, especially since the rules ban delving into reasons for doing things. In addition, although a few of the strengths mentioned probably will not be right, some comments will suggest talents you have previously been unaware of. This extra breadth and depth of knowledge can open new directions and practical vistas to you.

These comments will strengthen your self-confidence. They can deepen your self-understanding to such a degree that you can get rid of hangups that might have been blocking your progress.

This is what happened at one manager development conference. The new treasurer of a major company, a man in his mid-thirties, felt that he was the least successful of those present. He volunteered to be the first to have his strengths identified. All his promotions, he said, had come despite his not wanting them, even strenuously opposing them.

Six of his greatest achievements hid one common denominator: leadership responsibilities, but he could not remember assuming a leadership role before he was 12.

I pressed him on this point, insisting that his leadership skills must have been demonstrated at an earlier age. According to a study by Dr. Joseph Krieger, more than 94 percent of the "natural leaders" demonstrated their skills at an early age.

*Then I risked saying—and it is a risk that should be under-
taken only by professional psychologists—"There must be
something, even if it involved you in something mischie-
vous, or something of which you are not proud." He then
told about leading a fun-seeking gang. They would light
firecrackers on people's doorsteps, ring the bell, and hide to
watch the reactions.*

*The noise was not loud enough to satisfy the group, so he
had them empty powder from some of the fireworks into a
bag to which he had attached a fuse. The bag exploded in
his face before he could throw it. He wasn't proud of his
unhappy experience. He was injured and hospitalized for
months. "But," he concluded, "that's a leadership experience I'll remember for the rest of my life."*

*Our discussion of the incident showed what a deep impact
it had had on that man. He unconsciously avoided all
leadership opportunities and shunned promotions. He told
how promotions continued to come despite his opposition.
His boss had recently told him he was the new treasurer of
the company and that there would be no argument since his
name had already been painted on the door.*

*Deep down he had really wanted those promotions. His
pattern of leadership continued to emerge despite his
emotional block. Now, through group identification and
affirmation of his skills, he was able to surface the psychological block and challenge and overcome it.*

The team approach is enjoyable, instructive, and affirm-
ing. The materials needed are readily available: a dozen
sheets of letter-size (8 1/2″ x 11″) paper for each participant, a large sheet (about 20″ x 30″) of paper, a dark
crayon or marker, and a roll of masking tape. (As mentioned, four is the ideal number of participants. However,
as many as six can make up each team.)

If you followed the instructions in Chapter 3, you already
have done some of the following.

1. Each participant writes down a dozen or more of his or her achievements, using this definition: *An achievement is something you feel you have done well, that you also enjoyed doing, and of which you are proud.* Write down a few words about each.

2. Check the seven achievements you feel are of the greatest significance to you.

3. Identify the seven in order of their importance to you. Let "A" be the most important, or greatest; "B," the next; and so on.

4. If the seven include any you feel you just cannot talk about, substitute one from the remainder on your list and move the others up a notch.

5. Write your "seven" achievements on the large sheet of paper, using the crayon or marker. Be sure to start with your "A" item and list the others in sequence.

6. Select one member of the group to be the "up front" person.

7. This person attaches the large sheet of paper to a wall or door with the masking tape. The individual reads off first the "A" achievement, adding sufficient detail to indicate what the person did to make it happen, and what made it seem like an achievement. (Others in the group may ask the person up front for clarification, but, again, they may not ask *why* something was done.)

8. The individual before the group continues until at least four of the seven have been described.

9. The other participants listen carefully, writing down the skills they feel the one up front must have used to make the experiences happen. This writing should be done after each achievement is described.

10. Each participant now reads aloud his or her list of skills to the person up front.

11. The person before the group listens to all the readings and then collects all the skill sheets, possibly commenting briefly on what has been said.

12. Now the second person in the group goes up
front, and the game continues until each person
has had a turn up front. Then all in the group
discuss how they feel about the experience and
what they learned about themselves and one
another.

The person up front usually requires 15 to 20 minutes, so
the group should set aside two hours for the project.

Some groups prefer to have two persons up front one
afternoon or evening and two or three during a second
period over a weekend.

The team approach is recommended for any group of
people who want to get to know one another better and
increase respect for one another. Each participant is
expected to make only positive, honest suggestions on
skills. The fact that each member is an amateur in this
application of the System to Identify Motivated Skills
gives the person up front freedom to accept or reject any
suggestion. It also makes the participants feel freer to
make suggestions, even if they sometimes make mistakes.

What will you get out of it? You will get several objective
views of what skills you used to make your achievements
happen; these are likely to include some that you tend to
overlook. The suggestions are certain to stimulate your
thinking about your skills and achievements and your
understanding of them.

A few people are so hung up about modesty that it's hard
for them to participate in this exercise. Much value can be
derived from the project, especially when the group involves people who have completed the self-examination
recommended in Chapter 3. As the commercial said, "Try
it, you'll like it."

Using Functional Self-Analysis

The third way to enlarge your self-knowledge and deal
with reality is through *functional self-analysis* (FSA).
FSA is essential to goal setting because it enables you to
explore your career objective on paper and examine its
practicality.

John Jamison, a research project manager, once supervised as many as 15 scientists, subprofessionals, and an administrative staff. His greatest achievements depended primarily on persuasiveness, as shown in his briefing and liaison activities and in his negotiations for services and budget approvals. Other "greatest" achievements related to winning awards and competitions; developing reliable cost and operating data; and developing solutions to a wide variety of technical, interpersonal, and operating problems. In all these he worked independently, usually without supervision. He accomplished all the tasks assigned to him, as well as projects he himself initiated. One of his greatest achievements was a research project. None of the achievements mentioned supervision or management.

He performed his project management job well but said the administrative detail drove him up the wall. He often wished he were just an independent contributing researcher again, but he felt he couldn't afford to give up his status and salary level. Therefore, he maintained his supervisory role.

John had to believe—really believe—that his company wanted him to make the fullest use of his best skills and therefore would be willing to modify his job content from time to time. Only then did he become open to seeking another opportunity within the company.

He came to understand his motivated strengths, as differentiated from his formal training and experience. He had not seen, until then, how his doctorate could prepare him for anything other than some kind of research position. He accepted, albeit cautiously, the evidence that he would be buying more and more frustration as long as he pursued administration and research. He was deeply worried about status and salary.

He set tentative goals based on functions he believed and could prove he performed well and also enjoyed. These involved meeting people, solving scientific and technical problems, being persuasive, working out cost data, and being somewhat competitive. Through FSA he was able to prove that he had the required experience and the quality of results in each of these areas, even though the results were not always job-related.

The data he developed assured him that these skills could be valuable to the company. His task was to have his employer create a job where he could perform more effectively without suffering a reduction in salary or status.

He had a strong hangup about status. As far as he was concerned, the word "salesman" had no status. He discussed his problem with sympathetic executives who recognized the potential company benefits of his proposed move. They helped him make two lateral shifts, and he became one of the company's best marketing representatives.

This case history shows how the SIMS approach and FSA helped not only an individual but also a company. John was becoming disillusioned and unmotivated. His work was beginning to reflect his frustrations. He had been considering "running away" but was tied to his pay and title.

The process described here helped him reinvent himself, break away from his preoccupation with job titles, and become open to applying his best skills to responsibilities within the same company. He used techniques (described later in this book) to establish power contacts within his corporate structure. When the company agreed to help him, for his good as well as for its own, he patiently pursued his objectives. The payoff took two years of careful work and considerable self-study and planning.

When people know where they are going and feel comfortable about getting there, they usually will be patient in working things out. The higher up you are, the more patience it usually takes.

66 *When people know where they are going and feel comfortable about getting there, they usually will be patient in working things out. The higher up you are, the more patience it usually takes.* 99

Functional self-analysis will help you see where your present job is leading, how it relates to effective use of your motivated skills or strengths, whether there is good reason to consider a change, and what might be done to bring about the change. Beyond that, FSA enables you to discuss your career plans more intelligently with your superior, especially during your annual performance review.

Describing the Decisive Experience for Career Development

Now, describe the one experience you feel has contributed most toward your career development.

_____

_____

_____

_____

_____

_____

_____

_____

_____

_____

Listing More Strengths or Motivated Skills

List below three or more of your strengths or motivated skills. Don't be concerned if the items you list do not seem to be related to your present job.

1. _____

2. _____

3. _____

4. _____

5. _____

6. _____

Describing the Ideal Job

Now, taking into account all you have written in Chapter 3, try to describe briefly the next position you would like to have. You could, of course, want to keep your present one but expand your scope of responsibility.

_____

_____

_____

_____

_____

_____

Indicating Possible Blocks to That Job

Do you see any possibility that people, events, or other factors could stop you from getting that job? If so, write down the main details.

_____

_____

_____

_____

_____

_____

_____

Creating Function Sheets for the Ideal Job

Your "ideal" job would have certain responsibilities and functions or activities. List six or more functions that you feel must be in the job if you are to derive satisfaction from it.

1. _____

2. _____

3. _____

4. _____

5. _____

6. _____

7. _____

8. _____

9. _____

10. _____

Write each function on a separate sheet of blank, letter-size paper. Take one of these sheets and write on it two or more experiences that show your highest level of effectiveness related to that function. Give as many experiences as you like, using additional paper as needed.

For instance, if the function you are working on is writing, you might want to give examples like these:

1. The 20-page report I wrote on project X was not only commended by my boss but also duplicated and sent around to 200 policymakers in all divisions. I was given permission to modify it to conceal confidential data and submit it to a professional magazine. This is under way.

2. I am responsible for nearly all the technical correspondence of this division. This means up to 200 letters each month, rarely less than 50, most of them requiring intense concentration on highly complex details.

If the examples of writing were along the following lines, they would have very different implications; they probably would apply to a professional novelist or copywriter.

1. Finally completed the 400 pages of my book; it was edited and put into type, and I have just read the first page proofs. It is scheduled for publication about four months from now.

2. The 32-page brochure I wrote on subject X won tremendous acceptance at all levels of our agency and outside. The first printing of 100,000 already has been exhausted, and a second run is under way. Many compliments have been received for this job.

The statements can be of any length, but there should be at least two for each function. A loose-leaf binder may be helpful in this part of the project. For some functions, you may find no more than one example. For others, you may have four or more. Keeping the sheets in a separate binder will make it easy to refer to them and to add examples to each item.

For some functions the examples will be short; for others they will be quite long. For some functions, you will have to strain to find examples; for others the examples will come easily.

There is likely to be some overlap among the examples you put down for the different functions. For instance, the first example for writing, the 20-page report, could have been a study of the maintenance systems at five facilities. In such a case, this example—stated in different terms—also could fit into the functions of "field studies" and "maintenance management."

Organizing Your Function Sheets

When you have completed your statements on each of the "function pages," organize them so that the one with the most examples and statements is at the front, the others following according to the number of examples (the fewer the examples, the nearer to the back the sheet goes).

This arrangement will show where your preferences are, how much weight you give to each of your interests, in which areas you tend to expend your greatest efforts.

The FSA data also will indicate (perhaps by your omissions) your unmotivated skills, areas where you tend to give least effort, perhaps even where you need to be reinforced through education, training, private study, or experience.

This knowledge also gives you supporting facts for any requests you make for additional training or new opportunities.

When you are aware of your level of development in the different functions you ideally want in your job, you are much clearer on how you want to develop. Your new knowledge does not impose limitation; rather, it opens up more possibilities.

> 66 *When you are aware of your level of development in the different functions you ideally want in your job, you are much clearer on how you want to develop. Your new knowledge does not impose limitation; rather, it opens up more possibilities.* 99

This clarification is most important to you. Suppose your facts show a low level of performance in one function and the examples given are more than five years old. This could show that you really have been turned off from that function, and that you really have chosen not to be motivated in that area. Or it might show that you have been diverted from a strength activity.

In the latter case, recognize the difference and use the knowledge. When you demonstrate to yourself that you are unmotivated or turned off by a particular function, don't try to kid yourself that you might acquire a liking for it. You my want to work at that function; you may even need to work at it. But, if it turns you off, that's the way it is.

It is questionable whether the majority of managers and professional people are self-motivated. It is certain that too many of them are frustrated in their jobs. Sometimes the combination of talent, effectiveness, and a grateful boss can turn into disaster when an individual is not aware of one's own strengths and levels of competence. This happened to Bill, vice-president in charge of merchandising for a multimillion-dollar company.

Bill started as a trainee in an accounting department. He got into cost controls and systems. In six years he moved up fast. He devised inventory techniques that released substantial sums for profits and capital; created a salesperson's pay system that provided good incentives yet controlled spiraling salaries; and sold management on his new credit management system, which cut delinquencies. These were big things; and, as a reward, he was made vice-president of merchandising.

Bill had related well to people but had never supervised them. He had worked on problems, but they all had involved independent contributions. He could come up with ideas, but in the past they had always involved figures and systems. He wasn't so much challenged by the idea of being V.P. as he was hypnotized by the status and especially by the salary. After two years of increasing confusion, the company released him without realizing what had gone wrong.

Bill didn't know either. He felt "they" had done wrong by him. But the ultimate responsibility for success or failure is one's own.

When you talk about your career, the responsibility for its success, failure, or drift is with you. Other people and circumstances do have some influence; but when you prepare for your "good luck," you find it.

The FSA process you have been through gives you the ability to recognize the true location of your career payoff. It gives you the freedom to look for ways to change those parts of your job that turn you off, or at least to look for ways to reduce them. Later we discuss how to do this.

Understanding the Benefits of Functional Skills Analysis

Can you now see some of the benefits you gain through the increased knowledge provided by FSA? Here are some of them, not necessarily in order of their importance:

1. You know the key elements necessary for determining your career goals. (Chapter 5 explains this process in detail.)

2. This information will help you make better judgments about the educational courses, training, or experiences that would be most helpful to you in reaching your goals.

3. You know much better where and why you have been encountering many of your frustrations, and you will have some ideas on what can be done to improve the situation.

4. The essential elements for goal setting, knowledge of what you have to work with, come into sharper focus.

5. You are better able to compare your job as it really is against what you would like it to be.

6. You know how to use your strengths to get greater satisfaction from your job.

7. You can separate the reality of your potential or growth direction from the fantasies that lead so many people into job frustration.

8. You have the necessary data to support the career goals you will discuss with your boss during your appraisal interview.

Probably as important as any of these is your knowledge that your strengths are adaptable and are continuing to develop. They are flexible enough to meet the demands of new careers that accompany rapidly expanding knowledge and technology. You have increased your sensitivity to the kinds of activities that are likely to challenge you and make the best use of your strengths in the future.

Also, by omission, you are sensitive to the kinds of activities at which you risk doing poorly unless you work with extra effort and can put up with the dissatisfactions.

You can undertake high-risk functions, but you now are able to recognize the nature of the risks and, hopefully, gain commensurate rewards.

Overall, your heightened self-interest helps you make more intelligent career decisions and gives you the flexibility to change your mind when new opportunities come along.

> **66** *Overall, your heightened self-interest helps you make more intelligent career decisions and gives you the flexibility to change your mind when new opportunities come along.* **99**

After you complete your FSA pages, try to write a description of the kind of job that will use your strengths, that will enable you to be even more effective in the functions in which you are most competent.

Such a job might not exist. But perhaps it can be created. At worst, you may be able to modify your job description so that your job makes better use of what you have to offer and gives you more satisfaction and fewer frustrations.

Understanding your strengths and career style certainly points to your next as well as future career goals. But goal setting involves more than just your personal wishes. It includes many contingency items, such as company and department goals, your nonworking goals, and the concerns of your family. The next chapter shows you one practical way to intertwine these goals.

Consider these facts before moving on to the next chapter. It is possible to test on paper the kind of job you believe you want. First, you must be reasonably clear about your strengths. This chapter gave you three ways to clarify them, including a chart to develop a profile of them, and the EGO game concept.

With strengths sharply identified, you can make an educated guess about your ideal job and the obstacles that could be in the way of getting it. This analysis tends to reveal the kinds of education, training, and people relationships that may have to be acquired. It also leads to examination of the functions that must be performed in your "dream" job.

Carefully study your own experiences as they relate to the functions involved. Are you ready to fulfill your "dream" job requirements or make the modifications that practicality requires? Can you become a self-motivated professional or management person capable of meeting the challenges associated with job satisfaction and growth?

*The world steps aside, makes a path
for the man who knows where he's going.*

—David Starr Jordan
First President of Stanford University

Compare Your Goals with Others' Goals

Suppose you are in the advertising business with a great reputation for coming up with workable marketing ideas and plans. You are not happy about being just creative; you want to have more of a hand in making things happen—the kind of experience you listed as your greatest achievement. Your salary is good, so a change might involve some temporary drop in pay. You also would like to be less on call every hour of the day. Once in a while you'd like to have a six-week vacation, although you wouldn't mind doing a little business on the trip.

In brief, that's the outline of the goals set by a 40-year-old marketing executive with an M.B.A. The main functions he could do well included meeting people at all levels; persuading, selling, and negotiating; coming up with creative ideas that proved practical; organizing and planning marketing approaches; training personnel; and directing marketing operations.

Reshaping an Occupation

As a professional consultant himself, he knew the value of objective counsel, so he hired an executive career specialist to help him think things through. In his position he frequently heard about various types of job openings. Because his alumni association was active, he occasionally had been able to help others locate jobs. Among the 30 or so openings he knew about was one for a placement director at his graduate school.

His career consultant suggested that this might be a good job for him. "The quality of your alumni is recognized as the highest. There's considerable demand for men of that caliber," he said.

The marketing executive protested. "I don't know anything about placement work. I had only one course in personnel at graduate school."

"The problem is one of merchandising, or marketing," the consultant said. "With the quality of personnel you have to offer, all that is needed is to build up the demand for them. I see it as a classical merchandising problem."

"I think you're right. But I can't see the dean buying my services on that basis. I know him quite well, and he just won't buy that," was the response.

"I'm acquainted with him, too," said the consultant. "And I believe he will buy the idea if you approach him not on the basis of the placement job but on the basis of raising funds.

"If you create a demand—as you can—it will drive up the beginning salary potential of your graduating students. When it is known that the demand you created is largely responsible for their higher pay, the school could tap them sooner for contributions.

"View the job as that of a fund-raiser who uses marketing techniques to effect quick, high-pay placement of graduating students, as a result of which they make larger and quicker contributions to fund drives."

> *The marketing executive smiled slowly. "The dean will buy that." The man applied his strengths to a job he professed not to know. Some years later, he wrote a book on his success in college graduate placement.*

This case history shows that he could not have attained his own goals without full consideration of the goals of the dean, as well as the needs of the graduating students, who became his "merchandise."

He identified his goals and the goals of others in such a way that he could fill the requirements of a job he would otherwise not have considered. He changed many ways of fulfilling the job requirements; or, we might say, the job was changed—re-created—around his special skills. (This is one example of job enrichment or reevaluation.)

Because almost all management jobs are reshaped by their occupants and because it costs many thousands of dollars to recruit and train a manager, companies frequently are willing to reshape jobs to hold or get good people. But they must feel first that both the organization and the individual will benefit from job reshaping. The case history of the data processing company executive, discussed in an earlier chapter, also illustrates the willingness of organizations to reshape jobs.

Considering Your Own Goals

Your starting point must be your own goals. You need to determine what they are. Surely, you must consider company goals too. Essential to cooperation between you and your company is the recognition that your own goals don't stand alone, but you don't begin by trying to identify and meet the goals of others. Only after you have made up your mind about your own goals will you have the freedom to change direction.

Reviewing the Past

In order to be realistic, and also to dream, you need to

recognize what your goals are to be based on, what is the substructure of the building you plan to erect. As Shakespeare said, "The past is but prologue." There is a past; it is a prologue to your future goals. It is necessary to know the structure of that past so that you can build safely on it.

Too many people set goals without trying to find out what foundations they have established to support new developments. Many people try to base new goals merely on the avoidance of past mistakes. You already have done the necessary exploration. You already know the strong pillars of achievements and strengths that can support a structure of new goals.

> 66 *Too many people set goals without trying to find out what foundations they have established to support new developments. Many people try to base new goals merely on the avoidance of past mistakes.* 99

On Rectors and Vestries

In the Episcopal Church the man who might be called "manager" of a local self-supporting operation or "profit center" has the title *rector*. His job description usually includes responsibility for the operation of a small school system, sometimes for the construction of a facility costing maybe four hundred thousand dollars, and working out the financing for the facility. An ex-officio member of a board of directors called a *vestry*, he assists in problem solving for the 200 to 500 families in his region and is the liaison between his region and a number of outside agencies.

For most of this management work, he is given very little training. So, from time to time during his career, he needs to review how he is doing to determine what he could do better. Most clergymen and managers are in the same situation. Their jobs have grown around them, and these managers are learning as they struggle to keep up with progress. For most, goal setting and guessing have been almost synonymous.

Case History: A Rector and a Vestry

That brings us to the next case history. A couple of months after a rector had completed a career assessment and renewal seminar, he attended the annual meeting of his vestry.

A retired admiral on the board of directors said, "One thing we'd better do before we go very far. We'd better make note of all the damn fool mistakes we made last year so we make sure we won't do them again. I've been on this board for 16 years, and I must say we made some real bloopers in the past year."

The board members nodded in agreement. The rector, filled with the excitement of his seminar, said, "Suppose, before we do that, we look at the kind of foundation on which we can build, the areas where we know we have been effective, even successful. Suppose we first examine our achievements of the past year to see if we can identify the style of program we know we can handle and one in which our people will participate. Then we can set some goals for the new year and build in some protections against the mistakes we made last year."

The rector said that this turned out to be the first time in his ten years there that the annual vestry meeting had been completed in one afternoon. All the past ones had involved grumblings, blamings, accusations, and other varieties of confrontations over the course of three afternoons or more. Annual planning had resulted more from feelings of exhaustion—a "let's get it over with" attitude—than from enthusiastic, coordinated thinking. The following year turned out to be the most active one in a long time, and activities received the best support ever, both in the number of participants and in the amount of financial contributions.

The first step, then, to intelligent goal setting is a review of your past achievements. You probably want more like them, only better ones. You have already written down your greatest achievements, and it will take you less time to read them than to try to remember them. Reading them and also reidentifying the strengths you have listed will refresh your knowledge of the structure on which you have to build and also of the powers you have to take you where you want to go. Then you can start projecting your plans.

Projecting for the Future

Some men and women prefer to project for only a few months, some for a year, some for much longer—three to five years or more. You can use the principles that have helped every successful company. They apply both to the long and the short term. Here is the process for one-year goal setting.

A Pragmatic Process for One-Year Goal Setting

Initially, dream! Dream a year ahead. A year from now, what would you like to look back on as an accomplishment during the past 12 months? Let your dreams include work, family vacations and weekends, savings, career developments, hobbies, relationships, community activities—all aspects of your life. Use your career notebook. Label a fresh page "12-Month Goals." List your goals in a vertical column, using as many pages as needed. Allow ample time. The investment will pay off in achievement and help you surpass your goals.

If you're cynical about achieving your dreams, keep in mind that the concern with reality inherent in this process soon will establish a practical approach. You need to start with hopes and dreams. More of them may be attainable than you think if you set your goals creatively.

When you have completed your list (you can always add, delete, or modify goals), start a new page in your notebook. Head this page: "What I must accomplish in 6 months to have a realistic chance of meeting my 12-month goals."

Example: Goal of Saving $1,200 in One Year

The item "savings" will be used to illustrate the process. Assume that you hope to save $1,200 during the year, a monthly average of $100.

If you put down two vacations on your first list, you probably will take one during the first six months. That goes in. And, on the $1,200 saving plan, you'll need to list $600 for the first six months. But, as you think about it, you may remember insurance or other payments due in those first six months; you may not be able to save $600 during that period. You then examine how much you can save—let's say it is $400. Now you reexamine your 12-month goal of $1,200. A decision is needed to see whether you will be able to make up the $200 deficit in the six months remaining or whether you will have to lower your sights.

The same examination should be given to each item on your first list. You may not intend to do some of the things until the second half of the year. But you need to separate the items and see how far along you will need to be in each of them at the end of the first six months.

Another Example: Goal of Improving a Relationship

Not all the items involve money. Suppose, for instance, that one of your goals is an improved relationship with someone in your organization. In the first six months, you should have met with that person several times or at least talked with the individual often.

After you list the six-month bench marks, you need still another list, this one headed "What I must do in three months to be that far along toward my six-month goal." You reexamine your six-month list and compare it with your three-month list.

Other Examples

Will you have that first vacation in the first three months or the second? In which period is the car insurance payment due? How long should you wait before you make that contact to improve your personal relationship?

As you progress with your list for the first three months and revise the six- and twelve-month lists, you might remember a dividend arrival time, or a cash birthday gift, which could cause further revisions in your savings goal and timetable.

Your fourth list covers what you must accomplish in the first month if you are to attain your three-, six-, and twelve-month goals. Because the first-month list covers a limited period, you have to be realistic. If you want to save $1,200 in the year, you will need to establish a bank account in the first month and probably put $100 into it.

The Value of This Pragmatic Process

This pragmatic approach to the fulfillment of dreams avoids many disappointments. Further, it helps ensure not only that you reach your goals but also that you check on your progress from time to time during the year. The periodic review will indicate whether you should modify your goals. In other words, this process gives you greater freedom to change your mind when it is advantageous to do so. Where this process is used, nearly everyone surpasses goals in some way. Industry knows this process as *Program Evaluation and Review Technique* (PERT).

Considering Your Boss's Goals

It is important to remember that your goals don't stand alone, especially as they relate to your career. You need to be concerned also with the goals of your superiors. Thoroughly working out your own goals gives you a decided advantage. You are aware of some things no one else knows. You have a plan, and you know where you want to go.

> **66** *Thoroughly working out your own goals gives you a decided advantage. You are aware of some things no one else knows. You have a plan, and you know where you want to go.* **99**

You also know that it is virtually impossible for one person to guess accurately the goals of another. If you want to know your superior's goals in relation to your particular work, you will need to ask. But, because you are concerned with progress, you will also want to know your boss's goals for the department or division. Only when you know those goals can you make plans to cope with the differences, negotiate for modification of your job description, or take some other course of action.

One thing of which you can be sure is that your superior's goals and yours will not mesh in every respect. There will be parts of your job that you don't like. (Coping with them is the subject of the next chapter.)

In all instances both you and your boss have a common concern: to make the best use of your strengths (your boss may call it improved employee utilization) so that your superior's interests and those of the organization are served.

It is very rare for a boss to know all the strengths of subordinates. Because of job pressures, most likely your superior will have overlooked some of your talents and the areas where you are particularly effective. You may be given some frustrating tasks—tasks that do not greatly involve your motivated skills. These oversights are commonplace, almost normal, but they shouldn't or needn't be.

Now, through your self-examination, you have a key to changing this undesirable "normality."

Ways to Learn Your Boss's Goals

How are you to get the information you need from your superior? Do you merely say, "I would like to know what the objectives of this department are for the next year?" That could seem threatening. You might appear to be after your superior's job. You might even sound brash. No matter how your request is taken, you are sure to arouse your superior's interest.

A more diplomatic way to request the information would go something like this: "I've made an intensive study of my strengths and set some preliminary goals for myself. Would you be good enough to let me know the goals you have for me for the next year so that I can see how our goals mesh and make whatever adjustments may be needed?"

This is likely to stimulate not only your superior's cooperation but also interest in what you have done and how you went about it. Concern for you as a person will increase. This is a great opportunity to "publicize" your talents where you will likely get maximum results.

Being Persistent

Your boss does have objectives, whether or not they are on paper. Be quietly persistent in seeking them. Only then will you be able to relate the two or three sets of goals to get good clues on opportunities for development, as well as on where and how you may need to adapt yourself and your goals.

Reporting Your Strengths

If your superior asks for it, be ready to provide a report on your strengths—the functions at which you feel you are most competent. Be ready to provide also some examples to support your data.

Being Open to Different Views

Be open to expressions of disbelief. Some of your superior's opinions may differ from yours, even about the same experiences. As long as you believe your statements are accurate, and you probably can provide information to support your belief, any differences of opinion become opportunities for you to persuade your boss to take another look at the facts. No good executive knows everything that goes on in a department. No individual can be aware of all the details. Maybe you have some facts that could be helpful both to your superior and to you. There also is the probability that your boss has some facts you don't, and in turn those facts could change some of your data.

Being Open to Change

Either way, if you go to your superior with a willingness to be more helpful to the organization, and to change your mind in the face of new facts, the odds are that your boss will be open to cooperation.

Some Positive Consequences of Comparing Goals

Identifying your goals and comparing them with others' goals should have positive effects not only on your work experience but also on your life as a whole.

Promotion of Away-from-Work Activities

The comparison of goals will also point out where you could benefit by developing hobbies if you do not already have them. These away-from-work activities are much more than just a way of filling time. They contribute to your development into a well-rounded person.

Don't get the wrong idea. Not everything you do should have a precise, predetermined meaning. Your personal life cannot be divorced from your working life. Each part of your life makes up your total personality; each aspect of your life influences all the others.

> 66 *Your personal life cannot be divorced from your working life. Each part of your life makes up your total personality; each aspect of your life influences all the others.* 99

For instance, a very good day on your job, just like a very bad day, affects what you do later. The strengths and talents you are unable to use on the job need to be used some way in your personal life.

Increased Self-Expression in Community Affairs

Suppose that you have special strength in community affairs but your job provides no opportunity for using it. You might deliberately examine the possibility of political activity, perhaps for some civic purpose, locally or possibly on a broader scale. Family priorities enter the picture, just as they entered into the establishment of your goals. But the refrain of the song "I wanna be me, I gotta be me" always will be there.

You need to express your self-motivated skills. When they are not used, the energy they represent will find an outlet—almost always in the form of frustration and stress, as well as the illnesses they cause.

Awareness of the Need for More Education

Some people may find that the comparison of goals reveals special needs for education outside the areas supported by the employer, such as yoga, karate, or religion. Others may find they have extra strengths in activities unrelated to their jobs, but in areas where their jobs could be expanded. These, of course, are good points for discussion with your superior. But finding or creating an expanded job is likely to require patience and commitment from both you and your superior.

Once in a while you might find that your goals fit in with those of the organization but not with those of your superior. That's a tough one to deal with, and it is given specific attention in a later chapter.

Awareness of the Need to Change Jobs

For some people the data will indicate the need to change employers. After all, your employer does not have every kind of job and every combination of jobs available. There are times when conditions "conspire" to make job changing advisable. But there are many things to consider, even if this appears to be your logical alternative.

Beware of Being Held Captive as Deadwood

Always keep in mind that each person has a unique excellence that needs to be expressed. In other words, there are no "deadwood" people, but there are some who have so little opportunity where they are that *they seem* like deadwood.

> 66 *Always keep in mind that each person has a unique excellence that needs to be expressed. In other words, there are no "deadwood" people, but there are some who have so little opportunity where they are that* they seem *like deadwood.* 99

Here's a case in point. One man, in his fifties, some 30 years with the same great international company, had risen to the post of supervising custodian (with no assistants), earning less than $30,000 a year. The managers all liked his pleasing personality. He never was offered training because he had not completed high school. He had been shuffled around from one executive's payroll to another over the years. Now the company had a new president and tight budget controls. There was no payroll into which the custodian could be absorbed, so he had to go. The managers wanted to help him, so they sent him for career assessment—but had little hope for his improvement.

The SIMS approach revealed that the man had an excellent memory, that he was good with figures, and that he had informally studied inventory controls. All these years he had feared losing his income and sick leave benefits and had come to accept his hat-in-hand relationships with the people around him. He hadn't liked it, but he was doing better than many other people with the same basic education, he felt. Ambition? He had started with it, but had been advised to stay where he was, where he was liked, and where his bosses would protect him. So he became "deadwood."

Fortunately, the case continues. He was helped to overcome his resentment, which was based on losing the assurance of protection on the one hand and having to suppress his motivated skills on the other. He then began to look for a job in which he could use his real strengths. As long as he felt resentful, his attitude at job interviews gave him a negative image. He expected to be turned down, and he was, time and again. When he finally saw the possibility of being released from the structure of subservience, he took heart and obtained an inventory control job that enabled him to earn $35,000 for the first time in his life.

Those kindly corporate executives, and they could just as easily have been government or institutional executives, had "grown" an ambitious young man into corporate dead-wood by commonplace oversight. There are no deadwood people!

Beware of Quitting a Job Prematurely

You should not quit a job until you have explored and exhausted every possibility for opportunity where you are. Since nearly all executives have in their minds special jobs they need someone to do, there are sure to be many more opportunities available than are known at the personnel-related information centers.

Don't Rely Heavily on Personnel Offices

The central personnel operation in your organization should be seen as only one means of access to available opportunities. Most skills banks, where they exist, are narrowly concerned with "can do" skills and too frequently are not kept up-to-date.

Get a New Job before You Quit Your Current Job

Know this well! As long as you do a good job at what is assigned to you, the high probability is that your superior will keep you on the payroll—even if you don't like the job and it gives you ulcers. You should, of course, get another job before you quit your old one. Remember that your goal is to use your strengths and bring in income, not to have them wasted or misused while you are unemployed and searching for employment. The stresses of unemployment could be far worse than the frustrations with which you have been accustomed to coping.

Get Help from Your Self-Appraisal Team

You might consider asking your self-appraisal team to work with you on some of your goal-related problems. You all were helpful in identifying one another's strengths; you have respect for one another's areas of competence. The team members could, perhaps, help you rehearse or practice interviews with your superior. As one member took your superior's role while you played yourself, the rest of the team could suggest how to improve your presentation. This practice would help you learn how to get your boss's agreement on the functions you feel would best use your strengths.

Consider Staying and Coping with Your Current Job

A few people using this goals-and-strengths approach manage to get *all* they want from their supervisors. Chances are you will not get that much, but you will get more of what you want when you are clear about what it is and have a plan for getting it. At worst, you'll end up with a basically good job that has *some* parts you don't particularly like. But there are ways of coping with the parts you dislike, even getting rid of some; that is the subject of the next chapter.

Summary

Pragmatic goal setting requires that you know the materials or strengths with which you have to work and the foundation for goal setting.

The System to Identify Motivated Skills and the PERT system for goal setting and attainment given here help you gather the incremental information that makes good decisions possible.

Goal setting may be compared to planning a picnic. First you dream about what you want to do, where and when you want to go, and whom you want to invite. Then you identify their needs for food, transportation, and other essentials. Those involved have to be willing picnickers. You purchase and prepare what you want to take, get the people together, and go.

With career goal setting, you first get your own dreams and timing in order on a practical basis. Check with your superior on objectives to ensure that your goals and your superior's do not conflict sharply. Be clear about where your goals mesh and where you believe adjustments can be made. Discuss and work out things with your boss in the best possible way; be patient and check up at least quarterly as you move ahead; be open to modifying your goals when you see that it is to your advantage.

Always remember that you are one of many people in the organization, even when you are an individual contributor. You cannot have everything your own way; but if you take into account the objectives of others with whom you deal, and do your best to mesh your objectives with theirs for mutual benefit, you probably will attain and surpass your goals.

When work is soulless,
life stifles and dies.

—Albert Camus (1913–1960)
French novelist, essayist, dramatist

Coping with and Solving Career Problems

You'll find "spud peeling," conflicts, frustrations, and crises in every job. The System to Identify Motivated Skills, and the knowledge of your strengths gained through it, can help you cope with career difficulties and suggest positive alternative ways to solve your problems.

The Problem of Change

Change itself is a good place to start our discussion. The variety of changes affecting careers are accelerating almost daily. These include departmental and company mergers and divestitures, restructurings, technological advances, changed product lines, downsizings, and new corporate expectations and aspirations.

As long as you, like almost everyone else, base your identity on your job title, changes are likely to accentuate your fears and retard or stop your progress. But most of the identity crises arising from change can be avoided.

The following case history is probably outside your area of experience, so you may view it objectively.

A coal miner in Appalachia was out of work and had been unemployed for more than ten years. He and his family were on public welfare. He told a social worker, "My grandfather was a coal miner; my father was a coal miner; I was born a coal miner; and I'll die a coal miner."

The social worker said, "But your chances of getting a job in the mines are nil; the mining company doesn't need any more coal miners."

Clinging to his identity, the desperate man replied, "I was born a coal miner, and I'll die a coal miner."

He was talked into participating in a SIMS career assessment project. (As you read this, keep in mind that usually little value is ascribed to unpaid activities.)

The coal miner's greatest achievement was winning second prize for developing a special-color hybrid rose. Next was helping several members of his garden club arrange their gardens. Third was recognizing a color-change signal that warned of an impending mine explosion. On one occasion he got the mine cleared and saved many lives. His fourth achievement was winning his foreman's approval for high production and for cutting straight seams in the coal mine. Fifth, sixth, and seventh again related to his gardening activities. He had grown things since early childhood.

When he saw that his color sense had enabled him to observe the warning signal and grow the hybrid rose, that his love of physical activity had inspired him to work outdoors and to produce in the coal mines, that his sense of spatial relationships and orderliness had enabled him to arrange gardens and cut straight coal seams, he realized that he had inherited not just the coal miner "title." He learned to appreciate his special variety of motivated skills or strengths and felt that he could apply them in a new way. He adapted to a new career in gardening and tree care. He soon got off welfare and earned a good living.

A special word on change should be added for professional and management women if you feel that your managerial talents atrophied if you took time out from the workplace to raise a family. The SIMS process and functional self-analysis can help you see how you maintain most of your skills—even though you do not apply them to traditional employment activities. Your skills do not lose their identity when you change the way you apply them. The woman who organizes a car pool to transport the neighborhood kids to school applies her talent for organizing. The woman who volunteers to sit for a group of preschool children, gets them involved in learning games, and otherwise helps them develop demonstrates her strengths in teaching and directing and not just in child care.

The "bridging" quality in the System to Identify Motivated Skills also has proved helpful to overseas managers who have returned to the United States. The change problem in this situation is the very real difference between being part of the American colony abroad and returning to live in America. Many job and personal relationships are radically different, and often job content and title are different. These differences affect one's self-confidence and identity.

The Continuing Employment Principle

Another area of change with which managers must deal is firing people. That should be done with genuine kindness—not with money (the golden handshake), not just by keeping them on the payroll until they get a new job, not even by helping them find a similar job. Real kindness, and the minimizing of management's guilt feelings, is effected by what I call *continuing employment*.

Every person terminated, except for cause, tends to feel unwanted and to some degree useless. These feelings greatly hamper any chances of getting another job quickly, or of getting a better or different one. This is what happens when contracts are canceled and thousands are let go so that the organization may survive and continue to provide employment for the thousands who are left. It is what happens when men and women are part of a general reduction in force for whatever "good" reason. The only exception that comes to mind is a discharge from military service. Even then unemployment and loss of identifying title, however temporary, quickly cause feelings of being of less worth than employed persons.

The continuing employment principle helps terminated employees focus on their strengths and potential, not their limitations. It helps them recognize how these strengths can be organized so as to be valuable to other employers. It uncovers hidden talents that can make people more employable, trains them to find their own jobs, and shows them how to make the best use of available public and private placement services.

The Humble Oil Company and Exxon Corporation pioneered this approach. The results were widely publicized both in company publications and in publications of the National Association of Manufacturers and Research Institute of America. One-third of the first group of 44 released management and professional people were helped to change vocations without the need for retraining. They experienced really new starts in life, at pay levels averaging within 5 percent of their prior levels. Forty-three were in comparable jobs within a hundred days.

This is too close to perfection to expect repetition. But the SIMS and the continuing employment approaches to termination usually ensure 70 percent reemployment within 90 days. And more than one-third are able to change their vocations successfully without the need for retraining.

Any large organization can have in-house capability to effect the continuing employment principle. A group of companies could establish the facilities for providing such service for employers and employees in any city. The availability of this service to terminated employees would help managers cope with the distasteful task of firing.

Changes as Bridges to a Better Life

Resistance to change, being less fearful of the devil you know than of whatever devils may come with change, always will be present. Upgrading of the quality of management and professional life, any improvement, is change. Progress, which is one person's meat, can seem like poison to another, but it cannot be stopped. Improved ways need to be found to spread the benefits of progress. The System to Identify Motivated Skills is one way to turn changes into bridges to a generally higher quality of life. The coal miner-to-gardener bridge, detailed earlier in this chapter, is illustrative of such a bridge to a higher life.

Knowing your strengths can be advantageous in dealing with the parts of your job you dislike. First, the parts that do give you satisfaction will be aligned with your motivated skills. You can more easily identify these parts and therefore become aware of the other parts. Ordinarily, the parts you dislike will infrequently constitute more than a third of your "regular" job.

The confusion over motivated strengths and unmotivated ones can be illustrated by a case history. Plant management had just begun to move from Theory X management toward the Theory Y style of democratic management. The supervisors knew how to give orders, but not how to share responsibility. Wanting the new management style accelerated, the new vice-president asked headquarters to send a team of psychologists and trainers to train the supervisors in cooperative problem solving.

One of these professionals decided to apply the SIMS approach to the situation, working with groups of six supervisors at a time.

On the walls of the meeting room hung one large sheet of paper for each supervisor. After the introductions, the SIMS presenter asked, "Would you be able to identify the parts of your job you like so much that you wish you had more similar tasks?" The supervisors had expected to be asked what their problems were so they could be discussed and worked on jointly. It took some explaining to get them to understand—and believe—what was desired. Then they went to their own sheet and began to list five or more parts of the job they liked best.

It took a while, and they needed every bit of the encouragement given. When they had completed their lists, the SIMS presenter opened the meeting to discussion.

After a long silence, one supervisor exploded. "Joe," he shouted, turning to the man next to him, "we've worked side by side for more than eight years, and you never told me that you enjoyed training new employees. I hate that part of my job. If I had known, I'd have asked you to train some of mine, and I would gladly have taken over any part of the job you don't like."

Soon the participants were willing to discuss first the satisfying parts of their own job and then talk about the other parts. Next they began to help one another find solutions to their problems. By getting each to open up about job satisfactions and achievements first, thereby establishing each as competent in individual ways, the SIMS presenter made it possible for the supervisors to move on to problem solving or coping.

The Partnership of Excellence

There are four main ways people cope with parts of their jobs they dislike. The most popular approach is *to be sloppy*. Many people become careless when they have no interest in the things they have to do.

A second approach—nearly as popular—*is to ignore the task*, almost hoping that it will disappear through neglect, or that some "poor slob" with low self-esteem will take on the task.

A third style is *to be a perfectionist*. Such a person wants to be sure each part of a job is done perfectly, even if it kills the person—sometimes it does. (There are studies showing a clear relationship between doing frustrating, dissatisfying work and peptic ulcers, arthritis, and neuroses.) The perfectionist approach to disliked tasks is particularly grueling. Because people are so easily distracted from such jobs, they often take longer than seems reasonable. This approach often is used to please a supervisor and get a promotion. But, where there are good results, the person may get saddled with even more displeasing tasks and wind up in an unbreakable cycle.

The fourth style is to form *a partnership of excellence*. It seems to be the easiest choice, as well as the most effective one, when you have used the System to Identify Motivated Skills.

It begins with the recognition that there is excellence in each person and that there is dignity in every kind of work activity. There is no dirty work; there is no work that is demeaning to everyone. The activities that drive you up the wall are not enough to "drive anyone crazy," and they are not activities that only an idiot would do willingly. (Admittedly, some tasks have been oversimplified. Tightening nut nine on bolt nine all day long has dulled or hypnotized people doing well at that task. Now robots do such tasks in many organizations. Fortunately, large numbers of organizations are on the way to truly enriching such oversimplified tasks.)

Once you get the idea that different tasks use different forms of excellence in different people, you will not look down on those who enjoy doing work you find most unpleasant. When you reach that point, you begin to use the partnership-of-excellence concept.

> 66*Once you get the idea that different tasks use different forms of excellence in different people, you will not look down on those who enjoy doing work you find most unpleasant.*99

Assume you have identified those parts of your job that relate most closely to your strengths and have therefore isolated the parts you would rather be without. If there are 14 parts to your job, eight might directly apply your strengths. Two involve skills you don't particularly care about using, but you must do these tasks to perform your job. The other four you would rather drop, but cannot do so at the moment.

Going at it this way, you already have isolated the four most irritating parts of your job.

Your next move in the partnership-of-excellence approach is to look around for someone who would enjoy doing those four parts of your job as much as you enjoy the eight you have listed as satisfying. With your new attitude of respect for such persons—you might previously have looked down on them for taking on such tasks—you are likely to find someone more than willing to take over two of the parts. You may also learn that the person dislikes some parts of his or her job which you would enjoy doing. You may even be able, unofficially, to swap these job parts, and both may gain by it. The organization would gain two increasingly satisfied managers, and four tasks would be done more reliably—and probably more effectively.

This concept gives "aliveness" to job content. It also establishes relationships based on each person's respect for the competencies of others and enhances cooperation among those who share the approach. It makes a person both selfish and generous, in that the individual retains the favored parts of the job while giving someone else the opportunity to do more of what that person likes to do.

Shifting activities usually takes time, but the time can be shortened by cooperative planning with your supervisor. While the shift in your activities is in the planning stage, you may have to work harder at the tasks you dislike. Some of the frustration will be softened, however, because you can expect to find others who will more than willingly relieve you of some of them.

When you have arranged to switch some of your tasks with your coworkers, you'll of course need to let your boss in on what is going on and why. Your supervisor should be pleased with having your energies released for more productive application in the areas of your greatest strengths.

The Problem with Annual Reviews

This takes us into communication—the day-by-day contacts between managers and employees and annual reviews or appraisals. Annual review and problem-solving meetings will be dealt with here as "coping" elements.

In her book *Career Management* Marion Kellogg mentions the manager who says: "The appraisal data we collect on employees are just worthless." That is extreme, but it is not very far from the general condition reported: "Some managers won't say anything critical; others won't say anything specific."

Most managers view annual reviews as a waste of time. Their subordinates often share that view. At least one study indicates that these conferences, designed for a supervisor to "help" subordinates "improve," are usually followed by a drop in productivity for at least three months.

Positive Reinforcement vs. Dissatisfaction-Avoidance

Fortunately, the concepts of behavioral scientists are making some headway. Several organizations are reporting value in using B. F. Skinner's process of positively reinforcing (or praising) the behavior and outcomes a manager wants to be repeated. Increasingly they are applying the theories of Frederick Herzberg and Abraham Maslow, recognizing that most people are at a level of development where they want recognition, encouragement, and challenges to the best that is in them; that they are seekers, in Maslow's terminology, of self-actualization; and that there is little payoff (temporary at best) from traditional approaches to motivation, such as higher pay, improved working conditions, and other factors peripheral to the actual task. These are dissatisfaction-avoidance factors; they do not directly motivate. On the other hand, the research shows that satisfiers, or motivators, are such factors as achievement, recognition, responsibility, advancement, and other self-actualizing elements.

One company reported that the Skinner-Herzberg-Maslow approaches cut absenteeism of more than 1,000 employees from 11 percent to 4 1/2 percent in less than a year. These approaches helped another company cut its freight costs more than half a million dollars a year over a three-year period.

Identification of Excellence and Motivated Skills

Some behaviorists believe they can identify "nonmotivatable" workers. But this conflicts with my finding that each person does have excellence within and does have motivated skills. Undoubtedly most managerial problems come from those who would be classified as dissatisfied. Examination of the studies referred to indicates the failure to find ways to identify and release the skills people are motivated to use. It appears that the so-called nonmotivatable persons have temporarily given up efforts to develop or to find positions that turn them on.

I say "temporarily," because the SIMS process, especially when combined with the team approach, has proved effective in renewing and changing the careers of men and women on welfare rolls, hard-core unemployed youth, ex-convicts, early-retired persons, women long out of the workforce, as well as management and professional people. The great majority participating in SIMS seminars, whatever their reasons for doing so, have gained lasting renewal through learning more about themselves, expanding their perception of their usefulness, and realistically taking the blinders off and seeing new horizons.

An Approach to Career Renewal

Dissatisfied workers are not the only ones who bring problems to management. All people have problems, and most of them cannot be scratched away. One rarely used approach to people problem solving could be very helpful. It, too, uses SIMS techniques. The following example will show how it works.

A company sent two levels of managers to a SIMS career development workshop. Some of them were doing well and needed only a clearer understanding of their goals. Others were on the verge of being terminated if their attitudes and productivity didn't improve soon.

In the latter category, the career of one person—we'll call him Jim—had been sliding for two years. An assistant to a sales manager, Jim was seen as a comer and had performed like one ever since he had been hired out of college ten years earlier. Creative ideas and sales inventiveness were among his greatest strengths, but he hadn't been contributing in those areas for two years. He did what he was asked to, but no more. He passed the salt (but not the adjacent pepper) when asked for the salt.

Following the group identification process, he commented about his lack of contributions during the two years: "I guess I stopped giving ideas to my boss after he turned down one of my ideas. I got the feeling that he didn't want my ideas any more; so I figured if that's what he wants, that's what he'll get. I decided to do just what I was told, and no more. I can see now that I was only cheating myself. I have many ideas on how to improve things. Keeping them inside made me feel more and more guilty and is causing me to withdraw from relationships. I'm going to stop this stupid business."

And he did. Two months later, after he had done some outstanding work, his boss gave him a raise and told him that if he had not changed at just about that time, the raise could just as easily have been a pink slip.

An Alternative Approach: Informal Conversation

When it became clear this junior manager had become minimally cooperative, his supervisor, Bill, could have handled it on a personal basis:

BILL: Jim, I've noticed you seem to have something on your mind. I'm not going to pry, but I may have some suggestions that could help you get over those problems—whatever they are. Let's talk for half an hour, or have lunch.

(During this period, Bill would be very careful not to pry.)

BILL: I suppose you've had problems before in your life just like everyone else— and you've overcome or survived them. Right?

JIM: I've had my share of troubles.

BILL: Each of us has some inner strengths to help us overcome problems. I'm not going to give you any religious talk. I do want to help you remember the strengths you used to get by your troubles in the past. They might be helpful to you this time as well. Is that a possibility?

JIM: Could be. But I know myself pretty well.

BILL: Yes, but when we have heavy things on our minds, all of us tend to forget those strengths for a while. I'd like to get you remembering what your strengths are without asking you to answer any questions. I will ask you some questions, but I don't want you to give *me* the answers.

JIM: What's the big mystery?

BILL: I just want you to be aware of the strengths you have to help you overcome whatever problems you have. Your strengths, just like those of everyone else, are most likely to have been used when you do things you feel have been achievements. Right?

JIM: OK.

BILL: When you remember enough achievements— experiences when you did things well that you also enjoyed doing—you'll be able to see a pattern of your strengths. Now I'll ask you a few questions that I hope will help you see this pattern. It may enable you to know which strengths to use to overcome whatever may be bothering you now. The first question may seem unrelated, perhaps silly, but it will start you remembering things. Make a mental note of the earliest achievement you can recall, something, perhaps, you did before you were ten. [Pause]

Now, think about a few achievements you had during the past five years. [Pause]

Next, think about a couple of achievements during your college years—things that might or might not have been concerned with your studies. [Pause]

Now, think of three or four of your greatest achievements during the past ten years, achievements connected with any part of your life. [Pause]

Now, keeping them all in mind as best you can, try to see some skills that you used repeatedly to make those experiences happen. [Pause]

When you recognize the repeated skills— some of your motivated strengths—you'll be better able to overcome your present problem and whatever others may trouble you in the future.

Jim may or may not say anything. If he has nodded or signaled at all during these questions, he will have associated his achievements with Bill and will have partially regained the warmth of the old relationship. He will be sure to know that Bill sees him as a person with uniqueness, not just as someone else who takes orders. Jim will have been helped to stop feeling sorry for himself and reach a point where he knows he often has overcome difficulties and is an achiever. This boost to his self-confidence is likely to get him moving again.

The SIMS approach to people problem solving can safely be used by an amateur along the lines given in the preceding example. It very quickly moves the person from being a part of the problem to becoming a contributor to the solution. It helps the person help himself by looking at many past successful demonstrations of his abilities.

Because the System to Identify Motivated Skills helps in many areas, it is necessary to make clear once again that the SIMS approach is one contributing system, not a complete solution for all problems.

The SIMS Approach to Overcome Conflict

In this coping/problem-solving chapter, there is one more area to be covered: conflicts.

All behavioral approaches to conflict management point to the boss's opinion of subordinates' competence as contributing to conflicts. The manager who knows or suspects that someone is not competent will reveal sooner or later the judgment or opinion through personal actions. Such actions may involve bypassing, not consulting, ignoring, consulting on obviously minor elements, being brusque, and speaking adversely. The person treated like this may withdraw or, on the other extreme, become overly aggressive. Either way, conflict is stimulated. The manager and employee will, by their remarks and attitudes, mess up numerous conferences and efforts and block decisions and progress.

> 66*All behavioral approaches to conflict management point to the boss's opinion of subordinates' competence as contributing to conflicts.* 99

How can the SIMS approach contribute to overcoming this source of many conflicts?

Begin with the assumption that most people do not know all their strengths. We can reasonably assume that most people working together do not know one another's strengths. Initially, they have no experienced basis for making judgments about others' competence. It is common for people to probe for other people's weaknesses, to find out what they can get away with rather than probe for their strengths. It follows that such people will continue to be unaware of one another's strengths or areas of competence for a long time.

For instance, a large civic group elected to its board an aging man, Mike, who had been a member for many years. He was always willing to do some of the necessary chores. His election was more in recognition of his zest than of any special contribution he might make. At most meetings he was a listener and voted with the majority.

Mike, a mail room foreman with a large merchandising firm, participated with other members of the board in a SIMS team-building seminar, which included a group skills identification process. The others were quite surprised to learn that he had been a state running champion and, for 20 years, had organized and directed a variety of sports activities for youth in the metropolitan region.

Most board members were business owners, executives, or professionals. This news of Mike's competence as an organizer of highly successful youth programs (he was shy and always had avoided publicity associated with the athletic events) made this virtually ignored man very important to the current purposes of the association. In addition, each had learned something of the strengths of the other members. All became interested in Mike's opinions on matters related to his areas of competence, and he gained more respect from them. Perhaps equally important is the fact that the bickering for status practically ended. It was demonstrated that when people in a group can appreciate why they should respect one another, they organize and cooperate in different ways, and have less cause for conflicts.

Benefits of the SIMS Approach

Aside from the frustrations averted by this application of SIMS, other by-products include better organization for results, faster and better-deliberated decisions, fewer chip-on-the-shoulder attitudes, and more intelligent use of available strengths, as well as more willingness to request outside help with competencies not found among team members.

Today's behavioral psychologists and futurists, reports by the Departments of Labor, Health and Human Services, and Education, as well as numerous research studies, all appear to agree that workers must become more willfully adaptable. These adaptations or changes will bring identity crises, and preparing for them will reduce concomitant stresses and conflicts.

Summary

The SIMS approach brings into this area a new element for stability with changes—an awareness of one's strengths in ways that permit them to be combined and adapted differently without a loss of identity. Examples show how this releases men and women from job title attachment and gives them greater freedom to change obsolete vocations without undue anxiety.

Examples also show how managers may constructively overcome those deep guilt feelings usually associated with terminating subordinates. And they illustrate the partnership of excellence principle, which can help a manager cope with parts of a job he dislikes.

They show how the SIMS basic approach of looking for the best in each person helped one organization's managers to begin communicating again after many years of compartmentalization. In view of reports from some behavioral scientists, it is reasonable to say that all people have motivated skills and do become self-motivated when traditional barriers to the release of those skills are overcome. The examples also show how helping a person identify the best that is within him or her will strengthen the confidence so necessary for coping with and resolving problems.

Finally, the examples demonstrate how conflicts based on competence factors can be substantially reduced through team-building that uses the SIMS approach to help persons know and respect one another's strengths.

Money is never spent to so much advantage as when you have been cheated out of it: for at one stroke you have purchased prudence.

Arthur Schopenhauer (1788–1860)
German philosopher

Get a Raise

When is the last time you got a raise? We don't mean an increase in your salary because another year had gone by, or because it was company policy to give everyone a pay hike the first of each year, but a merit increase based on your real value to your organization. If you are like many people, your answer probably will be: "It's been a long time."

You have waited patiently without results. If you continue to wait, you probably will develop considerable skill in waiting, but not much else.

A Formula for Getting a Raise

A simple formula can get you out of the "routine" raise rut and bring serious consideration of you as a candidate for an "earned" pay increase. Notice, the formula is described as *simple*, not as *easy*.

Here is a four-step approach to help you get the raise you want and deserve:

1. Be sure you have earned it.

2. Be sure your boss knows you have earned it.

3. Be sure your boss knows that you know that you have earned it.

4. Be sure your boss knows that you know that your boss knows you know that you have earned it.

This may sound like double-talk, or at least a humorous approach to a very serious situation. It is neither. It is a system that works.

Nearly all the people who do not get earned raises have overlooked one or more of these steps. There's no accounting for those who get raises who do not seem to have earned them—their ranks are legion. Included in this latter category are people who did really important things that others didn't know about, as well as some who accumulated raises because of nepotism or favoritism.

There is also the "squeaky wheel" principle: If you make enough of a nuisance of yourself, the boss just might put through a raise to get you off his or her back for a while. This works some of the time.

The preceding rules, the first one in particular, are part of the SIMS benefits maintenance system. All good things need maintenance work—marriage, houses, jobs, kids, self-knowledge, computers, and so on. The increased self-knowledge gained through the SIMS approach needs to be kept up-to-date. Easy ways to do this have been developed. They will be presented from time to time throughout the rest of this book.

For now, the concern is limited to getting a raise while on your present job. For practical reasons, this must be assumed to be a change in your pay rate or other benefits. That is why it is necessary to go back to the time your last raise came through, or when you reached your present pay rate.

What were your real duties and responsibilities at that time? The word "real" is used because actual duties and responsibilities often are different from those outlined in job descriptions. In earlier chapters it was pointed out that almost every manager and professional person modifies a job within six months after being hired. The person's special styles—the ways the individual goes about doing things—change the job content in at least its points of emphasis.

You were paid what you are getting to do the type of job you were doing when your pay rate started. Employers may buy your future, but they are like bankers. They do their best to pay on the installment plan: After the work is done, with payment in *inflated dollars* on a value agreement arrived at in *noninflated terms*, the difference to bankers is added profits.

There are, of course, pay raises based on increases in the cost of living and raises associated with seniority. But the focus here is on the earned raise.

When your earned raise does come through, it should take inflation into account and be sufficiently above it to provide real reward for having earned that raise.

"Increased productivity" is a term that too often covers a variety of factors that should earn raises. These include cost reduction; ideas to save money or get desired results better or faster; and such intangibles as contributing to better morale, improved relationships, and a healthier environment.

Some Obstacles to Earned Raises

You need to be aware of a special problem, especially prevalent in larger organizations—groupism.

Groupism

When one person gets a raise, others in the same category or classification may feel they, too, should get a raise. This very business of classifying people, grouping them and taking away their individual identities, has created one of the many "Frankenstein monsters" that contribute to organizational arthritis. Some classification system is unavoidable, but it often has been permitted to smother creative individualism and encourage mediocrity.

When a manager must choose between approving a raise for only one person and having a discontented group, the manager generally opts for group harmony; and the earned raise is not given. Today's humanism, and even intelligent capitalism, requires that the person who earns rewards should get them. When that does not happen, when superior contributions are not rewarded, the high-talent person slows or stops personal contributions. B. F. Skinner's experiments have demonstrated that nonreward, even punishment for poor performance, begets adverse results.

> 66 *When a manager must choose between approving a raise for only one person and having a discontented group, the manager generally opts for group harmony; and the earned raise is not given.* 99

Management Excuses

All kinds of obstacles stand in the way of earned raises. "We consider people for raises once a year" is perhaps the most widespread obstacle. Today, with computerized payroll systems, this concept is reinforced by warnings of the chaos it would cause to be "changing the payroll data all of the time." Both approaches are "don't bother me" reactions of bosses who have other reasons for not giving a reward when it has been earned.

Management Preoccupation with Problems

Then there is the general feeling that "my boss knows what I'm doing, and therefore knows that I've earned a raise"; and its twin, a person's feeling that a reward will come eventually if he or she keeps the nose to the grindstone and just goes on doing a good job. The fact is that most managers continue to be fire fighters. They run to where things are going wrong and have little time left to give attention where things are going right. They are relieved by those persons whose work they don't have to worry about, who "don't need my attention."

> **66** *The fact is that most managers continue to be fire fighters. They run to where things are going wrong and have little time left to give attention where things are going right.* **99**

It has been said earlier that attention alone, as any mother will testify, is a kind of reward. Skinner proved that rewards tend to reinforce the behavior with which they are associated. The manager who gives most attention to problem makers is unquestionably encouraging more of the same.

Management Inertia

What these practices often add up to is a serious case of management inertia. Management believes that if it gives a raise to one, it must give corresponding raises to others, and it is cheaper to let one person suffer than raise the whole crew. It believes that if a superior person is doing a good job, that individual usually is no problem and so can be left alone. It believes that promoting a worker entails all sorts of training expenses and uncertainties, not to mention the paperwork, so why take the risk that the worker will fail? Laboring under this negative attitude, it is often loath to move at all.

> **66** *Management believes that if it gives a raise to one, it must give corresponding raises to others, and it is cheaper to let one person suffer than raise the whole crew.* **99**

Other Management Objections

Additional objections to raise giving include "The budget is tight," "We have an economy drive," "You're at the top of your salary range," and "Your timing isn't right." Of course, there are many more obstacles, but they all can be overcome by the person who has earned his or her raise.

Overcoming the Obstacles to Earned Raises

Too often a firm alternative job offer is used for bargaining purposes. That extreme approach tends to force an otherwise reluctant employer to give in, and it has too much potential for changing a good relationship into one that makes your boss wonder if you outsmarted or overpowered him. That attitude tends to stimulate attempts to even the score and could soon become counterproductive.

Alternatives to a Pay Increase

There are many ways to give a raise. The bonus is one; another is profit sharing; still another is some form of tax-free gift, which could be an expense account, special services like tax accounting or investment counseling, and extra vacation time.

A Pay Increase

But the age-old special reward for special services is usually a pay increase. This might be a sound approach, but day-to-day pressures combined with the scheduled times for consideration of pay increases often result in some deserving workers being overlooked.

Reward for performance is our concern here. Accordingly, "performance" should be provable. And it is.

Using the Four-Step Formula—A Case History

You will recall that the formula begins with being sure you have earned an increase. You can be sure of this when you know that the quality of the job expected of you when you reached your present pay level is higher now. Take the following example.

Bill, a maintenance supervisor, was responsible for machinery, equipment, offices, and similar items at the newest of the company's five facilities. The rumor mill was spreading the word that profits were slim and that there would be no salary increases that year. At 38, Bill had two engineering degrees and plenty of ambition. He felt his work gave him satisfaction; he believed he was worth more money; he doubted that he could have greater responsibility than he had at this new facility.

His search for greater income in the face of the no-increase rumor brought him to a career counselor. The SIMS study confirmed that he had chosen the right career. His counselor suggested staying with the company and pursuing a salary increase.

His achievements indicated he had gleaned preventive maintenance methods and systems not only from the company's other facilities but also from up-to-date sources in industry and that he had built these methods into the operation of the new facility. As the result of his actions, substantial savings were taking place each month.

"Does your management know about these savings?" he was asked.

His reply was: "They certainly should know about them. Installation of the new systems was approved by top management when the plant was in construction."

The counselor asked: "Does the same management team have responsibility for plant construction as the one that is responsible for plant operations?"

Bill responded: "The plant operations people are different, but they all report to top management."

Then, he paused and added, "What you're saying is that maybe the operations people to whom I report, and with whom I work, don't really know about my maintenance systems, even though they do know that the continuity of production at this facility is greater than at the other four."

"How are they to know if nobody tells them?" the counselor asked.

Bill began to think seriously about working out a way to get a raise from this employer, for whom he had worked eight years. There were several things Bill had going for him. He knew company politics, which managers had power and which only talked as if they had power. He had good working relations with most of the management and professional personnel. He had a good staff. Probably most important, he knew what the other maintenance managers were doing and what most of their problems were.

He completed the first step described earlier, writing down his duties and responsibilities at the time he was given his most recent salary increase. Then he headed another sheet, "My contributions since then," and listed them. He said it felt as if he were writing a "brag sheet." Yet it took three prodding consultations to develop a good list.

"How can you measure the value of preventive maintenance?" he wanted to know. He was able to get comparable costs from other sources for many of the same items. This showed him that his methods added up to combined manpower and reduced downtime and materials, and produced an annual savings of more than $200,000.

The total was very much of a surprise to him. "If you weren't aware, why should your vice-president be aware of your contributions to the firm?" the counselor asked. Only then, when he went beyond his feelings of self-value and learned the fact of it, had he moved from feeling he had earned a raise to being sure that he had earned a raise.

Savings add to profit directly: they amount to an increase in productivity. But the way in which they add is interesting. Very few corporations make a 10 percent profit on their sales. So a saving of $200,000 would about equal the earnings from the sale of two million dollars' worth of products. When Bill realized this, he began to think of asking for twice his $52,000 salary. That, of course, had to be revised realistically.

But now he had a new concept of his worth to the organization. He had come to recognize that he, like almost every good professional man or woman in management, is worth more than he or she thinks.

When Bill began to get annoyed about his "low rate of pay"—which previously had moderately satisfied him—the discussion moved on to how much of a raise would have pleased him before his self-appraisal. Ten percent would have been satisfactory, he said, in view of the company's low profits, but he really would have liked 15 percent. "But now, I'd be unhappy with less than 15 percent," he said.

"Suppose," the counselor suggested, "you aim at 20 to 25 percent and develop a plan with that expectation in mind. You've heard of people expecting trouble and finding it—the self-fulfilling prophecy bit? Well, you can just as easily use self-fulfilling prophecy to get something you want. When you move from wishful thinking to setting a goal and planning carefully to achieve it, there is a good chance you can succeed. Do your motivated skills indicate you should have a different title as well as a higher salary?"

"They're not going to make me a vice-president," he said. "I'm one of the five plant maintenance managers, and I'm already paid as much as the one who's been there longest, twice as long as I have."

"You seem to have a vice-presidency in mind," the counselor said. "Perhaps that could be a longer-range goal, especially since your achievement facts show you have worked on policy matters at several times in your life as well as on operations. Your concern for that status also should be kept in mind as you develop your plan for the pay increase."

They then began to work on the second step of the formula, making sure that his supervisor knew he had earned the raise. Fortunately, the third quarter of the company's fiscal year had barely begun. Timing is a major factor in getting a raise. The person who tries to get one just after the budget has been completed is likely to be disappointed; the same holds true for the person who plans for an increase just after the annual board meeting when the profits have been allocated. Nearly every employer has a schedule, written or unwritten, of its structured activities, the timetable the policymakers use to set guidelines for company performance.

In some organizations there is a set time for consideration of who should get raises and how much. If possible, you should begin to work on your plan for a raise three or four months before the company puts its budget together.

Bill developed a short list of key executives who would be interested in knowing about the maintenance cost savings, key people who could influence a decision on his pay increase.

He then worked up a concise report on his contributions since getting his last increase. Each of the four executives received the report with a cover letter, which said in part: "I have marked in red certain sections of this report that will be of particular interest to you." Bill timed the distribution of his report to coincide with the anniversary of his joining the firm. He indicated in his cover letter that he periodically examines his contributions to company effectiveness and that this time he felt his study was worth sharing with those who had been most helpful in achieving the results. He asked for their corrections, criticisms, and comments.

The sections marked for each executive's attention were very short. Short enough and factual enough it turned out to induce each of them to read all five pages. When they got back to him, which they did quickly, each was just as surprised as Bill had been and were pleased with him for sharing the report with them. One of the vice-presidents said, "If everyone were as conscientious as you in watching the dollar, we wouldn't be in a financial bind this year. We'll have to take care of you, even if nobody else gets a raise."

Bill was given a $15,000 increase, with an apology that there couldn't be an equivalent bonus with it. By far his raise was the highest of the few handed out that year.

Bill had completed the four steps. By making a list of his contributions, he made sure he had earned the raise. His report helped his bosses know he had earned it and that he knew he had. His letter requesting corrections and criticism—which he would have followed up within a week if he had not been called first—completed the fourth item, making sure that his bosses knew that he knew his bosses knew he had earned it.

Changing the Salary Range

Suppose you are at the top of your salary range. Or suppose you are not getting along too well with your boss, but nevertheless have earned that raise. What then?

In the first instance you need to change the salary range; in the second you have to change the conditions. Examples of how to handle each situation follow.

Jack was doing a very good job in a nonprofit research organization. He headed one of four departments, the one responsible for the highest proportion of the organization's income. His salary was comparable to that of a tenured professor, several of whom worked for him on a special project. It was well known that their university salaries were used as a standard for Jack's organization's pay scales. It also was well known that the university with which the professors were associated resented the fact that much younger men, however competent, were getting the equivalent of top university salaries.

Jack discussed this problem with some friends, indicating he would consider quitting if his salary could not be adjusted. After a while they came up with an idea to remove the professional pay choker from the neck of the salary scale. Twenty of the key faculty members were made special advisers to the research organization, with annual retainers of $1,000 each. Because of the special status this gave them, they dropped opposition to salary range changes, and Jack got a substantial raise, along with others in the organization.

Each situation is unique when it comes to effecting policy changes. What is the same is that solutions are available, and can be found, when conditions warrant changes. The need must be recognized, the salary increase must have been earned, and then some way usually can be found to provide it.

Overcoming "Cronyism"

Paul's case was very different. He had made good progress for seven of his ten years with a very large company. But he had received no increase for the past three years, and his frustrations continued to mount. Although he seemed to get along well with his coworkers, he felt like an outsider because the five other men and his boss always seemed to know more of what was going on than he did. His work was satisfactory, but no more. During the three years he had been in this department, he had seen others, no more effective than he, move ahead. "For some reason, which I cannot understand, my boss has it in for me," Paul said.

He went through the SIMS steps. The results showed he had been doing a good job, liked his company, and should have a good future there. But they also showed that his effectiveness had dwindled. He compensated for his employment frustrations by involving himself in community affairs in ways that continued to demonstrate his managerial effectiveness.

"Why do you feel you are an outsider?" he was asked.

Paul responded, "They have lunch together almost every day at the Princeton Club. I'm a Williams graduate."

It turned out that his boss was a Princeton man who turned to his old professor whenever he needed staff. Paul was the only "foreigner" in the department. The others hadn't intended to block him. It was just that the Princeton Club was the best place to eat; and while they lunched, they often talked shop. The information they exchanged informally also was available to Paul, but he didn't know what to ask for, and they all assumed he had the information.

When the reason for his "outsider" status became apparent, he developed a contributions-to-the-company report to discuss with his boss and also with the man who had hired him originally (by now that man was a vice-president). In his report he added a page on his contributions to the community; this showed he had not lost his ability to contribute ideas and leadership. Paul used his birthday as the peg for his report—there needs to be a time peg for such a report when it cannot be tied to an employment anniversary. He called the vice-president, reminding him of their early relationship, and asked for an opportunity to review his progress as justification for the original hiring.

Paul leveled with the vice-president. He suggested a three-way lunch to let his boss know how the informal "Princeton Club policy" was preventing the company from getting the best out of him. An open discussion, without recriminations, helped change conditions. In this case, Paul got an increase without having earned it because his boss had unintentionally kept him from doing those things that normally would have earned greater financial recognition.

Overcoming Unequal Pay for Women

This section would be incomplete without some reference to pay inequalities experienced by women. These inequalities are real, but they can be changed on an individual basis. The process is essentially the same, with the addition of some comparative data.

Mary, an account executive and copywriter in a small, growing advertising agency, handled substantial accounts. Only one other staff member handled more. His earnings exceeded $70,000 a year, partly because he was the president of the agency. Her salary was $35,000, just over half that of other account executives—all male.

She developed a brief schedule of her activities and results, along with the activities and results of two others doing the same work. The schedule made it clear that she was doing more work. She knew she was being paid much less for doing it.

She used her knowledge of advertising presentations to create a "show" of different parts of the schedule and asked the president to set aside half an hour for her presentation.

He congratulated her, said he knew she had been doing an excellent job, and assured her of a raise at the next regular time for such increases. Prepared for that response, she kept her cool.

"Don't you think the facts show I should be getting as much as the others?" she asked.

Some negotiation followed. She was given an immediate raise of 50 percent of the difference and assured of the balance within the year.

The point of Mary's story is that employers are nearly always willing to pay for what they are getting. Often, though, as with Paul and Bill, bosses simply do not know all that their subordinates are doing. Bosses rarely take time to identify the contributions of each manager or professional. They are content to accept progress and share some of the increased income without really examining who should get what proportion on the basis of his or her contribution. In the case of women's pay, an additional factor of custom or habit enters the picture.

Ensuring That Your Boss Knows Your Achievements

This leaves it up to the individual to make clear how much of a raise the person has earned. The actual amount, of course, will be decided by the boss. But when you go through the process outlined, you will have given your boss the facts needed for a reasonable decision.

It just doesn't make sense for a good manager to willfully deny a raise to someone known to have earned it. If you want the raise you have earned, be sure your boss knows you have earned it. Don't blame your boss if you haven't kept your superior informed and don't get the increase.

When you want a raise you have earned, get your facts. Be sure they are checkable and be open to correction if your view of the facts does not completely check out. Communicate.

When you keep your nose to the grindstone, when you just keep on doing a good job, that's when you can be sure that nobody needs to pay any attention to you—and nobody will!

Know your strengths.
The most important thing is
to know what you're good at.
Very few people know that.

—Peter Drucker to Bill Moyers
TV interview

Plan for the Future— Promotion and Advancement

Promotions too often are given to the wrong people. The reasons vary. They include nepotism; being in the right place at the wrong time; and the desire of a boss to keep a good assistant, therefore refusing to let that person move ahead.

Other "reasons" may be an inadequate system of information about available skills or discrimination against women, minority persons, younger workers who want to move up "too fast," older employees who are believed to be at an "over the hill" age, and those who haven't attended the "right" college or who didn't take the "right" courses.

You may be up against a boss who feels that you haven't earned a promotion unless you have been through trials like those the boss has experienced. Or you may be fighting a too-rigid formal structure for career advancement.

These conditions will continue, but they can be reduced substantially by men and women who are aware of their skills and growth potential, and who are ready to let their talents be appropriately known.

This chapter will explain how qualified persons can get an advancement that will benefit both them and their employer.

Employers Are People Too

The first factor to be appreciated is that employers are human, and therefore are not infallible. They make mistakes, most often in judging people's abilities, attitudes, and understandings. They have no crystal-ball competence in knowing everything that is going on. They often are isolated from communication with their most reliable employees because of problem areas that need attention.

Like everyone else, bosses are self-interested at heart. They want to enjoy what they are doing, get their work done, meet their responsibilities, and continue to grow and develop. They need new challenges or ways to sharpen their growing edge, and they want happiness.

Again, as with other people, the feelings and values of bosses influence and color their behavior and the way they see things. When you are aware of your own strengths, you become free to observe your own feelings and values, and gain an understanding of how they affect your behavior. Self-knowledge concerning your strengths also makes you more observant of the feelings, values, and behavior of others. But don't expect to be able to understand another person fully.

The relation of all this to career advancement can be seen in the case history of a woman who was a manager. She was performing well in a technical management job, earning a comfortable salary, and doing most of the things she wanted to do in her community and church. After completing a SIMS career renewal workshop, she decided to work toward a higher management position.

The data she presented to her immediate boss and his superior gained their support, and she was given a chance for greater variety in her work and more freedom in choosing her methods. At an appropriate time they approached the division manager, who had final authority for approving her promotion.

The top boss called her in, told her of his appreciation of her contributions, agreed they were increasingly valuable—but then denied her the promotion. He explained that in his engineering division higher management opportunities were limited to those who had demonstrated increased knowledge of the technology. She had made it clear that she was more concerned with maintaining relationships than with formal upgrading of her knowledge through college courses. But she was faced with a hard fact: managerial ability as such would not be rewarded without an increase in technological competence.

This gave her a choice: she could take some college courses, for which the organization would pay, or she could deny herself that opportunity and maintain her status, but with more respect from three levels of bosses.

She reexamined her values, the weight she put on community life, church activities, and the evenings and weekends she would have to devote to studying instead of spending the time with friends and neighbors. She elected to continue the life she had been enjoying, secure in the knowledge that she was free to change her mind.

Directing Your Own Career Advancement

Individuals must assume responsibility for their own career advancement, values, motivated skills, and concern with relationships—matters over which a boss has little influence. Individuals identify and understand these better when each person makes thorough use of the System to Identify Motivated Skills and of the forms on dates and relationships given later in this chapter.

For the moment, let's return to Bill, the maintenance manager discussed in the preceding chapter.

Bill's company experienced a turnaround the following year. It hit a good profit streak, and Bill's facility had the lowest maintenance cost of the five units.

The fact that it was the newest of the five was a contributing factor. Bill began to get eager for new and greater responsibilities. He could see no possibility for this in his present job. He knew he was the best paid of the five managers, but this only increased his problem. He returned for more career planning counseling.

He liked his company and his coworkers. His family liked where they lived. But he felt that if he stayed much longer, he would get stale and progress would bypass him.

The facts he had were clear enough. But because of his personal, family, and work climates, the counselor urged a look at the possibility of uncovering new facts. "What could happen," he asked, "to make the job more interesting, more challenging, and better paying?"

Bill said he couldn't see anything happening unless the company established a new position of coordinator or general manager of maintenance for all five plants. That move didn't seem to be in the cards; there was no thinking along those lines.

"Would creation of such a position have payoff for the company?" the counselor asked. Bill quickly saw some

areas where this would be possible. There would be both quick and long-range reductions in maintenance costs because of the establishment of uniformity in systems as much as the different plants would permit. The availability of a personnel interchange would give the firm a better-trained maintenance staff. A career upgrading system would cut the cost of personnel turnover.

"But," he added, "the plants were built at different times as the company expanded. They always have operated independently, so there's no likelihood that the post of general manager would be created."

"Since you have thought about it," the counselor said, "would you be willing to explore the possibility?"

Bill was dubious. "I wouldn't know where to begin. It doesn't make sense to simply go to the vice-president of manufacturing and ask him to create the job. I know him, and we get along fine, but I know him well enough to realize that his answer would be negative."

Bill and the counselor then brainstormed a plan that would lead to a reasonable approach to the vice-president. It was not a "quickie" approach. The beneficial manipulative aspects of it appealed to Bill.

First, he would write each of the maintenance managers, telling them he had incorporated some of their ideas into his facility and inviting them to see the ideas in action. If they would agree to come, he would try to get the vice-president to allow the time and expenses associated with such a visit.

When he had gotten positive responses from his four counterparts, he went to the vice-president and said he thought it would be beneficial for the company to have the others come in to suggest how plant operation could be improved. A two-day visit was approved and took place about a month later.

A report on their suggestions was written, indicating which seemed feasible, and forwarded to the vice-president. It was accompanied by a cover note recommending that Bill be permitted to explore on site how the suggestions were operating, and to pick up any additional information available. The note also pointed out how Bill had trained a backup man to carry on in his absence.

With the benefits of the group meeting in mind, the vice-president approved the serial visits in short order. Bill wrote each of the other managers saying he would like to visit them to see what else he could pick up, as well as exchange ideas of potentially mutual benefit.

On his trips he spoke to each of the managers about the benefits to be derived from increased communication among them. He also talked about the advantages of having a coordinator for such communication. When talking with one of the managers to whom he felt particularly close, he dropped the idea of a possible new position as general manager for maintenance, suggesting that he, Bill, would be an ideal man for the job. At each of the plants, Bill made notes on its maintenance procedures and discussed openly what he was doing at his facility as a result of the visit by the other maintenance managers.

When he got home, he compiled a procedural outline of each facility and sent it to the maintenance manager for review and correction. He suggested that all could benefit by circulation of the total set of procedures. When he was finished, he took a copy of his work to the vice-president with the suggestion that a new position be established to maintain and keep up-to-date the benefits that had resulted from his initiative. The vice-president took the matter under advisement, met with Bill, and called the different plant managers to discuss the proposal with them. About two months later the new position was created.

The entire project of creating that new position took eight months. It called not only for patience, planning, and the building of personal relationships but also for the proper timing of the various steps toward the goal. Also required were some not-so-obvious related activities, such as reading up on the latest maintenance techniques and active attendance at a national conference on plant maintenance.

Using Forms to Direct Your Own Promotion

A set of three forms will help you identify the basic factors Bill used, those that can be associated with your earned promotion.

The Position Requirements Form

The position requirements form should include the requirements of the position you believe you are qualified for. As demonstrated in the case of Bill, the maintenance manager, you need not limit your description to existing jobs; there could be some modifications you would prefer. Do not hesitate to suggest those modifications when you believe that they will benefit both you and your employer. Such changes may be seen as job-enrichment factors.

Position Requirements

1. General position title and description:

_____

_____

_____

2. Motivated skills needed in the following areas (list six or more):

_____

_____

_____

3. Personal relationships needed:

_____

_____

_____

4. Major work goals to be attained:

_____

_____

_____

5. Other general qualifications needed:

_____

_____

_____

6. After examining the previous requirements and the items in the Position Requirements form, what other training and experience are needed to qualify for this position?

_____

_____

_____

The Pattern of Contributions Form

The next form shows the pattern of your contributions within and outside the company that relate to your promotability. These almost certainly would include the achievements you listed in Chapter 3. They are needed at this stage, selectively, to assure you of your effectiveness in areas related to the advanced position you want and feel you have earned.

Pattern of Contributions

1. When did you join the company?

_____

_____

_____

2. How long have you been in your present job?

_____

_____

_____

Date started?

_____

Contributions and Outcomes   **Assignment/Dates**

_____   Job Title: _____

_____   _____

_____   Department: _____

_____   _____

_____

_____

Contributions and Outcomes   **Assignment/Dates**

_____   Job Title: _____

_____   _____

_____   Department: _____

_____   _____

_____

_____

The People Who Can Be Helpful Form

The third form should include the names of people who
can help you attain your goal of career advancement, and
their relationship to you or to that goal. It is important to
remember that no person works alone. Each individual is
related to others in some way, usually in very complex
ways. Very rarely does advancement result solely from
merit. It is due to a combination of circumstances, including knowing the right people in the right way, their awareness that your advancement could help them in some
manner, and elements of timing over which you may have
more control than you think. The case history of Bill also
demonstrated these factors.

> 66*Very rarely does advancement
> result solely from merit. It is due
> to a combination of circum-
> stances, including knowing the
> right people in the right way,
> their awareness that your ad-
> vancement could help them in
> some manner, and elements of
> timing over which you may have
> more control than you think.*99

It should be obvious that the third form is designed to
help you make sure you gain the cooperation of those
people who are most likely to be of assistance to you in
reaching your goal. Be sure that you identify the people
with power, as well as those who are related to what you
want on the organization chart. Very often, they are not
the same people.

People Who Can Be Helpful

	Name and Title	Data on Relationships: How They Can Be Helpful, When to See Them

_____   _____

_____   _____

_____   _____

_____   _____

_____   _____

_____   _____

_____   _____

_____   _____

_____   _____

_____   _____

_____   _____

_____   _____

_____   _____

_____   _____

_____   _____

_____   _____

_____   _____

_____   _____

_____   _____

Limitations of the Organization Chart

Tom, who worked in a well-known medium-size company, found his greatest ally in the man in charge of the executive development library. The library man also happened to be an assistant to the company president. At the time there was a rigid line of communication, which began with Tom's own boss, who wanted to keep Tom in his job for another couple of years. This may have stemmed from the fact that the boss, in his time, needed five years of "apprenticeship" before he was able to move up. Perhaps he now felt it appropriate for others to "wait their turn." But Tom believed he was ready for real progress and that his boss was in the way, although Tom liked him and had learned much from him.

Tom, 28, embarked on a strategy aimed at meeting the heads of five divisions, in the belief that what he could contribute would encourage them to open up a job for him. Identification of his motivated skills affirmed Tom's belief in his readiness. He identified some of his organization's "power lines" and worked at getting "plugged in."

He borrowed a book each week. When returning it, he tried to have a short talk with the "librarian" about it. The second time, he asked if it might be helpful to other readers if he wrote a two-page summary of the contents of each book he read. After the fifth book, he asked if he might be permitted to discuss one element in that book with a key person in a certain division.

The librarian changed hats, got permission from the president, and arranged a meeting with the appropriate division head. At that meeting Tom told about a field trip he was about to make for his own boss. "I'd like to return the favor for your helpfulness," he said, "and do something for you while I'm there—if it is feasible and doesn't take me away from my own task." The division head did have an assignment for him. Tom did it and reported back, and that relationship was established.

After he did this successfully a second time with another division manager, Tom took the librarian into his confidence and thereby gained another ally. By the time Tom reached the fifth divisional manager, he had been introduced to the president during one of his visits to the library. He knew it was just a matter of time before things would open up.

Tom's efforts required six months before the better job came along. In the meantime, he had prepared for his move by identifying a successor for his old job.

Of course Tom was playing politics. And, yes, he did "manipulate" others. Both words do have bad connotations. It is possible that someone better qualified than Tom was available when the job opened up. What is clear is that Tom had a goal, a plan, a strategy, and he made them work to benefit both the company and himself. It would have cost the company some $25,000 to replace him if he left—which is what the signs pointed to if he did not get the advancement he sought.

Most organizations do not have perfected career advancement information and selection programs. Rare indeed is the company with an open, progressive advancement plan. This makes it all the more imperative for each management and professional person to plan his or her own progress and develop the systems that make the goal reachable.

Nepotism Doesn't Always Win Out

It has been said that nepotism is the one obstacle that cannot be overcome. But self-interests of the boss and of the organization continue to be key factors, along with communication and relationships. You will see this demonstrated in the story of Lou.

Lou, age 36, was what amounts to a project manager in an advertising agency. He was one of six who reported to the production vice-president and thought of himself as a creative, good manager. His staff of three was supplemented by specialists. The production vice-president had a relative on his staff, a younger man who held a nebulous position and frequently required help from others. He wasn't exactly a dud, but the staff considered him to be the vice-president's fair-haired boy who could do no wrong.

The rumor mill indicated there would be a new position with the title Creative Ideas Manager and that the nephew would get it. Since Lou felt there was no hope and his future would be blocked, he sought counseling to discover what he had done wrong. (People always seem to be more concerned about what they did wrong than what they could do right.)

To be brief, Lou organized and installed a production control system that enabled him to see, day by day, the progress made by his staff on each of their accounts. He told the vice-president he could give him precise daily data instead of the generalizations customarily given him at the weekly staff meetings. At the next weekly staff meeting Lou gave a production report that was specific on where accounts stood, which ones were behind, and what was being done to make them current.

All five others and the vice-president jumped on him, insisting he couldn't be that specific in a creative environment like an advertising agency. Lou had anticipated the explosion. He quickly reaffirmed his report and invited the boss to check him and his staff.

The check took place, with the vice-president expressing doubt that the system would continue to work. When it had worked for three successive weeks, the vice-president asked Lou to explain his system to the other five. Two months later, because it was proved to be in the self-interest of the vice-president and the organization, Lou got the new job.

He had gained the respect of each person concerned, demonstrated his creativity and managerial skills, and made himself the logical choice for that number two position.

Of course, for every case of this kind, there probably are a dozen or more where nepotism wins out—especially in smaller organizations. But in those cases the organizations lose some of the employees who could contribute most effectively to company progress and growth.

Lateral Career Progress

Career progress is not always upward. It usually is that way with new and young employees, but not necessarily for the older ones. Sometimes it is blocked by the lack of employer planning or inefficiency on the part of the planners. Often the art of identifying those who will make good managers is not well developed. Progress also can be blocked by poor or inappropriate communication of skills between the manager and his subordinate.

Employers are always interested in knowing about those men and women who deserve promotions, in their own interest, as well as in the interest of the employee. But traditions of policy—traditions that may have been useful years ago but are humanly destructive these days—often block the recognition of qualified people.

One large government agency grants its upper-level employees up to two years' leave for job-related career development tasks. Jim, a top professional, saw the need for training foreign nationals in their home country to appreciate the workings and relationships of this agency.

He developed a plan, applied for a foundation grant, and was given two years' leave. He was effective, and he asked to serve as a consultant to his agency and represent it at an international conference in a nearby country. He sent back quarterly reports to his boss and otherwise maintained liaison during the two years.

When he returned, the day-to-day personal relationships that had prevailed before his leave could not be resumed. He was not up-to-date on internal personnel shifts in the agency. When he gave notice of his return, there was no job related to his experience available for him at his level. He was shunted to another job, as assistant to a reluctant boss, at his former salary. In his new surroundings he had to study hard to become reasonably familiar with his new tasks. He seemed unable to satisfy his boss.

After 20 good years with his organization, he began to lose confidence in himself. Reexamination of his contributions helped restore it. Careful inquiry revealed that his boss had wanted someone else for the job in which he was placed, but instead had been forced to give it to Jim.

Jim felt that his contributions abroad would be appreciated and would earn him a promotion. But he hadn't told anyone about those thoughts before leaving, while working abroad, or after returning. He felt that he was under fire and was the victim of circumstances. Although he couldn't afford to quit his well-paying job, he considered looking for another job elsewhere or trying to establish a new job within his agency.

The SIMS approach helped him prepare for the annual appraisal review with his supervisor. His report showed many years of substantial contributions to the agency but a scarcity of contributions during the past year. He asked his boss for help in getting him transferred to a new position where he could resume making worthwhile contributions while making room for someone who could do a more effective job for his current boss.

That openness understandably gained agreement. For the first time in almost a year, they really started to work together. Within two months Jim had a lateral shift into a newly created position with his former boss, coordinating the staff activities particularly as they related to dealings with foreign governments. He also aided in the development of trainees assigned to his agency by foreign governments. Within five months Jim's status was equal to that of the number two man in the department.

It would have been easy for Jim to charge into Personnel, claiming that he was a victim of management's poor judgment and demanding that management correct its error.

> *One virtually unbreakable rule of management is that personnel errors are covered up, usually with subtly forced resignations, golden handshakes, occasional firings, or meaningless "promotions" out of the way. Jim recognized that he would have to do his own career healing, but needed a little help from his friends and others who were concerned about his dilemma. He explored his achievements, identified where he wanted to go, and helped effect the creation of the job for him.*

Alternatives to Promotion

There are many ways of gaining career advancement. Ascending the management ladder is not passé, but it is not the only route.

Job Satisfaction in Your Current Position

The time has largely gone in the United States when people worked only for a living. Today, more and more people expect job satisfaction from their work, self-fulfillment, or self-actualization. These are modern phrases for a feeling that the work is giving one joy and opportunities for growth toward one's potential. It doesn't stop with the attainment of a goal. When one goal is attained, the next step is the attainment of another goal. Modern research also shows that most goals are not primarily financial ones, although financial rewards are usually included in the lower half of ten factors.

> 66 *The time has largely gone in the United States when people worked only for a living. Today, more and more people expect job satisfaction from their work, self-fulfillment, or self-actualization.* 99

Later Change in Vocation

This means, then, that advancement may involve a lateral shift within an organization, one that enlarges job satisfactions. It could mean a change in vocation as new fields of work come into being and old ones become obsolete. Sometimes the change requires substantial study; sometimes little or no additional training is needed. Change in any form brings its stresses. For these, the System to Identify Motivated Skills can prove to be a dependable cushion or bridge of stability.

Imagine, if you can, the stress faced by a medical doctor, a specialist in mastoidectomy, when he received news of a wonder drug that made his specialty obsolete almost overnight. In one instance a doctor returned to college for a year and specialized in gynecology, fully believing that population growth was a dependable factor—but even that isn't certain anymore.

Consider the Peace Corps Volunteer who helped a foreign community become self-supporting by getting it into the cattle breeding and marketing business. In the process he learned about artificial insemination, a specialty that wasn't much in demand when he returned home to the Bronx in New York. He, too, felt the stress of change. When the SIMS approach helped him separate his motivated skills from the name given to a temporary application of them, he was able to cushion that stress and move into a marketing position.

Becoming a Consultant

Sometimes specialization can lead to the outgrowing of one job and the need for movement into consultancy relationships—if growth and job satisfaction are to be maintained. In corporations experts often become internal consultants and, occasionally, consultants to customers and other firms. But it is not often thought of in religious vocations.

Reverend Wesley, a clergyman, had a pattern of achievements that revealed early and consistent concern with theatrical presentations and music. Not surprisingly he was a leader in movements to modernize liturgy, the formalities of church rituals. But one church has just so much room for innovation of liturgy. He complained that he didn't seem fulfilled. He had occasionally helped other churches of his denomination with their changes of liturgy. His counselor raised the question of expanding his consulting work for a fee.

Reverend Wesley hadn't considered that possibility. He explored the availability of his own church as a base, then began a year of planning and implementation toward a self-sustaining ministry as a liturgical specialist and consultant. Ten years of career, enjoyment, and increased income have followed. In the interim, he has written a book on liturgical experiences and has completed courses that enabled him to develop local and national religious television programs.

In this instance, the System to Identify Motivated Skills was a stability bridge to his "new career."

Assessment Centers for Identifying Promotable Personnel

Assessment centers are becoming increasingly accepted as an aid for identifying promotable personnel. Right now, more than a thousand small and large firms are using the centers. Regional conferences on new work ethics are enlarging this number constantly.

The assessment center starts with the conventional wisdom that upper management knows the right components of future jobs and that "trade tests" can be designed around those components. In large and medium-size companies, upper-level managers are trained carefully to be *assessors*, several of whom work together in a small team.

This approach holds great value to organizations, and especially to the managers who become assessors. They learn to observe and listen effectively and are given about three days to do so when assessing potential managers. They also learn to relate to one another much more closely than before, and to have differences of opinion without resorting to serious personal conflict. In their work together, the assessors almost form a semistructured human relations training laboratory in which they speak openly about their feelings toward the people being assessed, confer, and discuss their decisions.

The claim is made, and could very well be true, that assessment center identification of promotable personnel is more than three times as accurate as traditional systems.

Certainly the use of simulation exercises or games, combined with psychological tests, multiple interviews, and recommendations of superiors, is more likely to provide opportunity for demonstration of needed managerial skills than any one or a combination of the last three.

And it may be of historical interest to note that the assessment center process could be the first time that private industry has provided the lead in an innovating personnel selection process. In the past, innovations tended to originate in such old-line organizations as military and government agencies, and then were passed along to industry.

But there is an important area of oversight in the assessment center concept, as now practiced.

Every good manager in a new job changes its content in some way, occasionally in a major way, within six months after the person starts. The conventional wisdom which assumes that managers know future job components assumes also that people must reshape themselves to fit jobs. Yet almost every manager has hired someone who didn't fit a particular job description in certain ways, but who would add to its effectiveness because of special talents the individual brought into the picture. Job descriptions are flexible, often idealized, in their content.

It is true that assessment centers and the assessment process must begin with a reasonable appreciation of what is being looked for. But the oversight exists in the seeming assumptions that each person's pattern of skills cannot be identified prior to the assessment center project, that the boss alone may nominate those who have demonstrated promotability, and that simulation of business experiences is more a predictor of than a check on demonstrated skills.

Self-Nomination for Promotion

Self-nomination for potential manager training, based on a SIMS report, should be permitted and encouraged. A few companies now permit self-nomination for assessment center evaluation, but it does not appear that they provide potential nominees with a well-developed process for motivated skills identification.

This, then, is an area where the assessment center process can be improved and will be improved: each nominee, and others who want to participate, should be encouraged to use the procedures outlined in Chapters 3 and 4, write a report demonstrating actual and potential skills, and have this report data considered along with other data developed in the course of the assessment center process.

A Look at the Future

No one really knows what kinds of new jobs will exist in the future. A few already have become clear. There will be more astronauts and aquanauts as space and the sea are increasingly explored and used. There will be more leisure-time workers as the demands for physical and mental labor shrink and as weekends get longer and holidays more frequent. There is likely to be a movement toward hand-skill activities and artisanship, both as a means of preventing boredom and as a way of expressing creativity.

I have long forecast a general retirement option at age 50, accompanied by transferable pensions, as a means of enabling older persons to change into vocations that provide job satisfaction while they are young enough to enjoy many years of it. This retirement option would be accompanied by professional career counseling that would include the use of the SIMS approach and transition assistance to different jobs or careers.

My own belief is that a three-day week will become normal early in the 21st century, and that there will be double shifts—some working the first half of the week and others working the second half. In this way we can move toward the solution of two problems. The first involves the use of facilities. Obviously the overhead cost of facilities is reduced if they are used six days a week rather than the standard four or five. The second problem is unemployment.

Today, with the spread of flextime, part-time, rented, and temporary employees, and the four-day week of 32 to 40 hours, there are 120 million people employed and more than 8 million officially unemployed. If only a 4 percent increase in the number of employed could be engineered by adopting the three-day week by a small percentage of employers, there would remain barely a fringe of unemployed—primarily those who are changing jobs or careers. Other things would happen, too: human productivity would increase, partly because of reduced absenteeism; health would improve as a result of lessened work stress; and the crime rate would drop. The change would also spur research into how leisure-time activities could help enrich life personally and through community service. In addition, because barely a quarter of our highly intelligent young people get a college degree, there is the possibility that widespread use of the SIMS approach will bring to light thousands of geniuses (see Chapter 14) whose inventions and discoveries will lead to the start of new businesses. Cost-benefit equations haven't been worked out, but that can be done.

At the Paris conference of the World Council of Management Organizations (CIOS) in 1957, a Dutch economist forecast a new industrial revolution, with widespread unemployment as an outcome of automation. The reverse tended to happen as all countries of the world came closer and trade spurred industrial and agricultural expansion.

This enrichment of the world, which has not bypassed the developing nations, would have been impossible without automation. The rich probably will continue to get richer, but many more people are already seeking opportunities to help poorer nations make better use of their natural and human resources.

In this respect, it will be possible to use the System to Identify Motivated Skills to help people in poor nations leapfrog from agricultural-level careers to intermediate and high industrial production levels. Examples of how this would work are given in Chapters 9 and 14, along with some suggestions for assessment and career renewal, or the prevention of obsolescence.

Undeserved Promotions

Promotions do not always go to those who deserve them. A prime cause is that, being human, managers make mistakes. They have favorites, and the most deserving employee might not be around when decisions are being made. This drops responsibility for letting managers know about advancement potential into the laps of those who deserve advancement.

Open Posting of Jobs

In *Career Management* Marion Kellogg concurs and suggests open posting of jobs as a major means of reducing the chaos that often follows promotion of the wrong person.

Open posting is an aid, but it is no substitute for a system that helps the individual become aware of his or her own strengths and potential, as well as areas needing development in preparation for desired advancement.

The forms shown, and the examples given, help individuals become aware of their personal readiness for advancement, who can help them attain this goal, the elements of timing that enter the picture, and ways to increase the opportunities for gaining earned advancement and recognition.

Each is the maker of his own good fortune.

—Miguel de Cervantes (1547–1616)
Spanish writer

Develop or Renew Your Career

Our society is geared to the need for periodic renewal of our surroundings. We accept as a matter of course that our automobiles need periodic maintenance, and even an occasional overhaul. The appliances in our homes are repaired, modified, or even replaced when the job for which they were acquired changes and the old machines and methods no longer do the job satisfactorily.

It would seem to follow, then, that we should be both willing and able to extend this thinking to our own careers and even to our basic way of life.

To many people, the concept of change is frightening. Change is not to be taken lightly. It always leads into the unknown. And if the familiar is comfortable, it is possible that the unknown may be uncomfortable.

A widely held belief holds that maintaining familiar structures and systems will keep conditions the same. But so long as time goes on and people continue to grow, conditions cannot avoid changing. Thus people are faced with the paradox of the need to find stability in change.

Change can be seen as a renewal of your career. This chapter is designed to show you how to master the various changes you must cope with in your life and in your career.

Reviewing Your Career Style Periodically

Each individual develops a system of living to which the person becomes accustomed. We call it the person's lifestyle or *career style*. Every few years this career style needs maintenance; it may even require substantial overhaul. Unfortunately, too many people feel they can't be bothered with this effort.

Things sometimes go well early in careers. Progress may be fairly rapid through the lower economic levels. Many long in management and the professions probably have surpassed their original expectations and now tend to feel that a little slowing down is no cause for concern.

It isn't really, if—and it is a big if—everything else slows down, *if* young people who like to move ahead fast don't enter the job market, *if* they don't shove when they do, *if* things don't change as much in the future as they have in the past—and a long list of other *ifs*.

As people climb their career ladders, it is natural for them to become more concerned with maintenance of their job and status than with growth and change. The logical result is that they establish their own ruts. As their salaries and status increase, they realize they have more to lose. Thus they attempt to avoid risk and resist change. In short, they block progress and they bring on themselves the very disasters they sought to escape. "That which I feared has come upon me." Job foretold that thousands of years ago. Franklin D. Roosevelt put it another way: "The only thing we have to fear is fear itself." Today's psychologists call it a self-fulfilling prophecy.

Understanding How Your Career Style Can Change

Each person has a particular career style, and each adopts style changes for different occasions. Off the job your career style becomes your lifestyle, even though you may associate with many of the same people.

Affected by Type of Organization

Your career style is influenced by the environment of the organization within which you work. You may be part of a pyramid-type organization, with clear lines of responsibility and authority going up to the top. You may be in a more democratic structure, in which responsibility and authority are spread around. There are other types of organizations in which some divisions or departments operate under different organizational setups.

Traditional, Pyramid Organization

In the traditional, pyramid organization, the boss not only has the final word but also needs to hear all the right answers. The latter is impossible. Further it puts a crimp in the career style of someone who likes to act independently, particularly if the person must get prior approval before trying something a little different.

Democratic, Participative Organization

The democratic, or participative, management organization provides the individual with considerable freedom for action within guidelines the person has set with the help of a supervisor. The professional in these surroundings has more freedom to take risks and is encouraged to make positive changes to attain or surpass agreed-upon goals more efficiently. This system requires open personal relationships and communications, with freedom to disagree, to cross the often imaginary lines of organization.

Evident in Types of Career Styles

Most managers and professionals follow four main career styles. These categorizations are reported by Robert N. Rapaport in *Mid-Career Development*.

Maintainers

Some men and women become self-satisfied with what they have attained. They do as much as possible to resign from the rat race. They concern themselves with doing as little as necessary to maintain their hold on their jobs. These are the "maintainers." Unless protected by higher-ups, and this is temporary protection at best, they are prone to obsolescence and terminations.

Convergers

A second group can be called the "convergers." They move things along by pulling and putting things together in improved ways, by consolidation and coordination rather than through serious experimentation or radical change. They aim for smooth operations.

Impersonal Workers

A third group may be said to have an "impersonal" career style. They flourish in bureaucracies, both public and private. They are more concerned with manipulating their own progress, without particularly changing anything. They are attached to their organizations for fiscal, ideological, or other reasons; they aim for survival despite the coldness, impersonality, and even alienative qualities of their environments. The impersonal type hinders change with red tape and substitutes: the appearance of activity for progress.

Metamorphics (Changers)

The fourth group consists of "metamorphics," who are concerned with improvement. Rarely content with things as they are, they attempt to change them. They value creativity and like to leave their imprints on experiences. They seek self-actualization through growth where they are, through growth elsewhere if conditions are not right where they are, through changing their environments; sometimes they serve as consultants or operate their own businesses. Metamorphics are deeply concerned with good performance. They tend to be decisive and self-confident, taking risks and accepting the pain of losing. They usually are authoritarian, but are open to sharing power when it seems likely to help in achieving desired changes.

Styles Can Easily Change

Almost all organizations have people who fit each of the four styles or mixes of them. Each person expresses a style in his or her own way and changes that style to meet the needs of changed conditions. It is not too difficult to change your main career style. But it does require you to reexamine some of your behavior priorities.

A handsome man of 33 was trying to make a job change because his income had not been increasing at the same rate as that of others in his graduating class. He had a respectable Wall Street position and dressed impeccably, though in a somewhat peculiar fashion.

Fashion is part of career style because a person dresses according to his or her self-image. What this man regarded as one of his greatest achievements revealed the cause of his peculiar choice of clothes, which was an influencing factor in his financial status and a basic component of his maintainer career style.

The achievement was his election, years earlier, as the best-dressed college student. It had really hooked him at the time, and he resolved to stay on top. But although the business world was now his environment and structure, his emphasis on being the best-dressed college student re-mained unchanged—he looked and dressed like a college student.

The image conveyed by his appearance belied his actual age, competence, and knowledge and negatively affected customer relations. When he was helped to recognize the inappropriateness of his dress, he opted to seek self-actualization in his career rather than maintain a long-past structure of campus appearance. He soon was moving ahead on Wall Street.

Understanding How to Change a Career Style

This example is intended to illustrate how seemingly simple some of our hang-ups can be, how easily some of them can be recognized and overcome. It also demonstrates the basic process essential to modification of career style.

Examining Your Current Role(s)

Role disengagement is the first step in the process. This means examining carefully the many roles you play. The work you did in Chapters 3 and 4 will be helpful now in identifying those motivated skills that could be causing you problems. You then will be able to explore with an open mind how those skills may be applied differently to achieve your goals.

Testing New Behavior Patterns

The second step, and this is an aid to open-minded exploration, is to *try out the behavior patterns you would like to develop.*

There are many places around the country where you can investigate and try out new behavior and lifestyles. These places have a variety of names, as do the projects they conduct. Perhaps the term most often used is "human relations training."

Two nonprofit organizations that can recommend competent training leaders in your area are the National Training Laboratories in Arlington, Virginia, affiliated with the National Education Association, and the Association for Creative Change within Religious and Other Social Systems in Syracuse, New York. In seeking help from either organization, be sure to ask for the names of fully accredited professional members. Their members live in all parts of the country.

The projects in human relations training courses run from a long weekend to a week or longer. In them you meet people who have concerns similar to yours; they want to become more aware of how they feel about themselves and others, how others interpret their behavior. They also want to experiment with changed behavior and get feedback on how that comes across.

Although participants in the small groups are likely to be strangers to one another, they are expected to be open and trustful if the goals of the training are to be realized.

Combining Behavioral Testing with Other Methods

The procedures applied by competent professionals have been in use for many years. However, since the participants are experimenting, outcomes are not always what each person expects. Sometimes another experience, such as a conflict lab where participants are helped to learn how to cope with conflicts, would be useful. One thing is certain: few of the training lab participants will have had the benefit of familiarity with the SIMS process.

A few years ago about a hundred mid-career clergy and managers participated in a series of SIMS seminars led by the author and in human relations training led by the Association for Creative Change professionals. There were about ten of these sequential projects over a three-year period at the Virginia Theological Seminary.

The participants commented: "The human relations lab really lifted me and made me aware of my feelings, while SIMS clarified where I am right now in terms of my career" and "I can see where I'm going and what I have to take me there. I now have a means for changing my behavior to meet new conditions."

In response to a questionnaire, 97 percent said they felt renewed in their vocations; 92 percent said they felt freer to choose what they would do; 95 percent reported improved self-confidence, clearer goals, and better understanding of how to improve their interpersonal relations.

Perhaps of greater importance is the fact that nine years later most participants still were reporting current benefits from the combined projects.

This seems an appropriate moment to restate briefly the essence of the many SIMS programs, even though this may make the process sound simpler than it really is.

A Quick Review of the SIMS Process

A basic assumption is that each person has excellence within him or her. It is then theorized that this excellence is more likely to be demonstrated in experiences the person feels to be achievements rather than in other kinds of experiences. It is assumed, then, that the person's greatest achievements will show the greatest concentration of the elements of his or her excellence and that study of these elements is likely to reveal a pattern of skills used repeatedly in making several greatest achievements happen.

It follows that this pattern of excellence components is likely to appear in future "great" achievements of the individual. Heuristic studies with thousands of persons have shown that these components are self-motivated skills. The System to Identify Motivated Skills is the process that helps a person, usually in a small group with a professional leader, to become aware of the pattern of skills or talents that form the matrix of the individual's ever-growing excellence.

> **66** *The System to Identify Motivated Skills is the process that helps a person, usually in a small group with a professional leader, to become aware of the pattern of skills or talents that form the matrix of the individual's ever-growing excellence.* **99**

Benefits of the SIMS Process

With this additional self-understanding, all kinds of human relations and development programs gain in value. Risk taking is more intelligently recognized, handled, or refused. Experiences are more wisely accepted and evaluated because the purpose of the experiences can be more clearly identified—whether they are for fun, education, the experience itself, or other reasons.

Five years of research into the process, partly funded by the National Science Foundation, showed these outcomes for those who participate individually in a SIMS process group: They significantly enhance their self-esteem, their motivation to achieve, their sense of inner power, and their mental health and self-efficacy. All participants said they learned new things about themselves (increased their potential), and earlier research showed that their employability increased (three times as many obtained jobs in less than half the time required by others in control groups).

The latest research was conducted by the Dependable Strengths Project in the College of Education, University of Washington. Earlier research was reported by the U.S. Department of Labor in its magazine.

Strengths Valued More than Weaknesses

SIMS studies show that mistakes usually are the result of misuse, nonuse, or overconfidence in the use of motivated skills or strengths. When applied to a person, this knowledge gives a different understanding to the statement, "a chain is as strong as its weakest link." The traditional interpretation of that statement is wrong because it stresses the need to search for weakness rather than strength in an individual.

Many men and women who speak well cannot spell; many who write well are poor at arithmetic. There are those without hands who paint beautiful pictures, and survivors of heart attacks who have gone on to become active athletes.

People have the power to forge their own chains. If they wish, each link can be a motivated skill, one that ensures progress. But they cannot choose a link if they don't fully realize what it is.

Increased Awareness

The SIMS process helps people develop that awareness; it enables them to conspire with good fortune, to plan for and attain goals, and then to surpass even their greatest ambitions.

The system establishes facts and direction—both derived from learning through study of one's own experiences—which add to feelings and hopes that may be neither defined nor directed.

Results that Can Be Tested Objectively

An important SIMS contribution, not emphasized before, needs to be made clear—the data produced can be put on paper and tested against the widest range of uses.

Strength-pattern elements, for instance, can be identified and cross-checked. The way these motivated skills relate to effectiveness in present or projected assignments can be explored by using functional self-analysis. In other words, the standard risks associated with personnel selection, placement, acceptance of assignments, or new jobs can be evaluated on paper before they are accepted or before modifications are negotiated. This opens up a new form of job freedom because it allows a person to explore the viability of his or her own potential in relation to the content of the task under consideration.

When individuals have completed this exploration process, they will know if they are likely to be challenged and stretched by the task, if it is one they can do easily without challenge and still enjoy, or if it is one that will make little use of their motivated skills and therefore carry numerous risks and frustrations.

In the Reagan administration, Treasury Secretary George Schultz, speaking before the American Economic Association about investment in human capital, once said that increases in national output have been large in comparison with increases in land, man-hours, and physical reproducible capital. "Investment in human capital probably is the major explanation for this difference," he said.

Yet a 1973 report on manager selection procedures said that the best procedures, used by only a few employers in the 1970s, were more than twice as good as those of the 1960s. Early techniques had not made use of the SIMS process, which was believed to be a basic component of the "trade secret" system used by Exxon for early identification of its "comers."

The Inevitability of Change

The essence of this discussion is that no one is going to stop change. Most managers who are doing well will, because they are human, resist change. All managers and professionals, because they are potentially wise, will try to plan for their own changes. They now have a means of doing it that will be a help not only to them but also to their employers, families, and communities.

Psychologist Erik Erikson said: "Turbulence and reorganization occur at major points of transition." His life-cycle theory implies that development takes place by accumulation of knowledge or skills between stages, followed by transformations at critical points of growth. This process

is familiar to every student who graduates from one
school and moves into another, with its different culture
and different challenges. Attitude toward these differences and turbulence changes as one gets older.

The Constancy of Motivated Skills during Change

Things are changing too fast for comfort. This makes even
more important an awareness of the elements of continuity persisting in this climate of "discontinuity." When job
titles change, often with departmental changes, there are
new duties, new associates, and old relationships to be
loosened or dropped. This happens whether the move is
lateral or upward.

The elements of continuity, however, include your pattern
of motivated skills and your career style, even though
some adjustments may be needed in their application.
These are familiar accoutrements, stable and dependable
accompaniments to your song of life. They can be com-
panions when you feel yourself a stranger; they can be
your lifeline as you swing from one career crisis to another.

A New Career Style: Becoming a Dropout

Part of our changing world is a new career style, that of
the "dropout." The college student who leaves college
before graduating is a part of today's scene. That scene
includes a multiplicity of symptoms that reflect malaise in
prevailing organizational structures.

Among these symptoms are chronic complaints of poor
service and workability of products, heavy absenteeism
before and after weekends, increased frequency of complaints about job boredom and frustrations, strikes,
increasing refusal by strikers to accept first agreements
recommended by their leaders, and a slowing down in the
starting of large new businesses. But the people who care
little about the quality of their work constitute the highest number of dropouts.

Example of a Dropout
Who Nevertheless Displays Continuity

The Wall Street Journal *once reported on a magna cum laude graduate searching for deeper quality in life. Each of us wants a better quality for his or her life. But we have to work for it, to exchange our own labor for things we want. Money originally was designed to facilitate that exchange. But it has become a commodity of dubious worth on the scale of values.*

That honor graduate had been vice president of his class, editor of his college literary magazine, public speaking champion, and captain of his swim team. After graduation, he had acquired about four years' work experience as an editor. For some six months he had been living in an isolated village with about 200 residents, working at every kind of job to earn his keep. He enjoyed, he said, "good food and all the space I want." He added that it was the first place he didn't want to leave after a few days.

He made a special effort to get to know people who were bad because he had always been good. He developed skills in design and silk-screen processing to earn money. He raised most of his own vegetables. Mostly, he traded his labor for things he needed. He got his clothes at rummage sales and gathered bits of junk for which he might someday have use.

What we learned about him through the SIMS process was that he claimed to use none of the skills he had learned in school. Yet he was using the intelligence he developed and proved. He was using the versatility he developed in school. He was using his speaking and persuasive abilities, as well as his facility with words, all of which were demonstrated and applied in school. His concern with people, shown by his major in anthropology, also was being applied. His concern with physical activity and movement was demonstrated by his swim team activity in school and by his location shifts across the country. The limited data gave no background for his design and artistic skills, so no SIMS assumption could be made about precedents for them.

In brief, this former editor was very definitely making low-level application of several of his motivated skills and, consciously or not, was maintaining their continuity in what he did. He was even considering the use of his leadership skill through organization and direction of a skills center in the village.

Importance of Constancy of Motivated Skills

Motivated skills are constant; even preagricultural ones may be developed for industrial application. This has meaning not only to developing nations, but also to those whose occupations become obsolete because of a change in general needs or in technology.

For Workers Whose Jobs Become Obsolete

Many teachers are finding that their skills are not needed in teaching jobs, and many space scientists continue to find the labor market inhospitable. Retiring military officers, at only age 52, are in the same boat. These are professional people, many in middle management, who have to develop, however temporarily, new career styles; they *must* change.

For Developing Nations

Consider the possibilities for change provided by the SIMS approach when applied to developing nations. As an extreme case, consider a jungle tribesman who is unfamiliar with modern conveniences. Somehow a person has reached him, in his own idiom, and gleaned from him the following experiences as his greatest achievements. First, he makes necklaces for his village chief's ceremonial rites. He collects teeth and bits of bone and stones to trade with occasional visitors for shells and pieces of metal. He also makes necklaces, not as good of course, for two other village chiefs.

Second, for many years he has organized and led groups of youths on training-type hunting trips. Third, he has trained two younger apprentices in making necklaces. Fourth, he has been honored for creating a particular color of dye that he alone is able to make.

In explaining how he makes the necklaces, he speaks about having to shape some of the pieces, soften sharp edges, drill in the right places, then put them in the right order for stringing. He has to dye certain pieces and then arrange them in proper fashion to match the ceremonial robes.

To select and shape and drill the necklace bits, he applies design and spatial relations skills; he needs great hand skills and touch sensitivity and talent in the use of crude tools; he shows talent in recognition and use of colors; he arranges, or organizes, his materials. He is able to negotiate with other potential buyers for his necklaces. He is observant and skilled in physical movement. He is a leader of youth and an organizer and trainer of men.

If this man were shown a series of shapes on paper, then the going reality of a simple machine—first idle, then in use—it is highly probable he could quickly be trained to use it safely. He could then learn to train others, pick up organizational and management skills, and serve as foreman or better within a year. All this could be accomplished without the need for him to learn much more than a few signs or words relating to designs and operating practices. But he would want to be mobile and outdoors, and some way would have to be found to provide him with outlets for these motivated skills.

Fearful of change, this preagricultural man would tend to welcome opportunity to stretch and multiply the effectiveness of his skills if he could see the new tasks as a continuation of the ones with which he was familiar.

He doubtless would tend to resist if he were asked, "How would you like to try something new?" He probably would be interested if he were asked, "How would you like to make better use of the skills you have by using them in a different way?"

A Cushion to Change

A bridge or cushion to change, one that enables an individual to see stability and growth in changes, is the knowledge that his or her motivated skills continue to exist. Such knowledge helps an individual to be more accepting of changes, more adaptable, and more willing to cooperate in making changes happen.

A New Way to Learn: From Achievements instead of Mistakes

How are people affected by the traditional process, the old method, of learning from mistakes? You find out what you did wrong so that you never repeat that mistake. When you do find out and eliminate the cause of that particular error, however, nothing new is added to your experiences. The reduction of that something, the mistake, is important. But this may be compared to cleaning rust out of a machine. It operates better, but it continues to deteriorate.

A very different set of conditions develops when a person applies the humanistic process of learning from achievements. Under the new method, the individual studies the steps taken to reach peaks, with the basic concern of learning how to take the steps in more effective, easier, or faster ways. The person seeks to learn how to do something rather than be preoccupied with mistakes that caused pain and failure.

Although antitraditional, this study can be done with joy. It should lead to faster and more frequent reaching of peaks. In addition, when being at the peaks becomes more customary, the person looks for ways to raise them. Concern shifts from the avoidance of errors to the attainment of positive, useful changes. The measurement and release of this self-motivation, or inner motivation for change, has been largely overlooked by most behavioral scientists.

The System to Identify Motivated Skills adds the personal motivation factor to the organizational factors emphasized by Argyris, Marrow, Davis, and others. All behavioral scientists refer to inner motivation, but I have seen no references in the literature to procedures aimed at its release except through management-directed systems.

The process used by Exxon for early identification of personnel with managerial potential, which the company calls its *personnel development series* (PDS), has elements in it that are strikingly similar to the SIMS approach. However, PDS is used as a test by management to gain information about a person's potential, rather than as a means of helping that individual become aware of and develop potentials. Exxon regards PDS as an important proprietary asset and does not permit other organizations to use it.

Business Ownership— Changing a Career Style by Becoming an Entrepreneur

As many as 40 percent of managers and executives who lose their jobs express an interest in starting their own business, and many employed individuals have the same aspirations. In addition, a large percentage of working people are interested in moving up to more responsible management jobs. Yet, in spite of their aspirations, few people are well prepared for the rigors of self-employment, starting a business, or handling demanding jobs in management. And too many fail unnecessarily.

Need for a Way to Ensure Entrepreneurial Success

This combination of facts indicates the need for a way to prevent the start of career ventures that a few hours of self-examination could show are almost sure to fail for lack of self-motivation factors.

SIMS provides a pattern of facts to indicate the level of risk involved in an undertaking that requires known skills.

The operation of a business, for instance, requires ability to manage figures, operations or production, and people, and to make sales. It also requires motivation to own, to take moderate risks, to initiate activities, and to lead.

Examination of the kind of business contemplated will reveal other specific needs.

A Salesman without Number Skills

Frequently a person with just one of the four key strength elements—figures, production, rapport with people, and sales—decides to go into business alone. An excellent salesman and promoter did this. His achievements showed no trace of anything connected with figures. He lost his business when he didn't get things done on time, when he overlooked coordinating the delivery schedule of different elements of what he was selling, when he neglected to send out bills for completed work.

After his oversights came to light, he tried to get a figures-motivated partner or even a dependable employee who would handle that part of the operation. But because of his earlier failure, people had lost confidence in him.

Accountants without Sales and Managerial Skills

Accountants who are familiar with controls, costs, collections, and other figure matters often have failed in their own businesses because they lacked the ability to sell or to manage operations. Likewise, inventors, engineers, and production executives often have failed in their own businesses because they were not sufficiently self-motivated to drive themselves in the other key areas of business operation.

Roots of Entrepreneurship

One basic element of entrepreneurship is the self-motivation to own. Some of the entrepreneur's early motivation to own, found mainly but not exclusively in middle-class families, is rooted in the built-up newspaper or magazine route, which is treated as a property and sold, and in coin, stamp, and other collections, which may be kept up, traded, or sold. The serious coin collector also demonstrates motivation to work with figures and money. The serious stamp collector demonstrates motivations associated with travel and geography, as well as with design or some other art form.

Costs of Entrepreneurship

All ownership motivations have a price. Time must be given to them. The price of giving extra time—one that all successful entrepreneurs know about—is learned early by the youth or child who is a serious collector of stamps or coins or who handles a newspaper route.

Another price is isolation, as well as relationships for a purpose, relationships that could be called semi-manipulative. Don't let the word "manipulative" upset you. Babies "manipulate" by crying and making noises. Mothers "manipulate" by rocking cradles and appearing to make promises. Each person to some degree manipulates others.

Abraham Maslow once told me that benign manipulation is an essential element in human relations. What is unnecessary is destructive manipulation, which occurs when the person doing the manipulating is antagonistic.

When an Entrepreneur Lacks Necessary Skills

To get back to the entrepreneur, where early indicators of ownership motivation are absent and where indicators of any of the four major factors are absent, the entrepreneur should seriously consider abandoning the idea. If the individual decides to go ahead anyway, he or she should consider bringing in others (partners or strong employees) who can be relied on to provide the missing basic self-motivations essential to entrepreneurial successes.

If you think this is farfetched, consider the lessons provided by Exxon in its PDS program. Exxon reports that a study of the early lives of its good managers resulted in the creation of a biographical pattern that enables the company to identify the managerial potential of their college recruits.

Data from my own files may prove interesting at this point. I studied the biographical data of some 40 army managers with more than 20 years of service. From this was developed a profile to help identify new military officers who would be likely to stay around for more than 20 years. Earlier I developed a bio-profile that helped a company select new salespeople who outproduced prior new recruits by some 20 percent in the first year.

Using the SIMS Process to Identify Potentially Successful Entrepreneurs

The SIMS approach can be applied to the person who wants management status. In his dissertation at George Washington University, Joseph Krieger asked more than a hundred leading executives when—that is, how early—leadership potential could be observed. More than 95 percent said very early. SIMS has identified early "symptoms" of managerial skills. A key indicator, understandably, is demonstrated leadership. Others include demonstrated planning, organizing, human relations, and communication skills.

The Risks of Failure

When a person who never has been in a leadership role is put in charge of a group, the risk is not just of failure. The real risk is the impact of failure on the persons the individual is supposed to manage. What will they think about the person or organization that made the appointment? There also could be damage to the relations between manager and managed. What we have considered here so far is only the human side of an enterprise. The desired quality and quantity of output are also risked.

Too often people are given management responsibilities on the premise: "Just because the person hasn't done it before doesn't mean the person can't do it. The individual should be given a chance."

Early opportunities are available to almost all people to demonstrate many managerial skills. Class leadership in school, election to student government, business manager of a team or yearbook, running the annual dance, organizing a fair, planning a program, captaining the debating society, running the school office—these are among hundreds of different early-life examples that have been given by good managers in their thirties, forties, fifties, and sixties.

The man or woman who has *not* demonstrated the various forms of management skill in early life should consider carefully the risks associated with trying to adopt the behavior and responsibilities associated with management. The status may be fine, but it may not be worth the loss of respect from others who quickly spot inadequacies. It also may not be worth the guilt and frustrations that develop when a person feels inadequate to the tasks but does not think it would be proper to give up any of them. Research shows that these inner conflicts can lead to a variety of diseases.

How to Get a Different Position

Sometimes it is wise to bite the bullet. The manager who feels in trouble should collect data and organize it to determine personal career goals. If goals differ too widely from present responsibilities, the individual should look within the organization for something else that he or she would enjoy doing.

Next the individual should practice with a capable friend or professional counselor what might be said to a trusted higher-level associate when asking for advice on how to go about getting a different position or preparing for it, as well as what approach might be taken to the boss and to the person who could be the future boss. It really doesn't matter if the desired position is available. What does matter is that something close to what the person wants probably exists and that a plan to move into it can be initiated gracefully.

The relief of knowing such a change is in motion will remove much of the stress, and steps can be started promptly to eliminate, in full or in part, some sections of the present job that are responsible for the greatest stresses.

The very positive side to such change is the opportunity it affords people who have the potential for certain jobs but who have been bypassed for some reason. As detailed in the chapters on getting raises and advancement, there are many ways to use the SIMS process to help ensure that a person's motivated skills are no longer overlooked in the pressures of time and events.

Using the SIMS Process to Win

The System to Identify Motivated Skills is not the answer to all career problems. It enables you to develop reality patterns to help you choose the career battles you may be willing to lose and to identify those you have a very good chance of winning. After the diagnosis, judgment and values enter the picture. Sometimes the "doctor" is in a mood where the attitude is, "when in doubt, cut it out." But this may not be a desirable prescription for you at this time. Other times, the idea of letting it ride, or letting it burn itself out, may or may not be the right prescription.

> **66** *Actually, the only safe assumptions are that there will be frustrations in careers, and in the need to change careers; crises in careers will come more and more frequently.* **99**

Recognizing Motivated Skills: The Key to Stability with Increasing Change

Actually, the only safe assumptions are that there will be frustrations in careers, and in the need to change careers; crises in careers will come more and more frequently. Before these factors become unbearable is the best time to begin the diagnostic measures that help a person to cope, adjust, and adapt. Being human, people tend to wait until things get really bad, obsolescence sets in, or termination or illness results.

A few, of course, do a good job of coping and preparing for their growth. These few tend to be aware of their strengths and their impact on the careers in which they are doing well. These few—and they probably number not more than one in five—know the strength-stability factors that enable them to contribute to changes, to be in the flow of the changes, on top of them, and renewed through them.

More and more management and professional people are facing more frequent career changes. As changes in organizations become more necessary, career styles of men and women will need to change. Almost everyone resists change, while wanting its benefits. The stresses of these changes, which are affecting people all over the world as well as in the United States, call out for a mode of stability, something a person can hold onto while everything else seems to be moving around. Motivated skills can be a person's stability.

There may be times when an individual needs to think about demotion and lateral movement in a career, as well as times when the person sees opportunities for progress—opportunities that seem to require skills the individual hasn't used in the past. A coping mechanism is needed to meet such crises.

The SIMS process is a diagnostic tool to help the person recognize a central core of career stability and develop changes in career style and behavior that free him or her to adapt to the new demands. Reexamination of the SIMS motivated skills data affirms self-confidence and helps bring about renewal.

*When your job no longer demands more
than you have, do something else.*

— Harlan Cleveland, *The Future Executive*

Prepare for Your Career Future

During the next two decades most jobs will change in content and responsibility. These changes already are under way at an accelerating rate. It is appropriate to take a look toward the year 2005 and consider how the professional and management person can be prepared for changes that may take place.

The Current World of Work

Today, for an increasing number of people, work is a way of being. It takes up more than half the waking hours of some 120 million Americans. Its impact reaches into all parts of living. If it can be managed, work might just as well be enjoyable, satisfying, growth-building—self-actualizing.

Increased Number of Married Women Workers and Increased Imports

In the last half of the seventies, two major events influenced changes in thinking. These were acceleration of married women in the workforce and imports from Japan. In 1980, for the first time in the U.S., working wives outnumbered housewives. And the quality and pricing of Japanese imports made it necessary for executives to look into Japanese manufacturing processes, especially their concepts of human resource utilization.

Reduction in Job Satisfaction

In the mid-1970s the level of job satisfaction dropped sharply. By 1980, a report indicated that half would not stay in their jobs, given a chance to change. Actions to reverse this trend were implemented by government and private enterprise to bring radical changes to the "game plan" of work.

Foreign Employees

A Swedish automaker suddenly was faced with the possibility that it might be unable to get needed employees and managers. Employment statistics showed that very few of the people who had graduated from the country's high schools and colleges within the preceding three years had been hired by the company. Almost all the new personnel had been "imported" on one-, two-, and three-year contracts, the maximum time limit permitted by Swedish law.

The temporary nature of their employment made training and development costly and excessively expensive. The company studied its operations and the attitudes of potential new employees who were nationals. The findings convinced the company to make radical revisions in its management attitudes and in the work itself. As these improvements became known, local recruitment began to grow.

Several European countries have more than one foreign employee to eleven nationals, with Switzerland importing almost 30 percent of its employees. Virtually half the employees in many of the companies in these countries are foreigners. The foreign employees originally were regarded as "cheap labor," in much the same way high school dropouts are usually viewed in the United States. But just as in Sweden, the European countries now are finding costs higher than they appear on the surface. Such high costs have prompted companies to give a new, higher priority to the need for changing management systems.

Poor Working Conditions

In the United States, similar worker dissatisfaction was revealed when young, educated employees at "Lordstown," General Motors' most modern assembly facility, rebelled against the "inhuman" working conditions required by the plant's automated systems.

The Tarrytown (NY) facility of General Motors was on its list for potential closure, when a decision was made to use it as an experimental site for introduction of QC (quality control) circles or teams. These were semiautonomous teams of workers who focused on specific tasks and had shared responsibility for good-quality production. The idea was adapted from Japanese manufacturers. Within 18 months, the quality and output of that factory had moved from bottom to top in productivity of all GM plants.

Changes in Composition of Women Workers

The composition of women workers has also changed. There are six million children under six whose mothers work, usually because their pay is needed to make ends meet. And there are millions more working mothers of older children and teenagers. Women occupy two thirds of all part-time jobs (more than 11 million of the 17 million people who work less than 35 hours weekly). Some of them pair off and share full-time jobs. Control Data Corporation led the way in employing women part-time, with prorated benefits. Deep changes in how men and women work have been effected by the financial and personal needs of women to affirm and maintain their identities.

Legal Changes

> *And legal changes happened. In 1978 California passed a law that encourages companies in recession periods to retain employees by sharing the workload through a reduced workweek. Some of the lost pay is returned in the form of an unemployment (tax-free) benefit. Where one-fifth of the workweek (one day) is cut, the employees get one-fifth of a day's pay as an unemployment benefit. Under this law, 850 companies have been involved in this variety of part-time employment.*

These changes are by no means isolated examples. There already is momentum to change work, to change the kinds of managers who will coordinate the changes, and to change the specifications for personnel at all levels. The changes will not be static; they will be part of a continuing movement. Many men and women who try to resist this movement will be hurt after a relatively short time. Those prepared to recognize and manage these changes through cooperation with them will find more opportunities for fulfillment in their work.

Anticipating the Future

Forecasting the dimensions of human endeavor is, to say the least, an inexact art. Yet there are signs to show that professionals and managers can expect many things. For example, William Bridges wrote in *Fortune* magazine about "the end of jobs" as we have known them. Some of the changes will appear desirable; others may not. Let's look at a few.

Jobs More Complex and Management Altered

Virtually all jobs will tend to be more complex, have increased responsibility, and be more entrepreneurial. Leadership and decision making will be delegated downward, with the management layer becoming thinner and some levels of management even being eliminated.

Management style will be more and more participative. It will involve consultations among and with those doing the work as a means of arriving at better decisions on activities that affect all. A new influence will be much in evidence in both public and private organizations: the public interest and the ombudsman.

More Task Forces with Temporary Managers

There will be more task force approaches to getting things done, with temporary leaders for such groups. Sometimes these leaders will be appointed; sometimes they will be group-selected; sometimes self-selected. This will make leadership at some levels an occasional thing, with no impact of career backsliding when the task is completed and the leadership assignment ends. This occurs in the military when "spot promotions" are given officers while on a special assignment. When they complete the assignments they revert to their original grades.

Sometimes this kind of leadership will be a training experience; sometimes it will arise because of special expertise. But, as mentioned, it will not always be long-term or permanent leadership.

Trial Periods before Hiring

An American Management Association report indicates that new key executives may be increasingly hired for trial periods, perhaps three to six months, and continue on only if the "chemistry" of the relationship is mutually approved as satisfactory. If not, termination pay for a year would be paid to give the executive sufficient time to obtain other employment and to compensate for the inconvenience.

Career Ladders for Professional and Scientific Personnel

Professional and scientific personnel certainly will have a ladder of advancement that parallels that of management. It is likely to happen because the growing strength of employee organizations will cause this long-spoken promise of management to be fulfilled. The longer this action is delayed, the more surely management risks alienation of these key people. Their help is essential if present and future executives are to establish effective participative management and increase manpower utilization at all levels.

More Negotiation among Top Managers

At management, executive, and professional levels, there will be greater need for the ability to negotiate. Relationships will have to be established that stimulate the resolution of conflicts and the progress of work. Goals and intermediate objectives must be established in ways that encourage the attainment of goals as well as their modification if checks show this to be desirable. There needs to be more flexibility in acceptance of changing work demands and team organization to meet those demands. Openness is required in the use of work modules to permit team or task force members to adjust their times at work for new learning, or even just relaxing. Flextime work has become increasingly available.

Greater Acceptance of Part-Time Employees

Part-time employees will have to be accepted at all levels, occasionally because they have special skills, but more often because that is the mode of work they choose.

More Communication at Meetings

Throughout there will be increasing need for the ability to communicate at meetings and conferences in full knowledge that from time to time the breakthrough efforts or ideas will be "keyed-in" by independent contributors. Of course, with all these changes, there will be much experimentation in jobs. TV conferences are "in." Faxing, down-link conferencing, and online communicating have changed how people talk to each other.

Change in Responsibilities for Key Executives

The complexities will be ever enlarging for key executives, and their rewards probably will be limited financially. They also will be limited psychologically by the knowledge that they cannot take full credit for what happens—and must not— because to do so would tend to destroy the morale of those who contributed to their achievements. The job of executives will be orchestration, the catalysis of experts and other employees into a harmony of movement toward desired goals. This is not to say that there will be no discord. People somehow have a need to sharpen themselves through properly handled discord. The key executives will need to be masters at encouraging modification of the attitudes and behavior of people so that progress may be ensured. They will be masters of negotiation, compromise, coordination of efforts and ideas, and conflict management.

Greater Accountability for the Environment and to the Public

Tomorrow's leaders will be concerned with the environmental and public impact of their goals and decisions. They will need to cope with more uncertainties and make the best possible decisions on the basis of available expertise, data, and a dash of their own hunches. Because their decisions and activities will take place in an atmosphere of accelerating change, changes that seriously affect business and public life, they will need to be sharper in discerning their own strengths and weaknesses as well as those of others. But their emotional thrust will be to use their strengths optimistically rather than to remain inert because they fear their weaknesses. Since they will know that there is no one final system or set of techniques that "works," they will be open to experimentation, however cautious it may be.

More Conferences

The pace of change continues to be aided by scores of conferences on "changing work ethics," "work and productivity," "career changing," and "productivity." Associated conferences relate to "inflation," and productivity is a central component of those. Mostly they focus on tax write-offs of investments in capital goods, and rarely are concerns raised about the possibilities of human capital productivity. (In fact, the one federal agency avowedly concerned with human resource development, the National Commission of Productivity, is defunct. But there are two major organizations that continue to seek out and report on human resource development and productivity. They are the Work In America Institute in Scarsdale, New York, and the American Productivity Center in Houston, Texas.)

More Changes from Increased Education

The changes in attitude have been linked to increased education and to the communications media, particularly television and the Internet. With greater education and knowledge, neither of which necessarily implies wisdom, more people feel they would like a piece of the action. They want more say in the decisions that affect their lives.

Increased Worker Participation

They are getting their wish, and both government and business are finding that there is a cash payoff in enabling workers to participate in decision making. The same holds true in regard to redefining jobs to give employees increased responsibilities. Many leading corporations report that such changes, generally called job enrichment, substantially reduce absenteeism (often more than 50 percent); increase output and quality of work (many report more than a 20 percent rise in output); and increase morale, which tends to sustain the gains.

Against these facts are the results of polls conducted by Louis Harris and George Gallup. Their studies show that the great majority of employed persons say they are not interested in higher productivity. At the same time, most believe that they themselves could be more productive. They believe their productivity could rise between 20 and 50 percent.

More Participative Management

These studies and the recent experiences of corporations with job enrichment indicate that the heavy-handed boss who just gives orders is not the style of manager who gets cooperation from today's employees. Rather, the participative management style—which now affects fewer than 10 percent of U.S. employees and managers—is more likely to produce the cooperation and productivity that everyone desires.

However desirable the participative management style might sound, it is new territory for most professional and management people. It is tough to imagine being a team leader or manager on one task and later being a special contributor or team member on another. What about pay? What about employment security? What about career obsolescence? What about promotions? What about job titles?

There are no clear answers to these questions. Many companies already are facing them in small ways, and each is endeavoring to develop temporary answers. One thing is clear: new "answers" arrived at are themselves likely to change.

Only a few companies are known to be approaching the participative management/job enrichment systems from the viewpoint of the individual as well as the organization, task, or group. These organizations include the Nuclear Regulatory Commission, which has over 8,000 employees involved; Donnelly Mirrors Inc.; and SmithKline Corporation, which has several thousand employees involved.

In these organizations the individual is provided with the Management Excellence Kit, the Atomic Energy Commission Career Planning Manual, or personal counseling. Both the first two are based on the SIMS approach; all are designed to help the person identify strengths, develop personal goals, be prepared to coordinate the goals with those of his or her department or section, and otherwise contribute on the basis of self-knowledge to whatever job enrichment and organizational development process may be going on.

This program is seen by these organizations as adding a deeper level of involvement to the already reported job enrichment/participative management approaches.

How to Survive All of the Future Changes

All these changes will lead to more, which are as yet unknown. Throughout the changes, ordinary people with increasing levels of information and education will need to keep their cool as best they can. Many of those who resist the changes will lose their jobs and be forced to adapt. Some will be able to resist change and manipulate job maintenance. Most will be carried along by means of training and retraining, self- and formal-education programs, and sheer luck. Increasing numbers will press for job satisfaction, shorter workweeks, and flexible hours. Some, who use the procedures given in this book, will achieve the continuity, adaptability, and status fluidity needed for movement toward using and developing their potential—and attaining "self-actualization."

Men and women who know their strengths and are aware of the risks associated with not using them, or using too little of them, will tend to be alert to the training and educational programs they need for continued growth. They also will know that growth is not necessarily, or all the time, a matter of promotion or climbing the management ladder. They will have the security of knowing they are valued for who they are and for their contributions and achievements. They will live well and be self-actualizing persons. They probably will find it possible to give less time to the job and more time to community-enriching activities. "Community," in this sense, includes service anywhere in the United States and the world. They will find themselves enriching others, as well as being enriched by their varied experiences, which include their work and their family lives.

> 66*Men and women who know their strengths and are aware of the risks associated with not using them, or using too little of them, will tend to be alert to the training and educational programs they need for continued growth.*99

By 2005 there are likely to be, in my opinion, employers with two shifts of three-day-a-week workers, people who are highly productive because they find self-expression in what they are doing both on the job and outside it.

Many senior high schools now include in their curricula career planning courses along the lines of the SIMS process, to help students know themselves and select the courses that are most likely to fulfill them as persons and employees. Similar courses are available in many colleges, and both levels of education are offering—in many parts of the country—adult instruction in career renewal, job changing, second career development, and retirement planning. (Elementary, high school, and adult curricula are available through the Dependable Strengths Institute, 2821 Second Avenue, #1002, Seattle, WA 98121.)

Updating Your Achievement Data

Each four to seven years, alert employees will review their career achievements to clarify the direction for expanding job satisfaction and growth. Each year, between these thorough reexaminations, they will update their achievement data and establish new goals and intermediate objectives for the following year. The accompanying SIMS updating form will help you perform this annual reexamination with ease.

Filing Your Achievement Data

First, it is important to repeat what has been said about developing your original facts. Keep in a special file those facts you listed about your early and later achievements, the ones you felt were your greatest; the motivated skills that your work with a team helped you identify, as well as the ones you added; your functional self-analysis checkup; your goals and intermediate objectives; the relationships you recorded as needing development; and your training and educational needs.

These data show trends in your life, your enjoyable and inner-growth life, and will need to be supplemented by the facts gleaned from your annual reexamination. You will also need to glance at the data when you add your summary of achievements at the end of each quarter. These quarterly reports provide the data needed for your annual reexamination review.

It may seem as though there is too much paperwork to this career planning and adaptation business. Do it thoroughly once, in about 30 hours spread over a couple of weeks, and you have established a path to job satisfaction for the rest of your life. Most men and women give more time to examining an automobile's potential—with a steadily depreciating life of about 10 years—than they do to examining their own potential career with a probable life of 35 years of increasing worth.

SIMS ANNUAL UPDATING FORM

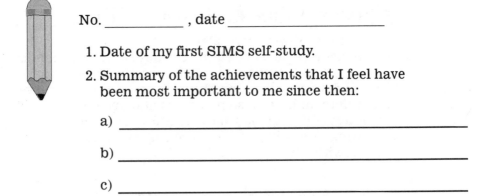

No. _____ , date _____

1. Date of my first SIMS self-study.

2. Summary of the achievements that I feel have been most important to me since then:

   a) _____

   b) _____

   c) _____

   d) _____

List additional achievements, as well as answers to the following questions, on separate pages.

3. Which of the achievements listed (a, b, c, d), if any, used skills associated with past greatest achievements? (On your separate pages, use the letters of the preceding achievements, and list the skills. Answer questions 3 to 8 on pages that can be added to your career development file. Record the date, the question number, and your answer.)

4. Which of these new achievements show development of my career or growth of my skills?

5. Notes I made after a consultation with my supervisor show that I agreed to do the following things.

6. In addition, I made notes on other things I want to accomplish, which are:

7. How closely, and in which items, have I come to matching or surpassing these objectives?

8. In view of my achievements during the past year, and the degree to which I matched or surpassed my written objectives, what should be reasonable objectives for me in the next year?

9. I have worked regularly with a small group (and followed through) in which we discussed each other's achievements. Yes_____ No_____

   a) If the answer is yes, have you benefited from the associations? Yes_____ No_____

   b) If the answer is no, have you spoken with others about the possible benefits of such a small group discussion? Yes_____ No_____

10. Chapter 5 gives instructions on goal planning. Reread that chapter and take the steps suggested. You will need several additional sheets of paper.

Creating for Yourself a Motivated Skills Report

In addition to the ten steps listed in the SIMS form, you should write a report to yourself indicating how you might make better use of your motivated skills. Consider giving this report to your supervisor and be sure to have supporting facts as well as the outcomes you expect for your team or organization as a result of the changes you suggest.

As part of your preparation for this updating activity, reread what you wrote down originally. That won't take long, and it will avoid the risk of overlooking some things.

That report you write, as well as the other data you have written, should go into your career file. A copy of your report should be kept available for easy reference because it will be needed for your review at least each quarter and as you consider the new things that are happening. It will help you to keep track of, and even take charge of, your career progress. Equally important, it will reinforce your feeling of freedom to cooperate with the changes that happen with increasing frequency, and will enable you to meet them without panicking.

Benefits of Self-Examination

Freedom and Stability

When you have identified your strengths, the strong threads of motivated skills, you will find they weave together into a lifeline that gives *job freedom* as you choose your changing career paths. This knowledge will give you *stability* when all around you the changes may cause shock waves and fear. Because you have objectives and relationships, you will have channels of communication that keep you informed on what you must do to anticipate and ride the crests of change.

Better Relationships

This is a *cybernetic*, a self-steering type of career freedom that enables you to relate to others openly. It helps you encourage them to use their best, as you expect to be encouraged to apply your best, your motivated skills.

More Freedom to Experiment

Some aspects of job freedom might not have occurred to you. Self-knowledge gives you *greater freedom to experiment*, to explore careers. If there is some job you are curious about—even if nothing in your background indicates that you really want to do it—give it a "taster's test"; try it out on a small scale. It could be tried as a night or weekend job, during a vacation period, as a volunteer or trainee, or through use of a sabbatical leave. (The safest way to experiment with a different career is to use functional self-analysis.)

Caution: Don't Judge Too Quickly

One caution: be sure you don't judge a job on the basis of a short-term reaction. Think of how you would enjoy the job on a steady basis. Before changing careers, get the help of your small group. This group, the one that helped you identify your skills, can be of continuing value to you as you consider changes, just as you can contribute ideas of value to other members of that group. It can be very supportive.

Suggestion: Meet Monthly with Your Group

Your group should meet at least once a month, with each individual displaying an achievement and motivated skills list as the person tells of further achievements since the last meeting. It has been found that each meeting invariably provides decision-making and problem-solving assistance to one or more members. This benefit is sure to get around to you sooner or later.

Use your group and let the members use your thoughts and ideas. Aside from the personal help you get from the others, you will be in line with an irreversible trend in American society—a trend toward mutual assistance, an interdependence that respects individuality, multiple inputs that stimulate wiser decision making, and the establishment of a trusting-relationship outlook that is increasingly needed in business and personal life. You will need the group to help you pass through many crises, whether or not you discuss them with the group.

The Threats of Worker Obsolescence and Forced Retirement

A U.S. Labor Secretary, James Hodgson, once said that although rapid obsolescence of talent is produced by the dynamics of today's enterprises, a credible goal for the future is self-realization through useful and interesting work.

Futurist Herman Kahn was tougher. He said there would be forced retraining or retirement of the American worker. *Fortune* editor Max Ways said that any specific job or skills can become obsolete.

The Need for "Career Insurance"

With such comments, there was mention of the probability that "career insurance" would be introduced. This would require organizations to counsel, retrain, and perhaps provide income-maintenance allowances to those whose skills have become obsolete.

The Need for Increased Community Concern

A Stanford Research Institute executive, Willis Harmon, warned of the sociocultural revolution that is making fast progress. It will require, he and many others said, that industry become more concerned with social responsibility and encourage its professionals, managers, and all other workers to become extensively involved in community concerns, as Xerox already has done. Harmon suggested that this might develop into a "humanistic capitalism," which includes the structuring of jobs to fit people.

The SIMS Process as a Hedge against Obsolescence

The person who completes the SIMS procedures outlined earlier will not only be able to make concrete suggestions on how his or her job should be restructured but probably also be ahead of the trend through self-restructuring of that job.

The Need for Better Understanding of Diversity

The change in value systems throughout the country, stimulated by more widespread education, TV, and other communication systems as well as by affluence and rising expectations, also contributes to the changes and uncertainties most people are experiencing. It now is clear to many that the United States is more of an amalgam of cultures from all parts of the world than a melting pot in which all are integrated. This point is proved by the success of periodic political appeals to ethnic groups. This sharper diversity in values is accentuated by global business, global tourism, and the crises of international trade and monetary rates. At the same time, different value systems are necessitating the need to collaborate, to interchange employees, to understand, to appreciate, and to learn from one another, especially in interglobal interactions.

The Goal of Improved Working Environments

All these factors affect employment and add to its complexity and pace of change. For some, they will mean a worse "rat race." But private and public employers can't afford the low productivity induced by the continuation of the rat race. Working environments will change, and are changing, to provide opportunity for each person to have greater job satisfaction. But in the main, as I have stated earlier, the thrust has been to hope the individual knows what is best for him or her and at the same time to be sure the organization does what it believes will be best for it and provide improvements for employees, which in turn will enhance the benefits to the organization.

This benevolent manipulation will be upgraded to true involvement as more and more organizations and persons use all the behavioral science and humanistic developments, including the SIMS process.

The Marriage of Technology with Spirituality

One of the interesting symptoms of the new social revolution is the "marriage" of technology with spirituality. It may be caused by rising complexities and frustrations, but there is no longer any doubt about a broad and rising interest in East-West religions, an appreciation of the mysteries that underlie natural forces like electricity, and mysteries associated with the different names given to God. The search for peace of mind, the search for meaning, and the search for scientific progress are being mentioned more and more frequently in the news and in public reports.

Chaos theory has stimulated science to include "mystery" in its considerations. M.I.T. professor Richard Lorenz used powerful computers to discover that, like a snowflake, nothing is ever quite repeated. The earth never orbits the sun in exactly the same ellipse twice; what is maintained is relationship, interdependence. Pattern is everywhere in nature. This "chaos" can be said to be ordered freedom.

The SIMS process focuses on uniqueness; patterns of motivated skills; strengths that team in work; relationships; community; and skills that respond to education, training, and change. It helps the person seek focus in wholeness as well as new possibilities.

It could be said that when a person looks for the best within and really tries to identify inner strengths and develop them, that individual is concerned with finding a way to let his or her own light shine. By encouraging others to look for the best in themselves, an individual is helping to forge a society in which each person may relate to the best in others.

> 66 *It could be said that when a person looks for the best within and really tries to identify inner strengths and develop them, that individual is concerned with finding a way to let his or her own light shine.* 99

This trend to include spirituality is on, and it has the blessings of the federal government as well as financial help from industry giants Ford, General Motors, AT&T, Exxon, Donnelly Mirrors, and a few hundred others. The person who can add self-understanding not only is moving with the tide but also is part of it.

Using the SIMS Process within a Team

A person can only do so much alone. This is why the small group and multiples of SIMS groups are important. The SIMS method enables a person to sort through the combined experiences of life, see clearly those parts that are worth repeating and improving, and try to forget the others. That's the kind of thing a good merchant does repeatedly. At least once a year, the merchant takes inventory to find out which items are out-of-date—the ones that will not produce a profit—and charges them off as losses either through special sales or in some other way. Not all items are seen as having equal value; that would be poor business. The write-offs enable the true assets to be valued. Everything else is charged off.

The SIMS method enables the person to apply that same business viewpoint to motivated skill assets. If the individual carries the weight of weaknesses on the books for a long time, and gives them equal or more attention ("Learn from your mistakes," "Find out what you did wrong," and so forth), the person will experience frustration and occupational bankruptcy.

The team approach prevents a person from lapsing into the rat race mentality, because it requires achievement experiences. It reinforces self-understanding and prevents fade-out of the benefits that come from knowing one's own motivated skills. The group prods the individual to look at new ways to adapt strengths and to investigate careers that support a sense of job freedom.

Using the SIMS Process beyond the Workplace

The SIMS process of looking for the best is not limited to the job. It is of tremendous value in all kinds of team efforts and conferences, including the team effort called "family," and the one called "vacation." As a kind of final word to the reader, the following three approaches are given with the intent that they stimulate you to develop more ways of applying the SIMS method to fit your own special conditions.

Group Exercises

The team that begins a task, whether it is a meeting or an activity, without first enabling each member to have reason for respecting the others is missing an opportunity. If the group is no larger than ten, each can be given two or three minutes to think about what possibly have been his or her own greatest achievements related to the purposes of the team. Then, in no more than two minutes, each should relate one of those experiences to the others. This establishes a climate in which all members of the team see themselves and the others as achievers and gain some idea of where and how they relate to the others as achievers.

Wherever this approach has been used, it has increased mutual respect, ensured cooperation, and led to improved productivity individually and collectively. The suggestion is that all team meetings should begin with this confidence- and respect-building climate.

Family Vacation Planning and Review

My wife and I have developed a SIMS approach to vacation planning. After each vacation, we separately write down those parts of it we enjoyed most and those we found obstacles to enjoyment, as well as the ones each of us felt were unique. We then exchange what we have written, find agreements, discuss the others to get mutual understanding, and abstract things we agree we would like to build into future vacations (and some we want to be sure to avoid). This has helped us have more enjoyable vacations and also plan with more intelligence the purchase of a vacation home.

Family Year-End Review and Planning

We also follow a similar approach as a "family team."
Each new year, we make our separate lists of happiest
individual experiences during the past year, happiest
experiences we believe we shared, and our greatest
achievements and disappointments of the year. Then we
exchange, read, and discuss.

Our discussions always have increased our understanding
and appreciation of each other. Each year we have
brought up things the other didn't know about, sometimes concealed hurts, sometimes unrecognized happiness. After we are through, we independently list our
preliminary goals for the year as the first steps to planning
for their attainment or modification. From time to time
during the year, we review progress, achievements, and
changes. Many times during the year we meet with a small
group to talk about achievements and reinforce each
other's progress.

The Need for Changes in Management

In an article I wrote for the *Harvard Business Review*,
"Pattern for Executive Placement" (Autumn 1947),
I stated: "Management is being compelled more and more
to consider the sociological results of its economic activities." The article suggested that management must shift
its mode from one of fitting people to positions to one of
fitting positions to people. It recommended the use of
techniques, the "birthing" of the SIMS method, which
"encourages a man to think of himself in a systematic way,
looking at his multiple experiences, taking a bit from here
and a bit from there, to prove he can perform an appar-
ently unrelated set of functions." It gave case histories to
show how such shifts were accomplished.

Using Motivated Skill Identification for Career Changing

There was choice then. But the time had not come when
men and women faced the "must change career" syndrome that is part of our present way of life. The shocks of
career obsolescence already have confronted a few million
people, including a goodly proportion of those in manage-

ment and the professions. Today, we have a system that helps people gain recognition of their unique skills.

It has cost industry and government billions of dollars to train and retrain those whose skills were made obsolete by technology and international trade, although the use of the SIMS process could have eliminated the need for nearly a third of that cost. The men and women themselves would have identified the kinds of jobs they could change to without training, or with minimum training.

The coming changes already have eliminated, on a small scale, many management jobs and have at the same time created some new ones. You cannot afford to risk being unprepared for these unknown changes. You will need to know your motivated skills so that you can influence your job changes from time to time within your organization. If you don't, you will be advised on the changes the organization wants and where it thinks you fit in. Of course, in the latter situation, you will be expected to make suggestions. But unless you have undertaken something like the SIMS process, your input will be based on only the hope that it will work out.

Including Others in the Search for Job Freedom

If you really want job freedom, you will need to want it for others around you as well as for yourself. You cannot have it just for yourself.

To paraphrase Abraham Lincoln, you cannot long have freedom and job satisfaction while others have rising expectations and lack it. You will need to be part of a win-win system, one that enlarges the pie so each may have a bigger piece, one in which the kind of competition that exists involves being your best more consistently and encouraging others, by your example, to do the same.

This does not mean harder work, but rather easier work and probably fewer hours. It will be work at which you are wiser in the application of your skills, so that you enjoy using them. Through this knowledge, you find the kind of growth you want, and you learn to live the quality of life you can value most.

These ten chapters have been devoted to the individual identification and appreciation of motivated skills. The final four chapters show managers how this knowledge can be applied from an organizational standpoint to help themselves, their employers, and their communities.

If you are a supervisor, read on and gain understanding of a management tool you may not have used before. Even if you are not a supervisor, read on so you understand what management plans to do with the information you may be providing.

*It is impossible for anyone to begin
to learn what he thinks he already knows.*

—Epictetus (ca A.D. 55–135)
Greek Stoic philosopher in Rome

Identify Employees' Motivated Skills

All supervisors are responsible for improved worker utilization. But supervisors cannot be expected to know everything about the people they manage. Why should they when few men and women know all their own skills? Accordingly, making the best use of people's potential becomes largely a matter of guesswork.

Easier Identification of Workforce Talent

So long as managers do not have a system that reliably identifies the self-motivating skills of men and women, their efforts to use people's potential will be far short of the optimum. They will, of course, seek and use improved ways to increase both efficiency and job satisfaction— such as job enrichment, management by objectives, and organizational development—but the work combinations that employees find self-actualizing will continue to be elusive.

> 66 *So long as managers do not have a system that reliably identifies the self-motivating skills of men and women, their efforts to use people's potential will be far short of the optimum.* 99

Much of the guesswork in the use of the labor force can be removed only by the subordinates themselves. It is true that most don't know all their skills and that most have hidden talents. But it is no longer true that the prime talents that move people to unique contributions must remain a mystery. The System to Identify Motivated Skills can clarify the existence of these prime talents, their present level of development, and their direction of growth or potential. Further, the SIMS process makes clear prime talents or strengths in ways that encourage the person to cooperate with technological and other changes taking place with increasing frequency.

Exxon (formerly Standard Oil of New Jersey) now is using something very much like the SIMS process to help identify early potential managers. The Department of Energy is using the SIMS process for the same purpose, and for employee upgrading and career planning.

The SIMS process can be viewed as a test. But it requires voluntary cooperation from the subordinate and cooperative exploration with the supervisor. It deals with selected biographical information from the person. It is concerned with clarifying the pattern of skills that has made achievements or successes happen. This combination of factors takes the SIMS process out of the realm of psychological and type testing and standardized scores, and goes beyond the limitations of bias.

Increased Productivity

Why should you be concerned with this? Isn't this all a function of the personnel or training department? Good questions for a manager to ask. The answer is that major concerns of a manager are performance, productivity, and quality in performance. All these are increasingly dependent on people and on knowing what makes people self-motivated. It is in this area that differences in workforce utilization will mean differences in organizational profitability or effectiveness.

In a national survey of some 200 executives in different leading corporations, most of them said that the productivity of their employees was less than 40 percent of what it could be at optimum. Productivity has gone up since, but mostly because of technological changes and huge investments.

Greater Organizational Effectiveness

Attitudes of people toward their work, and the attitudes of management toward recognition of their motivated skills, can make a big difference in the effectiveness of any organization, public or private.

> 66 *Attitudes of people toward their work, and the attitudes of management toward recognition of their motivated skills, can make a big difference in the effectiveness of any organization, public or private.* 99

Less Need for Workforce Training

There is a tremendous difference between motivated and unmotivated skills. Today that difference can be seen in any typing pool with 20 or more typists. Some do their work accurately, with ease, speed, and enjoyment. Others view their work as a chore; make too many mistakes—but not enough to get fired; type in fits and starts, a little sloppily; and are relatively uninterested in what they are doing. Those in the small first group are likely to be inner-motivated. Those in the second group are probably unmotivated, which means they would find themselves inner-motivated in other types of work. There also will be a middle group.

It usually is possible to make jobs more interesting and agreeable to employees, and this should be done as much as possible. But when the major effort is on job enrichment, it could mean that management has given up looking for inner-motivated persons. It also means that management is accepting responsibility for training and retraining its employees to meet changing job needs. A few hours of career planning conversation could make some of the training unnecessary and thus reduce costs.

How the SIMS Process Can Work for Managers

The following three examples will show how the SIMS process can work at several levels for managers. The examples will be followed by a summarized description of how the SIMS process works. The next chapter will provide some do's and don'ts that will be helpful to you in using the system.

An Unmotivated Soldier Back from Japan

A few years after a 29-year-old bachelor had returned from a tour of military duty in Japan, he had given up a short series of what he felt were dead-end jobs. He believed it more honest to quit than to stay bored and lapse into carelessness. He was asked to describe some of the experiences he felt he had done best and had enjoyed most.

His greatest achievement—this cum laude business school graduate said—happened after an off-duty drink when he was asked by a general if he had any idea of what he would like to do in Japan. He replied that he would like to find out what was behind the huge stacks of packing cases he saw on the docks in San Francisco and Tokyo, and on the decks of cargo ships all the way across the Pacific. He noted that most of the markings seemed to be identical.

His investigation revealed a costly foul-up in the military replacement order process and helped save many millions of dollars. He discovered that a specification had been misinterpreted and that five replacement parts had been ordered for each component of each airplane, even down to replacements for the screws and rivets.

Among his other achievements, he listed buying a wardrobe of 20 handmade suits of the highest quality in Hong Kong. The cheapest cost $25; the best $35. He couldn't understand why almost everyone else bought the cheapest suits. Even the best quality cost considerably less than the cheapest ready-made suit back home.

Another achievement was reorganizing his college fraternity house. He changed the meals, the social events, and the prices. For the first time, the organization became self-supporting.

His fourth achievement was planning and managing the yearbook so that it broke even for the first time in more than 20 years.

Each of the latter two achievements required him to conceive a management plan and gain the cooperation of others in agreeing on a budget, participating in activities, coordinating the timing of events, and maintaining the necessary records.

He was well able to do the detail work assigned to him in the accounting firms for which he had worked. He was skilled at it, but unmotivated. The achievement data on just these four of his experiences showed he was clearly motivated to express initiative in problem solving, to plan and organize, and to manage or control costs. He could gain the cooperation of coworkers and lead them. He demanded high quality. He was curious and observant about matters that might be overcostly, and he would look for ways to eliminate difficulties.

He stopped looking for a job that would use just his accounting training and experience, and began to look for one that offered him an opportunity to apply his problem-solving and managing skills and that used accounting as a tool. He quickly moved from assistant controller to controller of a leading manufacturing corporation. His salary doubled in the next three years because of his increased productivity, the rapidity with which he learned, and his corporate political skills.

The point of this for a manager is that a search for strengths or motivated skills in people can be done and that these strengths are the ones that produce a payoff for all kinds of organizations. This search for strengths is a far cry from the protective traditional approach of searching for weaknesses in order to avoid making mistakes in hiring. That approach hasn't worked, and human relations managers know it.

An Underachieving Pentagon Messenger

The second example involves a messenger in the Pentagon, a high school graduate.

I was training a group of Army specialists on the use of the SIMS process. One of their assignments was to interview a high-ranking military officer and a low-rated civilian employee. The pair who asked the messenger to complete the biographical questionnaire and then interviewed him were excited when reporting on it.

He was 18. His greatest achievement was being named a substitute high school mathematics teacher during the summer, although he had no college degree. Second on his list was his election as president of a community social club where almost everyone was more than twice his age. Third, he was president of the student council; fourth, he was valedictorian; and fifth, he was elected president of the junior class.

Why should a young man with such mathematical, leadership, communicating, and organizing talents be serving as a messenger? Why wasn't he in college? Simple. His sense of responsibility made him feel it essential to earn a living and help support the family. His father had died suddenly shortly after the youth had given his valedictory speech. This discovery led the officers being trained to arrange that the "messenger" get a college scholarship.

Again, the search for strengths, using the SIMS process, can and does reveal a pattern of self-motivating skills.

Beyond that, the pattern indicates the kinds of training a person will pick up quickly and what training will lift the total quality of the individual's performance.

An Unskilled Candidate for Welfare

The third example is at a totally different level—a relatively unskilled laborer who operated an old-fashioned polishing drum for some 35 years.

At 61 he believed he was too old to learn anything new that would provide him with a self-supporting income. He said at a SIMS reemployment workshop that he expected to become dependent on public welfare within a few months after he was terminated, when his savings would run out. He had been enrolled in the workshop by his company, which was about to terminate him because his job had been automated.

"If you feel that way," I said, "why did you volunteer for this workshop?"

"I'll be straight with you," he said. "I don't think this will help me get another job. I don't think anyone would hire me. But the company is paying for it, and I'm getting time off with pay, and you never know what good can come out of trying something."

The laborer, Joe, was asked to list his greatest achievement. He said it was fixing the broken stock on a rifle, "so good that the owner couldn't see where I'd repaired it."

"How did you do that?" he was asked. He told about his lathe and hand tools accumulated over more than 20 years. Sometimes he went hungry in order to buy a tool he wanted. His other achievements involved making well-structured cabinets and tables, paneling, and repairing wood products. Although he took no money for his labor, his work earned him high praise and respect.

"Perhaps you should be a cabinetmaker and repair furniture," he was told. He replied: "Nobody would give me a job like that because I've never worked for no one."

But he did get a job like that. And his rate of pay more than doubled. He was, and is, a self-motivated worker who gets joy from what he is doing.

In this instance, the point is that Joe was able to change careers without the need for spending any money on retraining. There were several byproducts: he is not collecting tax money through welfare checks; he is paying taxes; he is a self-respecting, joyful citizen rather than the despairing, dependent person he had anticipated becoming.

The Risks of an Informed Workforce

Can management afford to have employees know what their motivated skills are? Isn't it possible that people with that knowledge will be restless, create problems, and be more likely to quit? Anything is possible, of course. But management has been talking for a long time about the benefits of having the right person in the right job—how that would reduce absenteeism and sickness, increase productivity, improve human relationships, and otherwise contribute to cost reduction. All those benefits are bound to be accompanied by some problems. There are risks, and they deserve examination.

Perhaps some employees will get "bigheaded" when they know their motivated skills. That's a big "perhaps," because, if it happens, all kinds of problems could result. But one of the truisms in life is that people become modest when they know their skills are respected. This sometimes is said in another way: persons can "afford" to be conceited only until they are successful.

In an environment that encourages and helps employees to recognize their motivated skills, there is likely to be better communication between employees and supervisors, more understanding of department and organizational goals, and more cooperation toward achieving them.

How the SIMS Process Is Useful for Different Purposes

This must sound like the millennium. An explanation of how the SIMS process works—and the examples have oversimplified what happens—will make it clear that the process is not the answer to all personnel problems. The SIMS process is a tool that makes it easier to identify problems and solutions. This tool can be used for many different purposes.

In Working with Small Groups

The system can be used in small groups, and it is much less costly when used that way. It begins by assuming that there is excellence in each person and that there are many skills that make up this excellence. This combination of skills is more likely to be expressed in the experiences that a man or woman feels are his or her own achievements, rather than in other kinds of experiences; and these skills will tend to be most concentrated in what the individual feels are the greatest achievements.

The SIMS process helps a person remember many achievements and identify several of the greatest ones. The individual then is helped, usually with the assistance of a small group, to study these greatest achievements and to clarify which skills have most consistently been applied in making them happen. These are the individual's strengths—inner-motivated skills—and they are likely to be used when the person achieves again.

Without Job Titles

However, this process separates strengths from the names or titles given to different achievements—whether these be repairing a rifle stock, being valedictorian, or managing the yearbook. The process affirms the person's strengths—affirms that individual as having competencies. Because these competencies now are free from titles, they become more adaptable to combinations that fit other job titles. In other words, the individual tends to lose attachment to job titles and becomes freer to cooperate with change and contribute to it.

By Seeing and Encouraging the Best in Others

In addition, because the person knows the best that is within himself or herself, he or she can afford to look for and encourage the best in others. Such an attitude makes for more harmonious working relationships, especially when it comes to disagreements or conflicts. This is so because it then becomes possible for workers to respect one another's competencies, to learn from each other as they disagree while working toward solving a problem. In short, knowing the best within oneself aids teamwork.

In Handling Weaknesses

"What about weaknesses?" you might ask. Everybody has some. The SIMS process discloses weaknesses in two ways: first, by omission; and second, by clarifying the strength-weakness relationship.

When Leadership Skills Are Required but Missing in a Person

When physical labor and leadership do not show up in a person's motivated skills pattern, it is reasonable to assume a lack of motivation to do physical labor or to lead a group. This does not mean an inability to do these things; instead, it means that the individual probably will be uncomfortable and frustrated if these tasks constitute the bulk of his or her regular job.

When Leadership Skills Exist but Are Not Required on the Job

On the other hand, when leadership skills show up prominently in a person's achievements, but do not appear in that person's job, he or she will quickly become frustrated and try to use them—often in ways that raise problems.

Another example is a man who shows great strength in family relationships. If you ask him to take an important three-month business trip abroad without his family, you will find that his family relations "strength" becomes a "weakness" in regard to the organization's needs. Many more examples could be given of this strength-weakness relationship.

In Making Better Judgments about Using Employees

Much depends on where you sit as to what is weakness and what is strength. What is clear is that the knowledge of a person's motivated skills gives you more accurate information with which to make judgments on what to assign the person and how to present changes to the person in ways that gain his or her cooperation and support. You also can determine what assignments to avoid giving that person.

> **66** *What is clear is that the knowledge of a person's motivated skills gives you more accurate information with which to make judgments on what to assign the person and how to present changes to the person in ways that gain his or her cooperation and support.* **99**

These are advantages that make the manager's job easier. They afford the manager more time for leadership duties of greater importance. They enable the person to be more trustful of subordinates, and really more effective in utilizing the workforce.

The earlier chapters gave the steps an employee can use to identify self-motivated skills. It is not easy, and it does take time. But it may be the only way now available to add the important factor of self-motivation to other behavioral science approaches such as job enrichment, management by objectives, and the many strategies of organizational development.

The SIMS process should be administered by human resource departments. If it is, it can help establish new usefulness to those departments and give them a kind of credibility they long have needed.

The important thing is that we bring into play the full potential of all men.

—Crawford H. Greenewalt, *The Uncommon Man*

Maximize Employee Usefulness with the SIMS Process

Traditional attitudes toward the role and capabilities of the manager must be modified if the manager is to survive successfully the changes now under way in our society.

Most people believe that supervisors know all that is going on. If it were true, supervisors rarely would have problems. This unfounded belief only serves to multiply the problems.

Most employees also mistakenly believe that supervisors are aware of the best skills of those who work under them. If that assumption were true, there would be few problems of employee utilization and development. But again, the persistent but erroneous attribution of this talent to managers only compounds the problem.

The latter belief is changing rapidly, mainly because of the increasing number of younger people in the working world. They are more actively concerned with job satisfaction and self-actualization through work than are men and women over 40.

Younger employees complain more about being under-employed, that their best skills are not being used on the job. Too often they express their resentment against management by absenteeism, by stress-created illness, by carelessness, and sometimes by destructiveness. All these elements contribute to higher costs and lower productivity.

Making Better Use of Employee Energies

A modified approach by managers, team leaders, can ease these problems and even turn them into assets for the organization by making better use of the energies in-volved. The attitudes of managers will change anyway—in 8 to 10 years—because "now young" employees will become a major part of management by that time. However, waiting for progress to "ripen" in an organization is not one of the purposes of management.

Every good manager knows that employees are more responsive, more cooperative, and more productive when their strengths are challenged in their jobs and when they get quick recognition for jobs well done. Behavioral scientists call this "reinforcement." Good managers have been doing it for a long time. Now, however, it is easier for managers to improve their effectiveness by using recognition and reinforcement procedures in an organized way.

Paying attention to what employees are doing is not difficult, but it takes time. There is no way that a manager, relying only on observation, can know which part of a job employees feel they do best, or which part they enjoy doing, or whether they do a good job without enjoying any part of it. Finding out this information takes time and requires open, two-way communication with employees. Unfortunately, time usually is in short supply for managers.

The Value of Employee Data for Managers

Wouldn't it be helpful and timesaving if employees could provide a manager with reliable data on which parts of their jobs they do best and enjoy most—if they could reveal which are their most dependable skills (strengths); which, in their opinion, are their job achievements; which are their career goals, and why; and what training they feel would be most helpful to them and to their organization?

If they could provide this information, and a manager could hear it and be free to correct or confirm it, performance recognition and reinforcement would be taken off the back of the manager and would become a cooperative effort.

Interim and Annual Reports

A practical approach is for workers to develop an annual report as well as interim reports showing—from their viewpoint—how and when they are contributing to departmental goals, as well as how their work relates to their own growth, or lack of it. An annual report like this should be part of their own self-actualizing analysis. It can be an aid to the manager in planning each employee's career progress within the goals of the department.

An employee's first annual report along these lines probably will give data on outside activities, as well as on those related to the job. The employee doesn't expect the manager's blind acceptance of all the details that are new to him or her. The employee should be prepared for disagreement, somewhat prepared to attempt to prove a point, and even open to accept whatever the facts show.

Annual Report Conferences

Just for a few moments, review, as a manager, some of the major side effects of such a conference.

Gaining Better Knowledge of Each Other

Both of you will get to know each other better. The employee will know that you are aware of and appreciate his or her motivated skills. You will be more alert to the kinds of work the individual does best and enjoys most, and you will know that assigning such tasks will be an approach to achieving efficient performance. You will have two sets of information available, yours and the employee's. This can help you decide more wisely on where and what kinds of training money to spend, how to modify procedures so that department goals are achieved sooner and better, and what kinds of goals to set and what their intermediate objectives should be.

Improving Communication with Each Other

An additional side effect will be a better relationship, trust, and easier communication between you and the employee. You will be more likely to work together smoothly in problem solving. When disagreements occur, they probably will be impersonal, without any attempt by one side to "blame" the other. This leads to greater mutual understanding, which can be helpful to both the employee and you the supervisor.

Using Statements to Buy Time

As the manager at this conference, you will need to develop some "putting off" statements, phrases that will give you time to think about and examine the facts put forth by the employee. Such phrases might include "I'd like to think about that" or "That's a situation I'm going to look into; I didn't know about it."

These are not brush-off statements, nor are they put-downs. They should be made with the intent of conveying the idea that you need to think about what has been presented in the light of what is best for all concerned: the employee, the department, and the organization. You can make that intent clear by setting a time for another conference, a short one, in the relatively near future. Usually, a two-week delay is very acceptable. Sometimes a much longer delay is justified.

Taking Notes

At the first conference, you will need to take notes. You should ask for some time to go over the report, which the employee should be willing to leave with you. You should also take notes at other formal conferences with the employee because you need to refer to his or her wants and what you have said about those wishes. You should make no commitments at a first conference. Listen carefully, show interest, and suggest the second conference.

Protecting Your Own Interests

A well-prepared employee who has used the SIMS process along the lines suggested will be more alert to self-interests. The way the individual speaks could imply pressure. But, as the manager, you have to protect both your own self-interests and those of the organization. There is no need to yield to what might sound like pressure for quick action.

Encouraging the Use of Strengths

The employee will be talking about his or her strengths and self-motivated skills and, sometimes, about how they could be used more effectively. The use of these strengths on the job should be encouraged or reinforced because they bring about desired accomplishments. When they are used carelessly, or when nonstrengths must frequently be used on the job, mistakes and problems multiply.

Discouraging the Use of Unmotivated Skills

Sometimes people do things well by using unmotivated skills. This is especially true of men and women with higher intelligence who want to please their bosses, or want to test their versatility. But activities that mainly use unmotivated skills tend to turn off employees after a short period. For instance, a supervisor might be skilled at occasionally helping employees solve their personal problems. But if the supervisor had to do it all the time, as social workers must, it could drive him or her "nuts."

Ignoring an Employee's Weaknesses

When a manager thinks about improving the usefulness of an employee, the manager ordinarily should not consider that employee's weaknesses. When you put a spotlight on the weaknesses of a subordinate, you encourage that individual to think about yours. Even more important is the probability that the employee becomes resentful, turns off the "hearing aid," and gets psychologically unable to hear some good things you are saying. It is, of course, not possible or practical to ignore weaknesses that cause real trouble. These will be discussed later.

Providing Opportunities for All Employees

Managers will have to face a demand for upgrading employees and their skills. They also will have to produce employment systems that provide opportunities for full or partial self-support to persons who can work but have come out of public welfare, prison incarceration, drug treatment centers, etc.

The SIMS process can help translate some experiences of deprived and underemployed persons so their motivated skills may be seen. This helps change self-images of such persons from losers to possible winners; they become able to see themselves as sometime achievers. Here are two extreme examples.

A Person with a Prison Record

A man, now 38, who hasn't completed high school, is released from prison. He was put away because he was caught taking engines out of parked cars. He goes to a personnel department and applies for a job. The application asks if he ever was convicted. He checks the proper box and seals his fate. The employment interviewer catches that, gives him five minutes, says there is nothing available, but that he will be called when something opens up. The ex-offender knows he has wasted his time—again—in filling out the form.

He is enterprising, he really wants the job, and he will not accept the put-down. He calls the company and gets the name of a production manager. He then visits gas stations near the plant, asking what car the manager drives. He eventually gets the information.

One day, near closing time, he gets to the car, lets the air out of a tire, and happens to be around when the manager wants to start home. He offers to change the tire. The offer is accepted.

He works slowly, all the time telling the manager he is a capable mechanic who is very quick and has training in the assembly and repair of mechanical things like those the company makes. He asks the manager for the name of a foreman who might be willing to give him a test.

The next day he goes to see the foreman, saying the big boss said there might be a chance for him to demonstrate his skills. He makes it clear he would like to do a couple of jobs as a test to show he could do a good job; then he would go to personnel as the foreman suggested.

After passing the test, he tells the foreman what he believes to be his problem with personnel—being an ex-offender and maybe not fitting into the social scheme of the company. The foreman needs and wants good employees. He has to make a hard choice between desired productivity and the company climate.

Ex-offenders can be trained through the SIMS process to offer their skills—not necessarily in just this way—and they generally deserve a chance to renew their lives.

A Showoff Teenage Dropout

"Everyone in the mall knows me, and nobody would want to hire me," said Jim, a young man who was referred by the court to this alternative school. He dyed his hair jet black and wore it in a top knot; when he felt neglected, he shook his hair around until he gained attention. His greatest achievement, he said, was carving pictures and names into bits of wood that he gave to people he knew; "but there's no job like that." He got into trouble at school for doodling

during classes, sometimes drawing pictures, making designs, and showing them around. He would've had a collection of comic books, but once, when he was detained by the court, his family had thrown them out. He was good looking but sloppy in dress.

"I never did anything useful," he said, "except once when a kid in the lake looked like he was drowning, and I jumped in and pulled him out. His parents glared at me like I pushed him in, but I don't care." He also helped two neighbors move their furniture, "but that was nothing."

In our SIMS class at school, his team had said he had shown some artistic signs, he got along with people, he helped people, and he was very observant and dependable.

When the time came to create job contacts in the nearby mall, he came in looking clean, with a report on skills offered that said "Dependable, good at helping people, O.K. at carving names and pictures in wood, very observant." His report gave "evidence" of his skills like, "saw a kid gasping and floundering in the lake, jumped in and pulled him out though I couldn't swim." Also, "my friends like to see me carve their names on wood" and "helped some families move their furniture."

He took copies with him as he dropped in to the mall stores. In a jewelry store he said to the manager, "I don't expect you'll have a job, but do you think this report will help me to get one?" The manager asked if he ever carved on metal? "Naw," he said, "never tried that." The manager asked, "Would you like to try it?" He showed how to use an engraving tool, then offered it to Jim with a piece of metal. Jim engraved his own name; then the manager looked at it and asked, "Would you like to engrave people's names on jewelry they buy here?"

Soon Jim was offered an after-school job engraving; "Just having fun," he described it, "and being paid for it."

A properly led SIMS job-finding workshop has participants willing to offer their capabilities rather than just their experience.

The SIMS Process for Upgrading Employees

The basic SIMS concept is that each person has some excellence, which can be both identified and developed. Because the assumption is that skills exist, when even the person may not believe they do, the SIMS process often points the way to upgrading with little or even no need for training.

This can be quite a money saver for an organization concerned with meeting the upgrading problem at minimum cost—especially since this approach includes identification of self-actualizing, self-motivating skills that are always demanding opportunity for expression through good work. In management language, that translates into *high productivity*.

Focusing on Strengths rather than Weaknesses

The examples given add a different dimension to the meaning of weaknesses. Many weaknesses exist because people do not know, or do not know how, to communicate their strengths. People also demonstrate weaknesses because of an overconfidence in strength, which causes them to be careless. Witness the fable of the race between the tortoise and the hare. Weaknesses also appear to be an outcome of requiring a strength to be applied in an inhospitable climate. Consider the situation when an executive asks a pure researcher for a quick decision and the employee responds with a suggestion for a lengthy research process. This leads the executive to say that the person isn't decisive, thus attributing to the individual a weakness.

Weaknesses have an infinite number of causes, not necessarily related to productivity, while strengths are directly associated with it and are therefore more deserving of attention and reinforcement.

With greater knowledge of employee strengths, a manager can make better use of the workforce. But the manager must be patient in listening to what might at first seem irrelevant. It is easy and obvious enough when the experiences come through like those of the army messenger mentioned in the previous chapter.

But suppose a mother, inexperienced at job-hunting, comes to you and says that one of her greatest achievements is driving one day a week in the car pool for kids. It takes an effort to ask, "What made that seem like an achievement to you?"

She says, "I got fed up with chauffering every day, so I developed a schedule for working with four families in two blocks, with each of us driving our cars and picking up the kids one day a week. I felt it was quite an achievement to work it all out and get the others to cooperate."

Some of her other achievements were being in charge of several field trips for church teenagers. She got the parents and the youths together; helped them agree on a series of trips; worked out the scheduling; and then assigned the jobs so that someone got the tickets and others took responsibility for food, transportation, and related details. She took charge in the field to make sure that things kept moving as planned. In high school she was in charge of the senior prom. In college she served, very successfully, as chair of the graduation dance.

Such a woman might have a part-time word processing job, with no responsibility for organizing anything. This "new" data would reveal her talent for organizing, and a special task requiring that skill might be given to her. That certainly would be a way to make more effective use of available resources.

In this instance, it also might be suggested that she take some courses in business or public administration so that she could gain background and technology to support her organizing skills. Moves of this kind can not only be largely self-directed by the employee but also offer elements of job enrichment that could not take place without the facts an employee alone can provide.

It is not possible or reasonable for the new facts to effect changes overnight. When people are involved, changes require care and time. Almost all people resist change because they cannot know for sure what will follow. It is safer to stand still, we all tend to think, even though we know that the rest of the world will continue to move ahead.

Using the SIMS Process as a Bridge to Change

This contradiction in attitudes, and the related actions, worries managers. It is here that the SIMS process can help bridge the way to needed changes. It helps an individual know that a person's motivated skills are always with that person, no matter what the job title or assignment may be. This constancy, or stability, is a strong support to whatever career changes may be necessary. The person who knows his or her own strengths knows also that they can be applied in different ways.

In addition, knowledge of the person's strengths helps make clear the education or training essential or most helpful to a smooth transition.

There will be times when a person who has completed a SIMS strength-identification process comes up with a personal need for change that cannot be satisfied soon enough. There also will be times when the SIMS data will show that the person is unfit for the current job and that termination is the reasonable way out. These infrequent happenings face managers with the toughest part of their jobs, doing something that is almost certain to appear to the other person as harmful. Firing someone is almost like labeling the person "useless," and nobody likes to give or receive that label.

The SIMS process is a "guilt reducing" bridge here. It makes clear that the person has real strengths, real usefulness, even though an available job is not where those strengths can be best used.

In such situations the organization should help the individual obtain another position or become reemployed. This would reaffirm the person and also reinforce the manager who must make the unpleasant decision. There are effective guides to job finding in the form of books, audio cassettes, and manuals.

Using an Annual Review
to Regularize the SIMS Process

One way to regularize the use of the SIMS process is through the annual review. Nearly all major companies have arrangements for a formal review between supervisor and subordinate of the employee's career progress.

A variety of related contacts take place all through the year. But this is a time for pulling together the facts relating to progress or plateauing, and considering together what can be done to improve things or maintain progress in the following year. The purpose usually is along those lines, but most reviews are conducted in a very cursory manner, according to literature coming out of numerous companies.

The traditional annual review has reduced the credibility of managers and human relations officers and has contributed to disregard of performance requirements of jobs. This has been confirmed by several studies.

Two organizations report a turnaround in credibility, aided by the use of the SIMS process at annual reviews. At one organization, all employees are encouraged to use a specially designed "Handbook for Career Planning." It is given to them a month before the annual review. Each employee is told that the use of the handbook is optional. The individual also is told that the handbook is designed to help the employee gain a better appreciation of personal strengths and goals so that his or her own purposes may be fully considered at review time. A similar approach is used at a pharmaceuticals company in Philadelphia.

Both organizations use the SIMS process as a supplemental tool to get information not obtainable by ordinary means. The pharmaceuticals company also uses a wide range of other behavioral science systems, including job enrichment, organization development, T-labs, and management by objectives.

Credibility turnaround can be an important contribution to productivity and lower costs. It reduces absenteeism, raises job effectiveness, and cuts costly mistakes. Better morale and all-round cooperation for practical innovative progress are other benefits.

Some Potential Problems of the SIMS Process

The process does have some built-in problems for managers. Employees are accustomed to asking managers for all kinds of guidance and counsel, sometimes of a very personal nature. Managers frequently are helpful; this is part of their job. When SIMS makes strength data available, some employees are sure to ask the manager to do the interpreting. From deep and lengthy experience as a professional counselor, let me caution managers not to fall into that trap—because it is a trap, although not intentional.

Since each person sees facts in his or her own way, the manager is sure to view an employee's data in some ways with which the employee disagrees. For those situations, the manager will need a hedging statement. It could be something along these lines: "I'm not a professional counselor, so my approach is sure to be at least a little different from yours, and it certainly might not be on the nose." If something more must be said, phrases like this should be used: "It seems to me. . . ." or, "I'm not sure, but. . . ."

Resist efforts of a few employees to put the manager in the position of all-knowing father, while the employee plays the game of being child. Too often this is an unconscious effort to blame the manager when things don't go right. It is wise to resist the temptation—most of the time—to give depth counseling. Almost always that requires professional training in the use of the SIMS process and other behavioral and psychological systems.

The Value of the SIMS Process

Nevertheless, the manager will get considerable information from the SIMS data. Some of it will be important enough to the individual and the organization to be made part of the employee's personnel file or his computerized personnel data.

This process brings out the best in each person and provides ways for employees in small groups to help one another identify their strengths. Thus, it has the side

effect of causing more and more employees to seek and
encourage the best in others. This kind of climate is one
managers work hard to create. It's an environment that
encourages participation and discourages absenteeism. It
stimulates positive competition when each person tries to
do his or her best. Consider that in the light of a survey,
mentioned in the last chapter, which showed managers
believe that most people operate below 40 percent of their
optimum level of productivity.

Career and organizational job changes are happening
faster all the time. Most people now entering the job
market will change jobs and careers ten or more times,
according to the U.S. Labor Department. All managers
and employees will need to face up to what Alvin Toffler
calls future shock, or career shock. The newer movements
of managers, discussed in some detail in Chapter 10,
include systems that require much greater participation
in decision making by subordinates all the way down
the line.

Many managers will feel deprived of responsibilities;
others will welcome the additional time to do more
important things. Problem solving will become less of a
manager's responsibility; he or she will rely more on the
opinions and data of the employees concerned—while
keeping informed and available to pitch in if asked. There
probably will be more part-time or contract workers,
managers, and professionals.

Increased time for self-development and recreation will
create new types of working conditions. So will concepts
of work modules, with employees working in teams that
permit members to shuffle around their hours on the job.

There also will be earlier and later retirements, perhaps as
early as age 50. Some companies already permit retirement at 55; a few encourage it at 50. With job content
changes occurring every few years, sometimes radically,
everyone in a division or organization may suddenly have
to face the prospect of skills obsolescence. These realities
can already be seen here and there.

It is because these realities are here or clearly on the
horizon that this book was written. Anyone following the
procedures outlined will come to recognize that there is

continuity for each person through all the changes. The continuity of strengths will be a security track that eases stressful moves from one job or career to another.

There is good reason to fear the changes that are crowding in on us. But history provides substantial basis for hope and faith that they will be moving us toward the better things we want. The pessimistic predictions and turmoils of the Industrial Revolution slowly opened into twentieth-century growth and opportunity. The depression of the thirties moved more quickly, though accelerated by World War II, into the Western world's era of full employment. The feared prospect of automated unemployment in the 1950s did not materialize, although it did bring tremendous career and employment changes. The recessions of 1974 and 1979 were short-lived, even with inflation hammering at the growth curve.

During the '80s and '90s the world shrank into a global village. Any conflicts between countries rarely flared into violent war and generally were solved by negotiated agreements and trade agreements. European Union became a reality, the Soviet Union world threat was broken up, a bi-continent America has begun to exist, Asiatic nations have joint agreements, and India and China show strong signs of industrial and democratic growth.

There is more division, however, between the very rich and very poor. Some ways need to be found to house and educate the increasingly numerous poor so they too may participate in the growing prosperity of our global village. More training in the benefits of voluntarism and community-building, leisure-time activities, combined with a shorter work week, would help. There is a call for strengthening of neighborliness and peaceful relationships—despite an increased call for prisons and crime control.

SIMS-type programs have been developed, tested, and shown to be effective in schools, colleges, and many institutions, as well as with adults at all levels. The Dependable Strengths Institute of Seattle is concerned with training teachers and leaders in its procedures so that organizations of all kinds may have in-house capability to help their employees, students, and clients.

Currently there exists, for the first time in a long time, a worldwide acceptance of relations among all nations, despite frictions, wars, and threats of wars. In each country there is evidence that the principles of self-actualization and management by objectives are basic to individual growth of nations and persons, as well as to mutual understanding.

People have demonstrated very remarkable power to surmount obstacles as they learn to combine the uses of science with the powers of nature and with faith.

It is in this frame of reference that the SIMS process contributes a sliver of assurance for continuity, not ignoring the evils of which people are capable, but with faith that their interdependence and concern for one another as individuals—seeking the best for themselves—will become intelligent selfishness that provides a rainbow for progress.

Change can only be facilitated,
not decreed.

—Marilyn Ferguson
The Aquarian Conspiracy

Provide
Reemployment Counseling

The toughest job an executive has is terminating someone. Sometimes it is a department or a division, sometimes a general cutback or a reorganization caused by a
merger. Always men and women and personal relationships are involved. The termination act calls for inflicting
pain, and no one does that willfully or enjoys it. This
chapter outlines what can be done to alleviate and
shorten that pain and to reduce the executive's guilt
feelings associated with firing someone. (The term "reduction in force" does not diminish the impact of termination,
which employees call "firing"; it is just softer on the
tongue.)

A Case of Reemployment

Pain? In the middle of an industry-wide collapse, Bill, a vice-president of sales, was among those terminated when a division closed down. He was home before noon and told his wife. She was encouraging. He was depressed. A generous termination payment did not lessen his feeling of not being needed—almost of uselessness. A week later, this "enthusiastic and successful" executive meekly thanked his wife for not leaving him—a man who, at 52, said he was over the hill, unemployed, virtually a bum, who could no longer support the family he loved. He had always been a "good provider," he said, but no longer. And there were no job possibilities because the whole industry was depressed. "How could this happen to me, when I've worked continually since I was 14? Even in high school and college, I had jobs that found me! And I haven't missed a day through sickness all that time. I never had to ask for a job!"

His wife's assurances, a year's salary in hand—all these were insignificant in the face of his having no place to go to work, no way to earn a living. If anything did come along, he reasoned, he'd have to take a serious cut in the $60,000 salary he was accustomed to, and he'd have to start again at the bottom—that is, if anyone would even hire a middle-aged man with experience in only one industry. And he repeatedly sank into depression, not even playing the records he loved, not showing a sign of the toughness that had been his norm, not cracking jokes. He had become a man who had lost his identity and believed he would never recover it.

After two months and several relapses, all of them far from the first depression, Bill was reemployed in a different industry with plenty of opportunity at an annual salary of more than $48,000. Bill's boss initiated the reemployment counseling.

The Difference between Outplacement and Reemployment

There is a difference between what has come to be known as "outplacement" and reemployment. With *outplacement* as it is usually practiced, the concern is with assisting in placement of the person as fast as possible. With *reemployment counseling*, the concern is both with rebuilding the person's identity and with helping the person attract his or her next position. Reemployment takes no longer, usually costs less, and is often faster and more helpful than placement efforts. SIMS is one key difference; another is the dynamics associated with group process.

Side Effects of Reemployment Counseling

Important side effects of reemployment counseling include very fast release from guilt feelings for the executive who institutes the termination, and often a rise in productivity among retained employees. Usually more than two-thirds of those fully involved in reemployment counseling find jobs at comparable pay within 90 days, an outcome that frequently stops any potential rise in unemployment-tax payments for the company.

A Case of Reemployment Counseling

Let's return to Bill, the vice-president of sales. The chairman of the board, who fired him and knew him socially, offered to write his curriculum vitae or résumé and then reproduce it. (As Bill had written it, it was an uninspired listing of his education and work associations.) The chairman also insisted that Bill be counseled individually. Bill intensively studied his personal and work achievements and saw for the first time that he had enjoyed selling for 38 years, because at age 14 he was selling advertisements for his junior high school yearbook.

Making that connection helped him see his lifetime selling ability and began his turnaround. Functional self-analysis (Chapter 4) enabled him to test the reality of the strengths he had to offer his next employer, the areas in which he could prove dependable and productive; it also indicated his style as a sales executive. At that point he had lunch with his boss, the company chairman (visiting first with some former coworkers), and thanked him for the opportunity that had resulted from his being fired.

Then he wrote a report on his executive style and effectiveness. This report gave the reader facts that might not be easily discerned at an interview, and certainly would not be revealed on a chronological résumé or a job application form. It described him as an operating person, summarized his relevant background, then gave examples of his effectiveness in the areas of selling and sales management, policy-making, problem solving, personnel selection and development, and marketing strategy. It closed with personal and family data, education, and the names of companies with which he had been associated.

It was an easy-reading, one-page report revealing his strengths, which is all an employer really wants to pay for. Most of the counseling done to this point can be just as effectively done (sometimes more so) with a small group and at lower cost. But many executives value extreme privacy and pay the greater cost.

Bill resisted contacting his friends for help in finding a job—understandably. Throughout my career, I have advised professional and management people to avoid asking for jobs when they are actually seeking one. My researches have revealed that the person who says, "Do you have a job?" or "Could you refer me to a position?" quickly becomes persona non grata, forgotten, avoided. Bill instinctively shrank from this, but he knew no other way.

Top-flight executives are always "window shopping" for talent. One of their key responsibilities is finding people who can reliably get work done. And much of the time, they have projects on the back burner, waiting for the right time and the right people. Bill needed to circulate among such executives and let them "window shop" him. He was practiced in how to do this. (Members of groups practice with each other, under supervision and often with the aid of TV replays.) He began to see himself as the means by which one executive could help another to window-shop for a talented sales executive.

He also practiced building the climate for these window-shopping interviews by first visiting three executive friends. "I don't expect you to know of a position," he would say, "but I am looking for one. So I had an expert help me develop this report on my style and effectiveness. I've really never looked for a job before, so I'd like to know if you think this report will help my search." This approach invited them to criticize the "expert help."

They asked him lots of questions, admitted that they had learned from the report things that they hadn't previously known, and said that they thought the report would help him. (Two of them suggested that he also prepare a chronological résumé showing the times of his employment, his responsibilities, and his employers.) All of them said they would keep him in mind if they heard of something that could use his combination of talents. He said he expected to get something within six months, and that he'd keep them informed of his progress, if they didn't mind. They agreed.

Then he asked for an introduction to someone who might also be willing to keep him in mind for any possible openings in his line. To his surprise, he was given four contacts (one said he'd try to think of someone and would let Bill know), as well as permission to use the names of his other two friends. That opened window-shopping doors to executives he might otherwise never have met.

Obviously this contact-creating process established a climate in which he was constantly encouraged and could not be turned down flat. He began to see two new people each day, whenever possible. Between meetings he wrote thank-you notes to his contacts and helpers. Of course he also answered advertisements, registered with recruiters and appropriate private and governmental executive placement services, and collected tax-free unemployment compensation. The placement agencies pooh-poohed his report, but he was prepared for that.

Sixty pleasant contact interviews later (he often was invited to lunch and sometimes did the inviting), he started a series of job interviews which led to three offers, a negotiation of salary and benefits, and acceptance of the one that had the second-best base pay but that most closely matched his strengths and offered a good opportunity for growth.

Bill closed his job-finding project by writing to each of his window-shopping contacts, telling them of his new position, and thanking them for their encouragement and help. And a special letter went to the man who had terminated him.

Benefits of Reemployment Counseling

The "toughest job" of an executive will always be traumatic, but reemployment counseling can quickly alleviate the stress and pain, prevent added unemployment taxes, and restore goodwill, And the cost isn't much—usually about 10 percent of the terminated person's salary (with complete follow-through help until he or she gets an appropriate position), or about $1,500 in an individualized group with four months of follow-up (twice as long as needed by the average person).

An executive who feels guilty about meeting the need of an organization when it requires terminations will delay the required action and thereby hurt his organization. With reemployment counseling available, the humanitarian instincts of such an executive can be met in the best interests of all, on a cost-effective basis with maximum consideration for the persons involved.

There is always pain in terminating someone, just as there is some pain in all kinds of progress. Reemployment counseling (or continuing employment, as it was called in Chapter 6) is responsible social action that has tax, community, corporate, and personal benefits as well.

*The biggest human temptation
is not to ambition too much
but to settle for too little.*

—Thomas Merton (1915–1968)
Trappist monk, author

Identify Dependable Strengths: Key to Greater Productivity

There is an ever-increasing demand for higher productivity, greater employment of minority youth, and reduction of the underemployment that is prevalent in the economy. And it is hoped that many of these demands can be met without inflationary effects. In this chapter some ways to accomplish this are first illustrated by four examples and then explained.

A High School Class with Conflicts

Let's start with a conflict-ridden high school class. The teacher asks if students would like to know how to be more effective in solving whatever problems they have in life. He involves them in a small group process that enables them to perceive their own and each other's beginning strengths. Then the teacher helps them to recognize how it is possible to relate to the strengths of others so as to be more effective in solving or coping with problems. When this has been accomplished, each student knows that the others are aware of his or her strengths and what is behind those strengths. The need to prove oneself to others and to establish one's identity has been largely met. The one-upmanship that has prevailed until then becomes unnecessary, and the energy formerly given to conflict is largely transferred to improving strengths through learning and studying.

That scenario has occurred.

A Group of 58 People on Welfare

Now move to four groups of men and women on welfare, all of them over age 45. They are depressed and believe they are unwanted and have no future. They are in the "dead" files (never to be offered jobs) of a state employment office. Their speech is filled with "hopeless" terminology. Dr. Don Faith and Dr. Florence Bustamante worked with me on this project. Our task was first, moving them emotionally from the welfare culture to the employment culture, which was a culture-bridging problem; second, establishing them as productive and employable people; and third, enabling them to obtain good jobs. The language of employed people tends to be self-confident and hopeful; that of those in the welfare society is characterized by hopelessness and a lack of confidence.

Fourteen of the 58 poorly educated and virtually untrained men and women did not complete the process. Of the other 44, 60 percent (26) obtained jobs within eight weeks, and 90 percent of them held their jobs over the nine months of checking.

Dr. Rubin Krigsman, then with Xerox, used some of the findings of this project to help design that company's widely acclaimed minority recruitment program in Rochester, New York. When the process I designed was used in a controlled experiment for unemployed high school dropouts, Dr. Bustamante reported that three times as many of them obtained jobs (and in less than half the time) as those in the control groups.

Forest Service Employees

Twenty-five hundred U.S. Forest Service employees at all pay levels were involved in SIMS strengths-workshop seminars over twelve years. Virtually all (over 95 percent) said they learned new things about themselves: their potential had increased, all reported that their self-esteem had improved, and 82 percent said that they learned how to bring out the best in others.

A 1976 study of 200 professionals and managers who changed jobs and careers with the aid of the SIMS process showed these results: 95 percent said the process helped them to learn new things about themselves; 75 percent said it enabled them to be at least 20 percent more effective; and 29 percent said that their employers created new jobs for them, so as to use more fully their special capabilities.

Southeast Asian Refugees

The fourth example involves Southeast Asians—Vietnamese, Cambodians, and Laotians—who fled their respective troubled regions to come to the United States. In those cultures college graduates almost automatically get government jobs or work with family businesses. The other 95 percent grovel for "patrons" (potential employers), accept whatever is offered at whatever price, and usually live where they're told to live. They may not ask for raises or promotions, because asking reflects on the intelligence and generosity of the patron—something that could upset the patron's highly prized sense of harmony.

A system far different from ours! Using SIMS, we devised ways for Asians to translate their experiences at home into "American skills." Then the Asians were involved in a two-job process: the first at the beginning to help them learn English; the second, a better-paying job for applying their skills. This two-stage process helped them bridge the gap between their traditional semislavery and our concept of job freedom and upward mobility. Their counselors were taught how to use the procedures and ideas.

The Unlocking of Human Potential

What these examples show is the unlocking of potential in men, women, and youth. Dr. Margaret Mead said that people rarely use more than 10 percent of their potential. Psychologists in general are agreed that less than 20 percent of people's potential is used. Just suppose that in the case of minority high school dropouts, the figure really is Dr. Mead's 10 percent; it then becomes reasonable to assume that a portion of the 90 percent that remains unused could be found and used. If that amount were only 5 percent, it would mean a 45 percent rise in productivity! (Five percent of 90 percent is 4.5 percent. A 4.5 percent rise over a basic figure of 10 percent is a 45 percent increase in productivity.) Both employability and behavior would change.

With the general population, 5 percent of the 80 percent of unused capacity would be four points; which adds up to one fifth that might be added to the norm of 20 percent of potential productivity that is actually used. It is certain that new concepts, products, and businesses, as well as greater employment, would derive from a 20 percent rise in the number of geniuses and entrepreneurs!

The Limitations of Traditional Education for Unlocking Human Potential

Training and education usually enable people to do what they were trained and educated for. When prison psychologists approve the training of offenders to be barbers, that's what they know. But that form of barbering is obsolete: cutting hair is out; "styling" is in. Thus, training and education do not necessarily increase employability. Throughout the country, Ph.D.'s in the humanities know this all too well.

But human capital philosophers (such as economists Theodore Schultz and Gary Becker, who theorized that education, income, and jobs increase together) succeeded in having their ideas transformed into national policy. One very constructive outcome of their ideas—and there are many—is the community-college movement. Community colleges have indeed enlarged opportunities for millions.

Traditional human capital theories, however, were largely debunked by Dr. Ivar Berg in his book, *Education and Jobs: the Great Training Robbery.* Supported by Dr. Eli Ginzberg, director of Columbia University's Conservation of Human Resources Project, Berg gives data showing that the traditional view—"better educated workers are more productive"—is often not true. Dr. Berg points to the fact that research supporting the ideas of traditional human capital economists was extrapolated from studies of employed and highly talented people. I have already pointed out (in the story of the university placement director in Chapter 5) that demand for specifically educated people can be increased through marketing techniques, thus increasing their probable salaries. And in Chapter 2, I commented on a former chairman of AT&T who promoted the idea that executives come from the top 10 percent of college graduates—based also on elitist data.

"In every instance," Dr. Ginzberg states in his preface to Dr. Berg's book, "the data prove overwhelmingly that the critical determinants of performance are not increased educational achievement but other personality character-istics and environmental conditions."

Dependable Strengths Project Research over 48 Years

The last seven years of research at the Universities of Washington (College of Education) and Delaware and Seattle University involved four doctoral students. Some of the findings are that people in DSP seminars, classes, and workshops significantly enhance their self-esteem, motivation to achieve, internal locus of control, mental health, and self-efficacy. Participants reported that they learned new things about themselves (potential im-proved) and got along better with others (teamwork). These findings reinforced earlier studies reported by the U.S. Department of Labor, which showed that of those in DSP classes, three times as many persons got jobs in less than half the time required by matching control groups. Research funds came partly from the National Science Foundation.

Educators, Facilitators

In 1993, the Education Department of Idaho began stud-ies that resulted in the DSP becoming a part of Idaho's statewide education system at all levels. The first study involved 673 students, 95 controls, and 9 schools. The behavior of students after completing the DSP was signifi-cantly better (4.4 of 5); their attitude toward learning was significantly better (4.3 of 5); and the recommendation of the DSP to other schools was significant (4.6 of 5).

Population Diversity

From Harvard Business School graduates through recov-ering drug and alcohol addicts to prerelease and welfare dependents, the DSP has demonstrated high effective-ness. The Council of State Governments gave its highest 1993 award to a program applying the DSP (78 percent of 3,000 addicts and prisoners were employed or in training within 8 weeks, they earned almost 50 percent more than those not in DSP classes, and their recidivism was significantly lower).

Psychology

"Story" is now seen as at least as important as the "statistical" (test measurement) approach to knowing oneself. This constructivist view suggests that the person, through life stories, constructs his or her sense of what is "real." Stories of one's good and achievement experiences have been basic to the DSP for half a century. "Story" is basic in the lives of all ethnic groups. The Bible is full of stories. "Story" is central to modern qualitative research into the mystery of human behavior.

Chaos

The separation of religion and science has been ended by "chaos theory." It sees everything as connected to everything else, wholeness. We see order in our lives, but the unexpected happens: chaos, order. Chaos and creativity are two sides of the same coin. Predictability, order, and stability are good; but chaos, or disorder, exists too. And it can be good, not bad. The search for meaning in chaos leads to patterns within it. Faith that patterns exist in the million variables of daily life and thought leads to perception of strength patterns in a person's stories. Knowledge of the dependable strengths in these patterns enables a person to develop and combine them to meet changing conditions. Changes are part of future growth.

A Better Approach: Knowing What We Know

The unlocking of human potential requires knowing what we know, and that is difficult. Computers are helping to make a difference in many areas, but they've barely touched the unused potential in people. Knowing what we know, certainly knowing what we can do best, calls for setting priorities on the data in our minds, much of which is not easily recalled. The following case history is an illustration of this.

A man with two degrees in history studied computer technology to get a job. He was employed for six years as a programmer. He hated it but continued with it because it supported his life-style. Then, in despair, he paid a substantial fee for SIMS counseling. The activities he felt he enjoyed and did best went back 12 years to his military experience in Vietnam, where he was trained initially as a hospital orderly and ended up as the equivalent of a field hospital manager. His earliest achievement was splinting a dog's broken leg, and it healed. He told many stories of how he improved efficiency and saved lives by reinterpreting regulations, training volunteer hospital aides, organizing supply procedures, and—with the advice of doctors— changing schedules. He had no real authority to do these things, but he was accepted as acting "manager" because of his ideas and effectiveness.

After counseling, he was accepted by a large group-health organization as manager of paramedic activities, and suddenly a childhood dream came true. There is no place for "unauthorized activities you did well" on job application forms. Through his reanalysis of his own history (not because of added education), his potential changed radically; but a case like this has no space in traditional human capital theory.

Human capital theory needs reorientation to take into account the certainty that some of the hidden resources in people can be released and made available. When that happens, behavior changes as well as productivity.

What happens when, as revealed by the cases of the paramedic manager, the vermin exterminator, and the greeting card artist, a person becomes aware of the viability of skills or talents previously believed to be economically worthless? Who gains? Obviously, the individual does, and certainly employers do, as well as the communities they reach and serve—and Uncle Sam collects more taxes.

The Problem of Managerial Bias

But there is a management bias that needs to be appreciated. It is a very normal thing: in essence, "I like people like myself." The trouble comes when the manager needs someone who is unlike the manager. First, let us say, since the manager is a college graduate, the person would like an assistant to be a college graduate, too. When that is put into a job description, the term "college graduate" nearly always rules out nongraduates. When the person's major is added to the criteria, more people are ruled out. That makes it easier for the initial screener—usually the human resource department—but it has nothing to do with ruling in the person who has competence to offer but not the college or letters. So, the manager looking for competence tends to lose, at the same time the risks for first screeners are reduced. Clearly the manager loses when what I call "the Edison factor" (see page 36) is not considered. (Incidentally, young people who have IQs of 130 or higher drop out of school at more than three times the rate of less-gifted students!)

The Need for Selection Based on Likely Future Performance

Improved productivity and interpersonal relations are among the outcomes when people are selected on the basis of their likely future performance. How can the likelihood of an employee's performance and dependability be determined with reasonable certitude, particularly when change itself is so constant? It takes a bit of explaining, but it can be done.

Wrong Early Career Decisions

Let's start with an article in *Mademoiselle* (August 1980), which tells young women that college freshmen cannot be expected to decide on a major or a career. There is not enough evidence available, nor are sufficient clues possible at that time, the article says. But my studies indicate that a clear pattern of motivated skills (although in their early stages, to be sure) can be found in the great majority of people by age 18. Because wisdom usually hasn't been developed by then, young people can get hooked into making wrong decisions—by friends, well-meaning relatives, and some understandable fear of moving too fast from the culture of academe to that of the working world.

Poor Hiring Decisions

Most employers will lose half of their new college recruits in one to five years, which indicates many poor hiring decisions, some employee disappointments on the job, some erroneous career decisions, and a variety of other personal factors.

> **66** *Most employers will lose half of their new college recruits in one to five years, which indicates some poor hiring decisions, some employee disappointments on the job, some erroneous career decisions, and a variety of other personal factors.* **99**

The Problem of Obsolescence

Add to that the increasing executive and middle-management float from one employer to another in search of greener or more satisfying pastures. Then there is the obsolescence factor, in which developed skills become out of date faster and faster because of changing technology and scientific progress. What banker before 1973 could have been prepared for the rate of inflation that prevailed in 1979 and 1980? What engineer in the early 1970s could have been prepared for the manufacturing robots which are commonplace in the 1990s? What secretary using electronic, error-free, automatic-correction word processors fifteen years ago could have anticipated Pentium desktop publishing in Windows in the mid-1990s? What 1980 salespersons accustomed to flip charts and handwritten applications could have anticipated multimedia presentations and the uploading and downloading of data by a laptop?

The Limitations of Seminars and More Education

Of course there has been a tremendous increase in off-campus seminars and formal education to help management and professional people take advantage of advances in communication and technology. Many people who get that training are not aided by it, yet a manager does benefit by tracing the developing dependable skills and talents—the dependable strengths—of a person.

The Importance of Personal Motivation

First, a little self-verifying theory: suppose a person is involved in ten activities; if he or she drops two of them, the other eight can get more attention. "Can" is the important word. "Motivation" determines whether the other eight *will* actually get the attention.

The Importance of Repeated, Motivated Skills

Now transfer this bit of theory to a person's history of achievement. The experiences that brought the person achievement (as defined earlier in the book) include skills and talents that prove to be motivated because they were used to make many of those achievements happen and have been developed through those experiences. These repeated, motivated skills and talents are dependable strengths that are likely to be involved in making later achievements happen.

The Importance of Pleasure

More than that, they are related to low-stress activities that give pleasure and enjoyment. The "pleasure-pain" principle, in which we seek more of what gives us pleasure and try to avoid what gives us pain or high stress, also is at work on the job.

A Manager Who Aids the Recognition of Dependable Strengths

The manager who knows how to help a person recognize his or her pattern of motivated skills is also able to be clear about the kinds of experience, training, or education which will most benefit both that person and the organization for which he or she works. This becomes clearer when a manager recognizes the job freedom it gives himself or herself and the person. The person becomes more free to request that some unmotivated skill activities be taken out of the job, and perhaps that ones which use motivated skills be added. When unmotivated skill activities or duties are taken out of a job description, the energies associated with those activities are set free to flow into duties that are better fulfilled, more enjoyable, and less stressful to the person, and at the same time more useful to the employer—at a lower unit cost. Of course the manager is free not to change the job content or to change it very little or very much. The wise manager will, as soon as possible, make changes in the light of self-benefit, organization benefit, and employee benefit.

> **66** *The manager who knows how to help a person recognize his or her pattern of motivated skills is also able to be clear about the kinds of experience, training, or education which will most benefit both that person and the organization for which the individual works.* **99**

Such changes reduce costs associated with replacement hiring, with stress-related health problems, and with the employee's "most" productive work rather than "average" productivity. The person who knows his or her best self does not become a center of conflict; rather, the individual becomes a center for good relationships. And all because the manager is concerned with enabling the people on staff to know their meaningful dependable strengths in such a way as to make more of those strengths available.

Building a Bridge to a Different Culture

Managers know the effects of culture change but are rarely concerned with culture bridging. A culture bridge is necessary, for example, when a factory worker is promoted to supervisor. What usually happens then is that former friends tend to drop away—the worker is not invited to their homes and parties, because he or she has become a "boss." He or she has to learn a new language—that of management—and has to supervise, and perhaps correct, some former associates. These are big changes, and they cause stress. When they can be seen as a movement from one culture to another, the need for culture bridging becomes evident.

The Transition from High School to College—a Cultural Bridge

We are accustomed to think of culture change as being associated with movement from one country, with its own language and customs, to another. But one very deep culture change takes place when the "brightest" young people in a high school class go to college. There, they quickly find equally bright people from other schools, and find also that the brightest generally have their own "languages" and unique ways of working, and that they compete in different ways. These are among the marks of a different culture.

The Need for New Terminology

Again, specialists who become generalists have to learn new terminology (languages), relate to other generalists in new ways, and frequently adopt changed work habits. People on welfare for a long time have culture-change problems that are different from those of high school students who start work for the first time.

The Need for Maintaining One's Own Identity

Culture bridging, as I describe it, means movement from one culture to another—learning the new practices and speech without losing the best of what has gone before. It is a bicultural approach that helps to assure understanding and acceptance and also maintains and strengthens one's identity. People who fear losing their identity resist change, even when it's for the better.

Building on Strengths as the Bridge to Cultural Change

My concern with culture bridging centers on the loss of productivity, human values, and progress that results from resistance to change. Change itself is almost always resisted: it threatens to bring the unknown into the present, and who wants that? The person who can see that no matter how many ways strengths are applied, and no matter what they are called, they are all of a piece and continue to grow—such a person builds a personal bridge into whatever culture may be entered. Knowledge of what those dependable strengths are and how they are ordered anchors a person's self-confidence and sense of identity. It enables him or her to be relatively unshaken by whatever changes come about, and usually to act responsibly when change does occur. That person is able to accept guidance and correction and be relatively unhurt by but responsive to criticism. At the same time, because he or she exhibits stability in sometimes tough situations, that individual is likely to be a center of influence for calm effectiveness.

Case History: An Asian Fortune-Teller

The Asians I worked with included a fortune-teller who couldn't speak English, although he had learned to read and write English and Vietnamese before he was five and had picked up two more Asian languages in kitchens and markets before he was ten. In the market he often helped people speaking different languages to understand each other. Again as an infant he loved the garden and smelling and tasting all kinds of vegetables, grains, flowers, and herbs. He came to know where things would grow best and what growing things were likely to be close to other growing things. These skills enabled him and his group to forage and survive well during their hazardous hike from the interior to the coast of Vietnam. They also strengthened his power to observe reactions and helped develop his perceptiveness and ability to notice what went on in many places at once. In the market as a youth, he was known as "the ambassador" because of his mediating and language skills. Later on, these combined with other abilities to enable him to be an effective fortune-teller. The SIMS process was used to help him become aware of these developed skills. Knowing they went back into his life in Southeast Asia helped him build and cross his own culture bridge to selling work in the United States. That knowledge stimulated him to learn to speak English so that he could use his rediscovered and renamed talents.

Modesty and the Pursuit of Excellence

Professional or management people who get to know their own strengths are modest about what they can do, and don't need to boast or brag. As St. Thomas Aquinas said, a modest person is busy in quiet pursuit of excellence. The person who knows his or her dependable strengths tends to build culture bridges when they are required.

Redirecting Skills to Constructive Behavior

Like other creative children, Henry Ford got into trouble when his skills were not being used constructively. The dam design he drew at age 14 was implemented by a group of children he organized into a work crew. It flooded a lot of acreage—for which his parents were fined. For adults, the mischief often is suppressed and comes out as stress. The outgoing fortune-teller became a fearful and withdrawn man in a new country where his trade or profession is not listed in the *Dictionary of Occupational Titles*. He had virtually lost his identity, and he was depressed. Learning how he could translate the skills he had used as a fortune-teller into strengths that could be used in finding a job in America turned his life around. His old enthusiasm and confidence returned. He reached out to people again, as he had always done.

Requires New Insight

The story of the assistant sales executive was told in Chapter 6. He was a good contributor, but changed his attitude when he felt that his boss had stopped valuing his suggestions. He stopped contributing ideas. When he learned in a SIMS seminar that his self-suppression might be contributing to his holding-back attitude and his own feeling of burnout, and when he became fully aware that his ability to contribute ideas had always been one of his dependable strengths demanding expression, he realized the need to release that strength in a constructive way. He immediately began to give his boss suggestions that proved practical.

Requires New Focus

Behaviors change—voluntarily and not by manipulation—when people have freedom through knowledge to concentrate on using their strengths constructively in ways that continue to develop them. The behavior change can be compared to using a hose on the lawn: the more you focus, the more power and the greater reach you will have. When people acquire this knowledge, their behavior becomes more open to change, progress, and cooperative effort.

> **66** *The behavior change can be compared to using a hose on the lawn: the more you focus, the more power and the greater reach you will have.* **99**

Requires Identification of Strengths

For example, a very high percentage of students in high schools believe that teachers think that the students are there to be stuffed with information, and the students resist being stuffed. Resistance symptoms include the abuse of alcohol and drugs. It is well known that lack of self-esteem frequently leads to addiction and to other undisciplined activities. As was reported earlier, when a teacher introduced students to a team system that identified their strengths, they gained in self- and mutual respect. Like the fortune-teller, they became eager to use their strengths constructively and to learn how those strengths could be developed further. Communication replaced the "standard" practice of put-downs (as shown in Idaho's 1994 schools' research), and they began a continuing process of cooperation with their teachers and with the learning process.

Requires Self-Confident Cooperation

Similarly, management needs staff and workers who cooperate with and contribute to ongoing work and change. Wherever there is resistance because of personal stresses and frustrations of different kinds, there is a high probability that the person is not aware of his or her dependable strengths, and therefore is unlikely to be quietly self-confident. The behavior of self-confident people is different from that of people who lack self-esteem—and so is their productivity.

Of course, in a large organization it is not possible to get everyone all at once to appreciate his or her strengths. Even computers were introduced gradually, starting with the Navy in 1944. But it need not take 50 years to move effectively toward human resource development activities that bring out the best in all people by enabling them to appreciate and use their dependable strengths.

The Management of Dependable Strengths

John D. Rockefeller, Andrew Carnegie, and others emphasized that the highest responsibility of management is to identify and use the best in people. This strategy worked for them. In these changing times, many persons are concerned with their own individuality. This often does not, unfortunately, include knowing their patterns of

motivated skills, strengths that are a very real mark of the
person's uniqueness. This knowledge is needed in relationship to work, recreation, and leisure activities. In the
work area, it is management's responsibility to know and
coordinate the different strengths of people. The old-time
tradition of compensating for weaknesses and of trading
off strengths against weaknesses is just that—very much
out of tune with the times.

We are in an era when the assessment and management of
dependable strengths are essential for the maintenance of
living standards, growth, control of costs and inflation,
and reduction of stress and its resulting ailments.
Whether it is called the human resource development
phase of "postindustrialism" or something else, we should
move into it with alacrity and wisdom.

We are such stuff as
dreams are made of.

—Shakespeare

Be a Job Magnet
That Attracts Job Offers

When you work to attract jobs, they come easier and faster than when you go job hunting. Acting like a job magnet is a 2001 stratagem that fits today's conditions when mergers, restructurings, downsizings, and reorganizations are happening more often. It is based on fifty years of research and experience helping professionals and executives find and change jobs and careers.

It starts with the assurance that there is some kind of excellence in each person, and that employers get more benefit from using that excellence in ways which ensure greater job satisfaction. The problem is that most employers continue to say, "A good employee is hard to find."

Because of this belief, employers usually do not really try. Instead they generally rely on so-called "objective" means of measuring what activities an employee puts his or her heart into or loves.

For instance, employer job application forms don't ask, "What do you do best?" Human relations officers are known to say, among themselves, that "we give enough room for applicants to do a snow job, and asking that would just give them more snow job space." Government and private employment agency applications are no better. Their emphasis is on work history, formal education, and personal associations; it almost seems irrelevant to inquire about one's accomplishments associated with a sense of fulfillment.

For thousands of years, great teachers have pointed to the spiritual benefits of applying one's best talents. These have been given to a person to apply in ways that increase the good (work) in the world and support peaceful, growing relationships.

But let's be realistic and brief. Present-day reality demonstrates that job security is an uncertain idea. Employers have frequently demonstrated that job security is NOT their responsibility. However, income from the exchange or trading of services is a necessity.

Financial Capital and Human Capital

Financial capital produces things or products, visible and invisible (buildings, electricity, TV sets, TV and radio waves). Human capital produces ideas, attitudes, relationships, the means for machines and equipment to produce, etc. One needs the other!

The practice has been that financial capital hires human capital. The new practice will be that these different forms of capital will be traded, negotiated: employer capital will be open to attract human capital, and vice versa. Sometimes these connections will be for a longer time than others, but always the purpose will be for mutual benefit.

Growth will be central for both kinds of capital: in one case it will be personal growth, in the other financial growth. Each will be concerned with growth of the other.

Understanding Human Capital

Let's just look at the human capital side because there have been at least two centuries of university research into the employer capital side.

Know Your Own Human Capital

How can someone attract job offers? First, that person needs to know the pattern of his or her motivated skills or dependable strengths. Noted teacher-economist-author Peter Drucker says, "The most important thing is to know your strengths." He has said this in many books and articles, on television with Bill Moyers, and at numerous conferences.

"The most important thing is, know your strengths," said Peter Drucker to Bill Moyers, television interviewer. How to do that has been given in earlier chapters of this book. Motivated skills are dependable strengths. The first three steps are these: recall and list a dozen or more of your good experiences; identify and prioritize your top ten; and then describe those ten in order, reliving what you did in making them happen. Next, abstract from them the skills you applied repeatedly in making several of them happen. Then test those repeated skills or strengths for their reality. Follow that by writing a report on what has clearly become your human capital, including proof of their levels of development. Finally, use your report to test your effectiveness in communicating your potential for growth and adaptability in those areas of strength.

Joseph Campbell says it in these words, "Follow your bliss." The words used by Marsha Sinetar are "Know what you love."

When you know your strengths, the power pattern of how you are inwardly motivated to express them, you have knowledge of your human capital; you know what you have to offer and how you are likely to be most effective and productive.

> **❝**When you know your strengths,
> the power pattern of how you are
> inwardly motivated to express
> them, you have knowledge of
> your human capital; you know
> what you have to offer and how
> you are likely to be most effective
> and productive. **❞**

Then you are prepared to trade, just as you are better prepared to develop your strengths and adapt them to whatever changes are happening more frequently.

Of course, you now have developed your report on your motivated skills, dependable strengths, competences, capabilities, or skills/talents. You listed them in their order of powers or energies within you. And in that report are evidence of how they have been applied, some results of those applications, and other supportive data—including how and where they were applied.

When you know—really know—what you're good at, you have influence over how your strengths are applied and developed. You can see more clearly how to apply them to meet the demands of new situations. You are better able to accommodate to changes as they come along. This knowledge opens the way to better job interviews and to the creation of opportunities that use your unique combination of strengths. Employers create jobs for people who they feel will be productive.

Millions of job terminations at all levels have been part of the real-life economy during the past decade. It seems as if permanent jobs no longer exist, but lives and careers go on. Studies over the last half century show that continuing careers are associated with development and adaptation of people's strengths.

Tradition works against knowing your strengths— the best that is in you. Job application and evaluation forms relate to history rather than to areas of effectiveness.

Application forms don't ask, "What do you do best and enjoyably?" Evaluation forms are insistent on knowing the person's "weaknesses."

Your motivated skills or strengths are like energies demanding expression. The price paid for limiting their expression or applying them wrongly is known as stress, low self-esteem, and the various outcomes of those conditions.

Six Rules for Attracting Job Offers

Job hunting is a centuries-old tradition; now there are job attraction and "capital" trading. There are also six rules for attracting job offers. You need to know and practice these rules to be successful in attracting job offers.

1. Know That Employers Want Good Employees

Recognize that executives are always on the alert for especially good employees—both short term and longer term. I call this the human capital "window shopping" alertness of employers.

2. Present Yourself at Your Best

Dress your "window" as attractively as you can in a way that attracts attention. Your report should state briefly what you have to offer—your human capital, your motivated skills or strengths, and their supportive data. For instance, if you are concerned with a sales position requiring calling on people, and you are six-foot-seven in height, put that in your first or "description" paragraph. Or if your key concern is with finance, let the highest range of your effectiveness in finance be early in that paragraph. Or if "production" is your key concern, be sure that is strongly supported in your report's "description" paragraph. As long as the rest supports that opening paragraph, write only as little as needed to give good support under "Background," "Employers," and "Personal Data."

Don't fear the possibility that your report may be electronically scanned and that you could be "objectively" screened out. In any case, you should also have developed a functional résumé for reserve use; let your report be your first line of attraction. After all, it's offering you at your best and your future growth possibilities.

3. Know How Valuable You Can Be to an Employer

Keep in mind that the employer has a silent question behind everything that is said at an interview. That question is *"How can you be valuable to me?"* All your statements should be addressed to that question; otherwise, you miss the reality of what's involved in a job interview.

> 66 *Keep in mind that the employer has a silent question behind everything that is said at an interview. That question is* "How can you be valuable to me?" *All your statements should be addressed to that question; otherwise, you miss the reality of what's involved in a job interview.* 99

4. Know the Importance of Asking for Help or Advice

Never overlook the value of your ignorance or need for help. You cannot know where even casual relationships will lead to. For example, by *talking informally* with a counter clerk in a grocery store or hardware store where you occasionally shop, you may "accidentally" meet a relative of someone who may prove helpful to you.

Everyone tries to help a person who falls off a pier and cries for help. When *you ask another person for help*, the other person often regards your request as a compliment. For example, if you were to ask me for advice on a particular subject, I might think that you considered me knowledgeable about that subject; then I would take your request as a compliment. People respond favorably to compliments. Compliments can get you everywhere.

When you do ask for help, consider reality. For example, if you ask someone to look over your report because you think that person will help you get a job, that person, thinking that you are asking him or her for a job, may abruptly refuse your request. But if you first make it clear that you don't expect the other person to have a job for you, then ask that person to look over your report and advise you, that individual has no basis for rejecting you and may feel open to advising you. In other words, the person can look over your report and more easily come to link your skills with needs a relative or business associate may have mentioned recently—or may mention in the future.

When a contact knows your qualities and capabilities, you can *ask that person to keep you in mind if a position requiring such capabilities becomes available*. You will have established yourself as a potentially useful person— someone whom a "window shopping" executive may find valuable.

Employers are eager to find really capable and motivated employees. Employers are always on the lookout for people with capabilities who enjoy work in which they are competent. Most job descriptions fit earlier holders of those jobs; therefore, employers are willing to modify them for someone new who may have more to offer. Employers offer short- and longer-term jobs or tasks, not lifetime careers. Employers have a secret question behind all that goes on at interviews: "How can you be valuable to me?" You can trade your motivated skills or strengths when you know what they are. The report on your capabilities, strengths, or competencies does reveal how you might best be of value to an employer.

5. Get Yourself Remembered

After you have established that you are valuable to an employer, *get yourself remembered for a month or two*. Ask a clerk, dentist, clergyperson, police officer, or someone else to keep your capabilities in mind for a couple of months in case an opening becomes known. This gives you time enough to hear through a relative or contact about a job or position that needs the qualities you offer. Because you have asked someone else to listen only for a bit, there's nothing difficult about agreeing to that. The other person, therefore, usually will agree.

What really has happened is that your previously unknown contact—or even a known one—has entered you into his or her *chain of helpfulness*, a chain where one person may be helpful to others. At this point, you have stopped being a potential job hunter and have become a possible means by which a favor may be earned by recommending your capabilities.

You need to know the tested and different approaches which let you be part of a chain of helpfulness that attracts job offers to you. There is a flow to your dependable strength energies. They demand expression. Your uniqueness is a natural expression of the best that is in you.

Until you know the best you have to give, you remain tied to the traditional selection process: telling your employment history, listing your credentials, and hoping to receive a line on the payroll. I can't resist mentioning, however, the Bible's comment that "it is better to give than to receive." Happiness lies more giving than in receiving.

With knowledge of your strengths and proofs of their application, you can go not only to those whom you don't know but also to your friends, supporters, relatives, and others who feel they know you best. You can be sure they will see you in a new light.

The chain of helpfulness is a number of people who will gladly help another person if they can, especially if they themselves might later benefit from the helpfulness of that "other" person. It's the "I'll scratch your back and you scratch mine" syndrome, or the idea that "I'll do you a favor, and maybe you'll do me a favor." It's really an attitude, a kind of neighborliness, but not a requirement or an expectation.

The chain of helpfulness is helpful to both a job magnet person and an executive who is window shopping for a "hard-to-find" employee.

This is the key: when you organize yourself into the chain of helpfulness, participants in the chain know and focus on your motivated skills, or strengths, and become willing to let possible beneficiaries know about your availability. It's a different way—very different—but the most successful way to get into the employment game.

As you know, most job applications and résumés find their way into circular files. But something of potential value stays in the active basket. Your report, perhaps with résumé attached, gets into the future value basket.

Now if you can get that contact to refer you to someone else, without a feeling of obligation, you will have gained another possible "advisor" who may see your capabilities as a way of earning a return favor.

Obviously, this approach shows you how to influence the way someone, known to you or not, thinks of you as a valuable person. Step five ends when you suggest, "I'll let you know of my progress from time to time." It's a statement, not a query. And usually a person will indicate in some way that "I'll be glad to know how my advice has worked." For you, this is a matter of your obtaining "permission" to call in a couple of weeks and remind him or her you are still looking—if that is so. The call is not intended to be more than "please continue to keep me in mind as a potentially valuable person."

6. Enlarge the Chain of Helpfulness

Now that you are seen as a valuable worker, find out whether a person would be willing to direct you to someone else. Do this without suggesting that the other person might have a job opening. You might say, "I wonder if you know someone who might hear of an opportunity for my capabilities in the next couple of months? I wouldn't expect that person to know of a job now." In other words, "I know I'm a valuable person to someone, and I could be just the one whom you might use as a means of earning a favor from that person."

This might add a link to the favor chain associated with helping an employer find just the person the employer needs.

In reality, this approach results, three times out of five, in the new or old contact referring you to an acquaintance.

A Review of the Six Rules as Steps

And there you go through the same six steps. First, keep in mind that good employers are always window shopping for good employees; second, develop an attractive report that reveals your potential, backed by evidence. Third, in responding to interview questions, keep in mind the silent question, "How can you be valuable to me." (Doing this will be covered a few paragraphs later.) Fourth, because even your closest friend or relative is not fully aware of all you have to offer, remember that anyone can be a contact for you. Fifth, get yourself remembered for a month or two. Sixth, seek a referral, or enlarge the chain of people keeping your values in mind in case they hear of possible uses for your capabilities.

Now what's been going on? By now you have created a way that avoids your being turned down, and ensures that you are seen as a valuable person worth remembering and being referred. And you will, at this level, feel comfortable in seeing two or more such contacts daily—all the while seeking to enlarge the chain of helpfulness that you have initiated. If you see only ten such contacts a week, in four weeks these contacts can add up to forty people keeping you in mind as a valuable person. And within four weeks, it has been found, information of some kind of job or task opening will be made known to you through those forty contacts.

Using a Script to Speed Employment

Here is the script many thousands have used to speed their employment—people who have shown they are effective at all levels, as well as those who've been told they have no valuable experience.

First, be realistic: Good jobs are hard to find, and most people looking for jobs in traditional ways face a number of turndowns before they finally pass through all the hoops and land on a payroll. You've been through the motivated skills process; know the best you have to offer, and know that you can do better.

You are not looking for turndowns, but for entry into the chain of helpfulness where others refer you to potential employers. Those in the chain are unlikely to know initially of an opening, or to have one. The following process and script is known as the Job Magnet Approach.

1. *"I don't expect you to have a job or to know of one. But I am looking. Will you look over this report on my capabilities and tell me if you think it could help me get a job?" (Give the person a copy of your report. You might suggest, "Please ask me some questions?")*

2. *After the person has given some comments, say, "Will you keep me in mind for a couple of months in case you hear of an opening that would use my strengths?" (A nod or affirmative comment carries this forward.)*

3. *"Thank you. I'll let you know how I'm doing from time to time." (Immediately continue with . . .)*

4. *"By any chance do you know someone who might hear of an opening in the next month or two, one who might use my strengths?" (Listen quietly, attentively, expectantly. Three times out of five, when the person has thought silently for a bit, he or she will answer positively. This leads you to say the following.)*

5. *"Would you give me that person's phone and address? I wouldn't expect him (her) to know of a job right now, just get to know about my strengths that would help a potential employer." (Listen and write accurately the response.)*

6. *"Thank you very much for your time and advice."*

Now examine for a moment what this kind of conversation does. You present your strengths, and these indicate that you have human capital of value to offer. Nearly all people like the idea of associating with persons of value. Then you essentially ask for advice. This takes only a little time, involves no money, and is something most people will give—especially if you make it clear that you do NOT expect them to know of job openings.

In addition, when you said you'd let him or her know of your progress, and there was no negative suggestion, you received permission to phone and tell how you're doing about two weeks after your meeting. Your call serves as a reminder that you want the person to continue to keep you in mind, though all you might need to do is say, "I'm still looking" or "Nothing has opening up yet and thanks for keeping me in mind."

(Use this script with your report, which you may now want to call your "Human Capital Report." In this case your "description" paragraph may be a simple listing of your key motivated skills or dependable strengths. The list might start with what you feel are your most powerful two or three strengths. If so, you might use "Key Strengths" as the title of your list.)

Testing the Job Magnet Approach

You should test this Job Magnet Approach with five people: three whom you know, and two you don't know. The last two tests should be casual but purposeful meetings with persons who you think cannot be of help— perhaps a store clerk, a policeman, a dentist, or someone like that. You cannot know where that contact might lead you, but you should expect good outcomes.

When you follow these same six steps with each job magnet contact you make, and since this process involves no rejections but only encouragement and mostly referrals, you can schedule at least two of these contacts a day, or ten a week. We have found that just four weeks of these contacts bring openings to you. This is reasonable because in four weeks you will have made 40 job magnet contacts. Each of them is likely to have seen 20 other people during a month, so the outreach of 40 may extend to 800 (40 x 20). If one of those mentioned a need for someone with your capabilities, your job magnet contact could remember your strengths and your worth and refer them to you. A job opening with focus on your strengths would come to you.

All contacts are job magnet ones, unless you know a specific opening is there. This allows you to enlarge your contacts to those you don't know, even those who you may feel could not possibly give you a referral. The check-out person in a grocery or hardware store, for instance, may be related to the son or daughter of the very person who would love to interview you. You cannot know who knows whom, or who meets whom. The checkout person, for instance, knows the assistant manger, who knows the salespeople who stock the store's shelves; and salespeople know their products' managers and executives, etc. So don't overlook the usefulness of people you don't know!

Maximizing the Job Interview

The same principles are involved in the job interview (which is where your job magnet interviews will lead you). It is important to know how to ensure the same focus on your strengths during job interviews.

When you know your strengths after going through the steps given earlier in this book, you can give clear, positive proof of your effectiveness. So that you can check the reality of your strengths, the process required you to describe two or more experiences that showed your highest level of effectiveness as proof. Always, when illustrating a particular area of strength, give one or more of those examples.

Keep the Interview Focused on Your Strengths

Keep interviews focused on the worthwhile strengths you are offering, your best human capital, and your future growth. Hold off any attempt to query you on what pay you might want. This lets you put a light on your worth and likely contributions. And this makes it difficult for an employer to suggest that you start at the bottom of a pay scale.

Tell an Employer about Yourself

If an interviewer asks you to talk about yourself, you have prepared for just this moment by going through the Motivated Skills or Dependable Strengths process, including Functional Self-Analysis or Reality Testing, and writing your Report on Capabilities or Competence. You have identified those few activities or strength areas where you are at your best, and have written down things you've done that show your highest levels of effectiveness. Therefore, you are prepared to respond:

> I'm particularly effective in a number of areas. Three of them are organizing, writing, and researching. Which one would you like hear about first?

Let's examine what this statement to your contacts and interviewers accomplishes for you. First of all, it provides an adequate response to your interviewer. Next it shows that you are a good producer in several areas, three of which you name. Then you give control back to the interviewer and ask him or her to suggest where you proceed. All along, however, you keep the focus on your areas of strength, not only areas where you work best but also areas for which you have prepared good stories to demonstrate your effectiveness.

In other words, you have responded to the silent question, the one that is rarely voiced but is behind every word that interviewers speak. That thought is, "How can you be valuable to me and to our organization?"

If the interviewer names one of your areas of strength for you to talk about—say, organizing—you give an example showing your highest level of effectiveness, to date, in that area. Telling a story that shows your capability should take no more than two minutes; interviewers rarely are willing to hear a story for longer than two minutes. Then, after a moment of silence, you say, "Is that the kind of information you want? Would you like me to give another example of my organizing ability, or should I talk about another area where I'm effective, perhaps writing, re-search, or teamwork?" (This enables you to repeat two areas of strength you have already mentioned, and to add another one. So you are keeping the focus on areas where you can be of most value, and you have started to show how valuable you can be. All these facts you wrote down while working on your Functional Self-Analysis or Reality Test.)

You thus steer the interview from talk about your chrono-logical past to consideration of YOUR FUTURE potential effectiveness—that is, to your greatest strength areas. Remember, an employer can hire only your future! (It's paid for by the hour, day, week, or month AFTER your future is delivered.)

By following this procedure, you are giving the interviewer more information than can be gleaned from a traditional application form or résumé. You are helping to make clear what the employer may gain from hiring you—for either a short-term task or a long-term affiliation.

More than that, you are making it clear that you do have effective skills to offer and that you know where you can be especially valuable. This opens the possibility that the interviewer may become a contact who refers you to other potential employers, even if "this" interview doesn't turn into a position. (In that case, at the end of the interview, you open that contact possibility: "You've come to know a lot about what I have to offer, and I'd appreciate it if you'll keep me in mind for a couple of months in case you hear of an organization or person who may be able to use my strengths." That can be followed with the job magnet approach outlined earlier in this chapter for attracting job offers.)

Any person you see or contact is a possible source through which a good job might be referred to you. An-other source of unknown contacts is reached through e-mail and the computer.

As the interviewer comes to see the benefit of letting you demonstrate the areas of your greatest effectiveness, it becomes clear that you are prepared to give of yourself in a position that calls for the best that is in you. This opens the possibility that there could be a modification of the "established job description" in order to use more of what you have to offer, or that you could fit into a better position. In any case, the organization would know more about your possibilities than your work history and education could possibly show. The way you are talking about yourself shows not only your strengths but also how you are motivated—that is, the spirit behind what you are offering.

Tell an Employer about Your Background

During an interview, the interviewer may say to you, "Tell me about your background." If this happens, you might respond with words such as these: "I do a number of things well. Three of them are organizing, writing, and researching. Which would you like to hear about first?" After the interviewer names one, you tell in less than two minutes a story that demonstrates your highest level of effectiveness in that activity. Following that, you ask, "Would you like another example in that area, or would you prefer an example of my effectiveness in writing, research, or teamwork?" This tosses management of the interview back into the lap of the interviewer.

He or she, perceiving that you have developed a way of providing facts and proof of your effectiveness, is likely to encourage continued presentation of your strengths and the stories that demonstrate their level of application

If you are not asked to comment about your past, you can take the initiative and suggest, "I suppose you'll want to know something of my background?" The response to that will ordinarily be positive. Then you say, "There are a number of things I'm good at. These include (and you name three of your areas of strength)." Then you ask, "Which of these do you want me to tell you about first?"

While this strategy ensures focus on your strengths and provides proof of their level of effectiveness, it also shows that you are someone who is likely to give of your best. (You *are* offering your best.)

This doesn't mean that an offer will always follow, but the possibility is there. Many times in my experience, the content of a job has been changed to make better use of a person's motivated skills; then job creation takes place.

The Final Hiring Decision

The final decision on hiring is, of course, in the hands of the interviewer. When the decision is positive, what must follow are a discussion of job or task responsibilities and possibilities of growth, and the matter of how you get paid—salary or fee and associated benefits, insurance, vacation, pension, savings, and others, which may include education, training, attendance at conferences, etc.

If there is a negative decision, a suggestion was given seven paragraphs earlier on how to handle it. Essentially, the interviewer or executive becomes a possible Job Magnet contact: one who, as described earlier, is encouraged to remember what you have to offer, keeps you in mind for a couple of months in case he or she hears of an opportunity that would use your motivated skills, and refers you to someone else who might find it useful to know about you.

The Success of the Job Magnet Approach

When used with the aid of a one-on-one counseling organization, this process may be called *a Remember and Referral Interview*. It has been effective for hundreds of thousands of professional and management people for almost fifty years, starting with officers of all military services in 1946. In recent years this process has been effective for individuals in groups and has become known as the *Job Magnet Approach*. In groups, people are known to reduce their job-finding time by more than a third.

The concept of attracting job offers by offering to trade the best that's in you has usually resulted in all kinds of people attracting jobs within four to eight weeks. In tests with high school seniors and new college graduates, four weeks is as long as it takes for most to get jobs. When

Dependable Strengths (Motivated Skills) training is given to men and women completing prison terms, records show they earn on average 40 percent more in the first year than those who were not so trained.

The National Science Foundation helped to fund five years of research of this process in the College of Education at the University of Washington. Before-and-after tests showed that people in our classes, workshops, or seminars significantly increased their self-esteem, motivation to achieve, sense of power over circumstances, mental health, and self-efficacy. In addition, a great majority said they learned new things about themselves, tapped into their potential, and could see themselves getting along better with others.

I continue to be surprised by new stories I hear from counselors and teachers I have trained to apply these techniques with integrity. People become taxpayers instead of being long dependent on welfare; Harvard Graduate School alumni get the highest average rate of starting pay on graduation; many people find they are qualified for different careers after feeling limited by their formal degrees; women and disabled persons find new possibilities in themselves and gain success in careers; and schools and colleges of the entire State of Idaho use the processes in these pages to teach people of all ages how to bridge from school to employment.

Closing Thoughts

I've written this book as a contribution to meet the needs of opportunity and fulfillment that are felt by everyone. At almost 85, and after 50 years of good counseling service, I may be writing my last book.

I know there is excellence in each person everywhere, and it is seeking expression. At this time employed people face unknowns of mergers and downsizings; and millions of unemployed find hope fading. I know from experience that procedures in these pages can assure renewal for people: renewal in their appreciation of how deep are the strengths within them, renewal of the possibilities they can see from the mountains they climbed while exploring for their motivated skills, and renewal of hope for their futures.

Bernard Haldane

More Good Books from JIST Works, Inc.

Dare to Change Your Job and Your Life
Carole Kanchier, Ph.D.

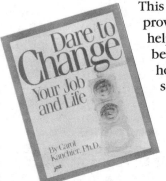

This significant, life-changing book provides readers with the tools to help them identify and change the behaviors or beliefs that might be holding them back from true satisfaction.

ISBN 1-56370-224-X

$14.95

Order Code J224X

The PIE Method for Career Success
A Unique Way to Find Your Ideal Job
Daniel Porot

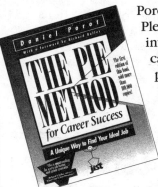

Porot's method combines elements of Pleasure, Information, and Employment into a uniquely useful and motivating career planning and job search approach. This new edition presents Porot's concepts in a graphic and memorable way.

ISBN 1-56370-182-0

$14.95

Order Code J1820

Look for these and other fine books from JIST Works at your full-service bookstore, or contact us for additional information.

More Good Books from JIST Works, Inc.

The Very Quick Job Search, *Revised Edition*

Get a Better Job in Less Time

J. Michael Farr

The techniques in this book are proven to cut your job search time in half! It was selected as one of the top job search books ever and a "must have" by career counselors.

ISBN 1-56370-181-2

$14.95

Order Code J1812

The Resume Solution, *Revised Edition*

How to Write (and Use) a Resume That Gets Results

David Swanson

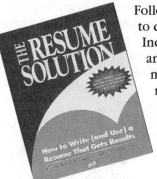

Follow the step-by-step directions to complete a SUPERIOR resume. Includes more than 50 well-written and designed resumes plus tips to make your resume stand out and get noticed.

ISBN 1-56370-180-4

$12.95

Order Code J1804

Look for these and other fine books from JIST Works at your full-service bookstore, or contact us for additional information.

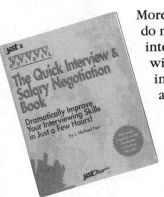

More Good Books from JIST Works, Inc.

Gallery of Best Resumes

A Collection of Quality Resumes by Professional Resume Writers

David F. Noble, Ph.D.

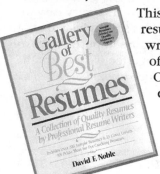

This is a showcase collection of quality resumes written by professional resume writers. Includes resumes for a variety of occupations grouped by category. One of the best resume collections ever assembled.

Using WordPerfect in Your Job Search

David F. Noble, Ph.D.

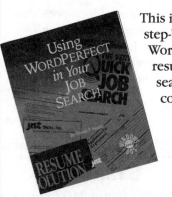

This innovative book illustrates, step-by-step, how to use the power of WordPerfect to create outstanding resumes, cover letters, and other job search documents. Also tips on conducting a successful job search.

Look for these and other fine books from JIST Works at your full-service bookstore, or contact us for additional information.

More Good Books from JIST Works, Inc.

America's 50 Fastest Growing Jobs, 3rd Edition

Official Information on the Best Jobs in Our Economy

J. Michael Farr

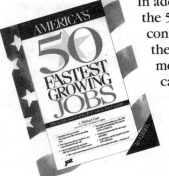

In addition to thorough descriptions of the 50 fastest growing jobs, this edition contains all new information based on the latest data available from government sources. Good for students, career changers, and job seekers.

Using the Internet in Your Job Search

An Easy Guide to Online Job Seeking and Career Information

Fred E. Jandt and Mary B. Nemnich

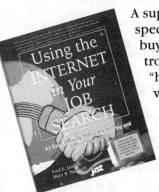

A superb book that covers the entire spectrum of online job search, from buying a computer to writing an electronic resume. It is the definitive "hands-on" guide for job seekers with access to the Internet.

Look for these and other fine books from JIST Works at your full-service bookstore, or contact us for additional information.

Here are just some of the many positive reviews of and quotes on previous editions of Career Satisfaction and Success:

From **Best's Review**: *"Those on the management level can learn to clarify each employee's strengths and weaknesses, devise job enrichment programs, boost morale and productivity, and eliminate personality conflicts . . ."*

— — — — — — — — — — — — — — — — —

From **Supervision** *Magazine*: *"This one-of-a-kind book presents a practical approach for overcoming job discontent . . ."*

— — — — — — — — — — — — — — — — —

From **Personnel Journal**: *". . .* (Career Satisfaction and Success) *helps you get the most out of your career potential by demonstrating how subordinates can keep growing and increase productivity by using their strengths."*

— — — — — — — — — — — — — — — — —

From **Quality Progress** *Magazine:* "Career Satisfaction and Success *is a book no manager or professional person can do without."*

— — — — — — — — — — — — — — — — —

From **Dr. Harold Sheppard:** *"A much needed, wise, and practical guide for managers and employees searching for a more satisfying and rewarding work life . . ."*
—**Researcher, W.E. Upjohn Institute for Employment Research**

— — — — — — — — — — — — — — — — —

From **Dr. Stokes Carrigan:** *"An important book not only for individuals, but also for organizations which realize that strong, self-confident employees are their most important asset."*—**Corporate Training and Development Manager, Smith Kline Corporation**